Hugh Mackay AO is a social psychologist and bestselling author. His non-fiction covers social analysis, psychology, communication and ethics, and he is also the author of nine novels. He has had a sixty-year career in social research and was a weekly newspaper columnist for twenty-five years. Hugh is a fellow of the Australian Psychological Society and the Royal Society of New South Wales and has been awarded honorary doctorates by five Australian universities. He was appointed an Officer of the Order of Australia in 2015 and is currently an honorary professor in the School of Medicine and Psychology at the Australian National University. He lives in Canberra.

The
Way
We Are

Also by Hugh Mackay

Non-fiction
Reinventing Australia
Why Don't People Listen?
Generations
Turning Point
Media Mania
Right & Wrong
Advance Australia . . . Where?
What Makes Us Tick
The Good Life
The Art of Belonging
Beyond Belief
Australia Reimagined
The Inner Self
The Kindness Revolution

Fiction
Little Lies
House Guest
The Spin
Winter Close
Ways of Escape
Infidelity
Selling the Dream
The Question of Love
The Therapist

The Way We Are

Lessons from a lifetime of listening

HUGH MACKAY

ALLEN&UNWIN
SYDNEY • MELBOURNE • AUCKLAND • LONDON

First published in 2024

Allen & Unwin
Cammeraygal Country
83 Alexander Street
Crows Nest NSW 2065
Australia
Phone: (61 2) 8425 0100
Email: info@allenandunwin.com
Web: www.allenandunwin.com

Allen & Unwin acknowledges the Traditional Owners of the Country
on which we live and work. We pay our respects to all Aboriginal and
Torres Strait Islander Elders, past and present.

 A catalogue record for this
book is available from the
National Library of Australia

ISBN 978 1 76147 005 9

Index by Garry Cousins
Set in 12/17 pt Sabon LT Pro by Midland Typesetters, Australia
Printed and bound in Australia by the Opus Group

10 9 8 7 6 5

The paper in this book is FSC® certified.
FSC® promotes environmentally responsible,
socially beneficial and economically viable
management of the world's forests.

To Sheila

And to my grandchildren:
Luke, Kate, Hannah, Charlotte, Rebecca,
William, Emma, Megan, Claudia, Alex

CONTENTS

CONTENTS

PREFACE

Our society needs healing . . .
and we know how to do it!

The Way We Are is a reflection on the state of Australian society as we are about to enter the second quarter of the twenty-first century. For most of the first quarter, we experienced such steady economic growth that many of us were lulled into thinking that a healthy economy meant a healthy society. But history tells us that, in the case of individuals and societies—and even economies—dream runs can be dangerous; we need occasional setbacks and challenges if we are to develop our resilience.

Over the five years since 2019, we've been experiencing our share of setbacks and challenges. We've also experienced unprecedented use of the word 'unprecedented' in response to the sustained and devastating bushfire season of 2019–20; the floods that engulfed entire towns; and the COVID-19 pandemic, with its wave after wave of infections punctuated by lockdowns, mask wearing, physical distancing, home-schooling, working remotely and all the other changes to our lives that increased the risk of social isolation—plus, tragically, the more than 21,000 COVID-related deaths. By late 2023, the pandemic was far from over, and Australia had become a 'hotspot' with the world's highest reported death rate per capita from COVID. But the persistent, impatient talk of getting 'back to normal' was a worrying sign of flagging resilience, as if we were not as well equipped as previous generations to deal with such a sustained challenge.

When you consider what pre-COVID 'normal' was, it's a wonder anyone would want to go back there. Yes, we were a more prosperous nation; yes, we had more personal freedom; yes, we were jumping onto aircraft and flying thither and yon in record numbers. But there were other things going on in our society that, from the perspective of the mid-2020s, don't seem quite so attractive.

In fact, we were becoming a rather troubled, wounded society: more lonely, more anxious, more depressed than ever; more medicated; more sleep deprived; more gambling addicted; more economically unequal. In many ways, we seemed less sure of ourselves—still fighting old battles over ethnicity, gender, religion and politics, becoming more aggressively individualistic, and placing ever-stricter boundaries around 'acceptable' attitudes and values, while seeming powerless to address such relatively simple problems as homelessness and poverty. (Yes, *simple*. Not complex. Not mysterious. We need to give homeless people secure housing, and poor people more money, and we need to pay more tax to fund such healing measures.)

In this past quarter-century, we've also been doing some disgraceful things.

Violating our human rights obligations by treating asylum-seekers in our offshore detention centres as if they were criminals and, even when they come to the mainland, denying them permanent residency; steadily eroding our public education system by pouring billions of dollars of *public* money into private schools, year after year; participating in an ill-conceived and disastrous invasion of Iraq; allegedly committing war crimes in Afghanistan. We've continued the mad talk of tax cuts that would confer most benefit on the wealthy; we've poured half a billion dollars into extending the Australian War Memorial instead of asking ourselves, as the anti-gambling ads suggest, 'What else could you do with that money?' . . . to say nothing of committing ourselves to spending $368 billion on eight nuclear-powered submarines that may or may not finally be in service by the 2050s, and may or may not be fit for purpose, especially if remote-controlled submersibles have by then replaced crewed vessels, or if spy satellites can by then scan the ocean's floor as well as they now scan its surface.

We've brought insufficient energy, imagination and commitment to the problems besetting First Nations peoples created by the collision of our cultures. From the very beginning of European settlement, we failed to acknowledge our kinship—the humanity we share—with the people of the nations who had been here for up to 65,000 years before the British colonists arrived. Although the 2023 referendum on the Indigenous Voice to parliament failed (largely because it was politicised), the referendum process increased national awareness of the gap between Indigenous and non-Indigenous Australians on such indicators as life expectancy, health, education, living standards and incarceration rates.

In the aftermath of the referendum, both sides of the argument spoke of the need to redouble our efforts to close the gap, using existing channels of legislation and influence. So the referendum result may, paradoxically, have been a catalyst for the fresh energy and insight needed to accelerate the process of reconciliation. This may yet turn out to be a period in which, to quote Seamus Heaney, 'justice can rise up, and hope and history rhyme'.

***

It's tempting to resort to hand-wringing over many of those failures, shortcomings and disappointments. And yet . . . look around you. All over Australia, every day, people are performing acts of kindness for friends, neighbours and total strangers; making sacrifices—large and small—for the common good; quietly finding ways of helping to make the world a better place. *In general*, people mean well. *In general*, we understand our obligation to contribute to social harmony. *In general*, we understand the idea of community and connectedness and we appreciate our need of each other.

A pleasant part of my professional duty as a social scientist is to point that out. A less pleasant duty is to alert us to some alarming trends that really do threaten to rip the fabric of our society. I'll describe those trends—some of which amount to self-inflicted wounds—in 'The Context' that follows. For now, I'll just say this: whether it's climate change, artificial intelligence, addiction to social media, increasing inequality, the rise of individualism or any other perceived threat to our social health and wellbeing, we each need to ponder the consequences of our own actions very carefully. This is not a time to be reckless. It is not a time to be too assertive about 'Me'. It's a time for fresh commitment to the noble purpose of living more selflessly, in a spirit of greater kindness and respect towards each other.

***

In January 1955, at the age of sixteen, I started work in the fledgling Australian public opinion research industry. Pre-computers, pre-television, pre-commercial jet aircraft, pre-latte and, of course, pre-mobile phones (though Chester Gould, the creator of the popular Dick Tracy comic strip, had equipped his detective with a 'two-way wristwatch radio', so the idea was in our heads). Australia at that time was a very conservative, male-supremacist culture, but that changed rapidly as we moved through the 1960s and 1970s and began to embrace the notion of a pluralistic society, and to respond to the early stirrings of the gender revolution.

What a privilege it has been to have lived through, and helped document, the changes that have been almost continuously reshaping Australian society over those seventy years. I wish I could be around for the next seventy, or even the next twenty-five . . .

Actually, I don't say that lightly. I am deeply curious about the next twenty-five years and am inclined to be optimistic about what will happen. We have reached a critical period in our social evolution—we've become more fragmented, more divided and less cohesive over this past quarter-century, but we are at last beginning to recognise the harmful effects of individualism on people who belong to a social species. Because I believe in the power of human nature—our essentially cooperative, communitarian nature—to bring us back from the brink of chaos, I am hopeful that we will soon reverse some of the present trends or at least start to repair the damage they've inflicted on us.

The crucial first step is to rebuild our sense of community, starting with the local neighbourhood. Our personal encounters—with friends, neighbours, dog-walkers, posties, tradies, shopkeepers and even strangers on a bus—are the building blocks we need.

A wounded society can only be healed when enough of us choose to live differently. The good news is that we're dreamers and storytellers: our dreams of a better world can inspire us, and the stories we tell each other can show us how to translate those dreams into action. I hope some of the material in these pages might encourage you to contribute to the healing process. It's urgent work.

THE CONTEXT

Born to connect, but lonelier than ever

Let's start with a statement so blindingly self-evident you might feel it's hardly worth mentioning. Yet it both frames and underpins everything you're going to read in the following pages . . .

Whenever we talk about human attitudes and behaviour— the way we think, the way we feel, the things we do, the way we respond to each other—we need to remind ourselves that we humans belong to a social species. We're herd animals. Communitarians by nature. Hopeless in isolation. *Hopeless*. Can't function. Can't flourish. We need each other. We need families, neighbourhoods, friendship circles, work colleagues, choirs, book clubs, sporting teams, groups and communities— 'herds' of all kinds—to nurture and sustain us, and give us that all-important sense of *belonging* that is so fundamental to the mental and emotional health of members of a social species.

Most of the fine and noble aspects of human nature cast shadows, and there's a dark side to belonging, too. It can be seen in the ugly excesses of tribalism, nationalism, religious sectarianism and group-based fanaticism.

But whether our motives are noble or dark, we can't help connecting, congregating, communicating. That's the kind of creatures we are. We are born to cooperate. Literally, *born* to cooperate. Neuroscientists can point to the cooperative centre in the human brain. Of course they can: what else would you expect to find in the brains of members of a species whose very survival depends on its ability to cooperate?

To put it another way: we're innately equipped to participate in the Grand Human Project, which is to create and maintain social harmony—and harmony between us and the vast ecosystem of which we are a part—since that's the only way our species can survive, let alone thrive. Chaos, driven by everyone trying to please themselves, is the alternative.

Those same neuroscientists tell us there is no 'competitive centre' in the human brain. We learn to compete, in all kinds of situations. But the so-called 'competitive instinct' is not instinctive at all: it's a socially conditioned form of behaviour that's actually at odds with our essentially cooperative human nature. Even sport, that most intensely competitive theatre of human activity, is actually a showcase for human cooperation at its best: from the beginning, we learn to cooperate not only with teammates but also with our opponents in playing in accordance with the rules and spirit of the game.

To say that we're built to cooperate doesn't mean we spring from the womb exhibiting all the qualities we need to bring that innate capacity to fruition. I'm talking about qualities like kindness, compassion, mutual respect, tolerance, inclusiveness, generosity and, above all, a willingness to make personal sacrifices for the common good. All those qualities need to be nurtured, encouraged and reinforced. But the raw material is there, inside us all.

Just like language. There's a language centre in the brain, too, but that doesn't mean we're born able to speak the mother tongue. Though we have the innate *capacity* for language, we can only become 'native speakers' as a result of careful and repetitive instruction, example, nurture, encouragement and reinforcement.

***

Being a member of a social species is good and bad news.

Here's the good news: you are not alone! Being born into a social species means we are all part of a greater whole. We're all in this thing together. We're hardwired for helpfulness. We exist in a shimmering, vibrating web of interdependence and interconnectedness. *Beautiful.*

Here's the bad news: we all need to play our part to keep that web vibrating, to maintain our connectedness. Whether we feel like it or not, we're obliged to cooperate. (I'd even say *morally* obliged—in this case, as in many others, morality seems to be a by-product of biology: the survival of our species demands that we live cooperatively, so our moral code evolves to encourage cooperative behaviour) Whether we feel like it or not, we need to show kindness and respect towards each other, for the health and wellbeing of our species. Whether we feel like it or not, we'll find ourselves obliged to make sacrifices for the common good, to miss out on something *we* want in the interests of the wellbeing of others—especially those who are disadvantaged, marginalised, poor or in some other way in need of our help and support. Notice that being human *entails* providing such support. The poor, the disadvantaged, the homeless, the marginalised don't have to justify their claim on us; their situation is eloquent enough. We are obliged to relieve poverty, for example, simply because it exists.

That's what 'belonging to a cooperative species' means, and sometimes it is a tough call. Sometimes we want to curl up into a little ball and just be left alone. Sometimes we crave silence. Sometimes we want our own private space for rest, reading, reflection, meditation, prayer, recreation. In fact, we all *do* need such periods of solitude as a way of recharging our batteries, of replenishing our resources for the demanding task of being human. So our quiet times, our alone times, our 'me times', can be seen as the very opposite of selfish: they are actually something we must do to keep ourselves fit for the good life—the life of goodness—the life lived for others. There's a community out there that needs us. Needs our engagement, our participation, our support. Being born human means we have to get out there on that stage and play our part.

Here's the beautiful symmetry of the human condition: we need communities and communities need us. We need them to nurture us and to preserve our sense of belonging; they need our engagement and participation if they are to survive.

Naturally, we will sometimes choose to please ourselves, but always with the caveat: being human means we ought not please ourselves at the expense of others. We might demand the 'right' to free speech but, being human, we know that free speech has its limits, and those limits are set by our responsibility to be respectful and courteous towards each other. We might hurt or offend someone unintentionally, and that can be sorted out by a heartfelt apology. But *deliberately* hurting or offending someone diminishes our own humanity because it goes against our true nature.

Sometimes we feel like ignoring, attacking, humiliating or otherwise demeaning other people, because we think they're boorish, offensive, stupid or 'beneath' us. Sorry: they're human, too. They're part of us, too. If we get what the Grand Human Project is about, we'll know that we must treat everyone as we ourselves would wish to be treated—even those whose views might irritate, offend or infuriate us. (Being human can be a tough gig.)

So what went wrong?

Considering what it means to be human—considering our deep need of community—it's sobering to ponder what's been happening to our society, and societies like ours, over the past thirty or forty years. Because of the choices we've been making about how to live, we've been generating a series of big-scale social trends—'trends' is the polite word; 'disruptions' might be more accurate—that have been pushing us in precisely the opposite direction from the one that is healthiest for members of a social species. Far from promoting social harmony, increasing social cohesion and encouraging the spirit of cooperation, these trends have had the cumulative effect of increasing social fragmentation, eroding social cohesion and encouraging a competitive ethos based on the primacy of the individual rather than the community.

It's been a peculiar stage in the process of our social evolution, because it seems as if we're making choices against our own long-term interests. Here's a quick reminder of seven current trends that, cumulatively, tend to erode social cohesion and lead to social fragmentation. I'm saying 'reminder' because we're all familiar with these trends: after all, we ourselves have driven them by the life choices we've been making. They're *our* trends—things we've done to ourselves, not things that have been done to us.

***

Shrinking households are a bit like the demographic equivalent of climate change. We've seen it coming, we know its causes, we know the likely long-term negative consequences for our society, yet we don't seem to know what to do about it ... and many people don't think we need to do *anything* about it.

Our households have been gradually shrinking for a hundred years. In that time, Australia's population has increased roughly fivefold while the number of dwellings has increased roughly tenfold, so we've been creating households at twice the rate we've been growing the population. In other words, we've been shrinking our households (while, weirdly, increasing the size of our houses, thanks to Australia's absurd tax arrangements that encourage over-investment in the principal place of residence). The average Australian household now comprises just 2.5 people—a national figure that would be even lower were it not boosted by Sydney, where the average is 2.8 persons per household.

Let's look at that another way: nationally, one in every four households now contains just one person. You didn't grow up in a society like that, and neither did any of our forebears. Caution: this does not mean that one in every four *people* are living alone: there are obviously more people living in larger households, though the second most common household type after the single-person household is the two-person household. One- and two-person households together account for well over 50 per cent of all Australian households.

One-third of women over the age of sixty-five now live alone. (For men, the figure is one in five.) If they reach the stage where coping on their own is too much of a challenge—physically or emotionally—older people are unlikely to be reabsorbed into family households. Given our society's current propensity to warehouse the elderly (and, indeed, the young), they are more likely to be consigned to an aged-care facility.

Not everyone who lives alone is lonely. And, conversely, not everyone who is lonely lives alone: loneliness is a state of mind, and I'll say more about that in a moment.

But a society in which every fourth household contains just one person is a society living with a heightened *risk* of loneliness on a massive scale.

Plenty of solo householders love living alone. They've chosen to do so, and they may see their solo-householder status as a symbol of freedom and independence. 'I have family members, friends, work colleagues, neighbours,' they may say, 'so I have as much social contact as I want. But I love nothing more than coming home to my personal, private sanctuary. I shut the door, punch the air, and say: *Alone at last! Peace and quiet! No one to criticise what I eat, or read, or watch on TV. No one to tell me when to go to bed or when to get up.'*

On one occasion when I was speaking publicly about the societal impact of shrinking households, one person in the audience loudly objected to my suggestion that this was a worrying trend. She lived alone, loved it, definitely regarded it as a symbol of her freedom and independence and claimed her solo-householder status was a key contributor to her 'self-actualisation'—a term borrowed from the US psychologist Abraham Maslow—which she regarded as the most important goal of her life.

Maslow's theory of a pyramid structure of human needs was published in 1943 and became highly fashionable, especially in business schools and marketing courses, during the increasingly egocentric latter years of the twentieth century. His seductive proposition that 'self-actualisation' sits at the very top of the hierarchy of human needs has worked as a strong reinforcer—and justifier—of a rather romanticised individualism and, for some people, unbridled selfishness. My own view, presented in *What Makes Us Tick*, is that once our basic survival needs are met, there is no *hierarchy* of psychological needs, but a dynamic interplay between the ten primary social desires that drive us: the desire to be taken seriously, the desire for 'my place', the desire for something to believe in, the desire to connect, the desire to be useful, the desire to belong, the desire for more (of whatever we enjoy), the desire for control, the desire for something to happen and the desire for love.

***

14

But back to solo households. In contemporary Western societies, living alone is an attractive option for a growing number of people, and many of them love the experience—even if only for a short time.

Others hate it, and experience aloneness as loneliness. They're likely to be people who never chose to live alone but were pitchforked into solo-householder status by a change in their circumstances: bereavement, divorce or other relationship breakdown, the flight from violence or some other intolerable domestic situation, relocation to a new town or city for work . . . there are many reasons why people become solo householders without choosing or wanting to. Not all of them hate it, but many of them feel uneasy, or insecure, or anxious. Far from shutting the door and punching the air when they arrive home to an empty house, they report an aching loneliness. Some of them turn lights and television on before they go out, so they won't be so conscious of the silence, the emptiness, when they return.

Such people ask themselves 'Are we meant to live alone?', or 'Is this a natural way for people to live?', and you sense that the strongly implied answer to both questions is a wistful 'no'.

Some solo households ring with the laughter of friends and neighbours streaming through the place; others are so quiet, the silence can feel like a reproach to the householder. Some feel like a refuge; others like a prison. Some are furnished lovingly and lushly; others reek of neglect and despair. So let's resist the temptation to generalise (the besetting sin of social researchers).

There are many factors propelling the trend towards smaller households: increasing longevity, a falling birth rate, a high rate of relationship breakdown, the fashion for nuclear-family rather than multigenerational households (a fashion that took hold in the 1930s), introversion, the rise of individualism . . . and there are many different responses to the experience of living alone. But the *societal* impact is clear: this is one of the main drivers of social isolation and a key contributor to the epidemic of loneliness that, as we are about to see, now has us in its grip.

There have always been hermits and isolates, people who prefer their own company and even people who are disturbed by the very idea of social contact. But these have been a tiny minority. Until the second quarter of the twentieth century, most people lived in 'herd households' where—like it or not—they had to learn to live with others in domestic intimacy. The 'others' might have included parents, siblings, perhaps a cousin, a grandparent or two, an unmarried aunt or uncle, a lodger, a housekeeper, or other permanent or casual members of the household. That was good for everyone's sense of belonging, and it was good preparation for being engaged members of the local neighbourhood and the wider community.

I've devoted this much space to the phenomenon of shrinking households because I can't think of another social trend that so dramatically illustrates the shifts in the character of our society and the direction in which it seems to be heading.

Now to the other six . . .

***

I've already mentioned our **high rate of relationship breakdown** as a factor in household shrinkage, but it's also a big contributor to social fragmentation more generally. When a couple splits, a two-person household may well become two single-person households, at least for a while. But there's more to it than that. In a society where between 35 and 40 per cent of contemporary marriages are likely to end in divorce, there's a lot of pain out there as couples decide to terminate their relationship; there's a lot of disruption of families, friendship circles, neighbourhoods and other communities the couple may have jointly participated in; and there's a lot of adjustment, rearrangement and adaptation to the new circumstances—no matter how desperately the partners might have desired the split or how much better their lives may become as a result of having separated.

If children are involved, the pain, the adjustments and the rearrangements are significantly tougher challenges for all concerned. About 20 per cent of dependent children in Australia are living with only one of their natural parents and some families manage these arrangements relatively seamlessly. But many find it tough going, especially in the beginning. Even when parents are determined to put the children's interests ahead of their own, it can be hard to insulate their children from the tensions of the parental warzone.

***

While we're on the subject of children, I'd add the **falling birth rate** to my list of disruptors. But first, let me stress that I am not in favour of *increasing* the birth rate. There are already far too many people on this planet for the resources available to sustain them; if Australia wants to increase its population significantly, immigration rather than an increased birth rate is the way to go. I am simply observing the contribution a low birth rate has made to our becoming a very different kind of society from the one many of us—and most of our parents and grandparents—were born into.

At around 1.6 babies per woman, the birth rate is way below the replacement rate of 2.1 babies per woman. It will probably fall further: many of the countries of Western Europe have birth rates lower than ours. If you happen to be a post-war Baby Boomer reading this, you probably know that when you were born, the birth rate was around 3.6 babies per woman.

Why has the birth rate fallen so dramatically? A vast improvement in the education of women is probably the biggest factor: all over the world, a rising standard of education for women is associated with falling birth rates. This doesn't mean that well-educated women are too smart to have kids; it means they are more likely to pursue a career and to give that a higher priority than their mothers or grandmothers did. One or two children might fit into that scenario, but four or five probably wouldn't. (As ever, there are many exceptions to that pattern.)

There are plenty of other factors involved in the falling birth rate, of course: improved contraception; a radically changed attitude towards marriage itself (more conditional, less institutional); a reluctance to bring more children into an already over-populated world; and a more materialistic (or, sometimes, more pragmatic) attitude, which sees children either as a drain on limited financial resources or simply an unaffordable option. There is also a generational ethos that encourages the postponement of commitment: 'Let's wait and see', 'Let's keep our options open', 'Let's not rush into anything'—where 'anything' can include a stable intimate relationship (let alone marriage), babies, a mortgage, or commitment to a single career or a single employer. No wonder the average age of the mother at the birth of the first child has risen from twenty-three to thirty-one in the past half-century. When it comes to postponing conception, nature often steps in and declares that time is up, so that's another contributor to the falling birth rate—and to the rising demand for IVF.

But why include the falling birth rate on the list of contributors to social fragmentation? Simply because children have traditionally played the role of social lubricant in local neighbourhoods and communities. A family moved into a new locality, the children got to know other children (on the school bus, in the playground, in the classroom) and gradually the kids' social network came to include their parents. Children would often get to know 'the kids next door' before the adults had connected.

Now that, relative to total population, we are producing the smallest generation of children Australia has produced since records began, that social lubricant is in shorter supply than ever: there are relatively fewer kids around than there have ever been.

We're finding ways of compensating, of course—notably through pet ownership. There are now more pets than people in Australia: 26 million of us and 28 million of them. If you doubt that many of them—especially dogs—are child substitutes, just observe the names they are given: Nigella, Sophie, Roger, Ian, Hugh (yes, I recently heard of a canine Hugh) . . .

it's hard to find a Fido, Smudge or Spot these days. The dog park is a great place for pet owners to meet and chat, but it's doubtful whether such contacts are the equivalent of families connecting via their children.

***

Fourth on this list: **the sharp decline in religious faith and practice.** The loosening attachment to organised religion over the past fifty years has had a huge impact on the character of our society—both positive and negative.

For context, we should note that about 60 per cent of Australians still identify with some religion, but the number who identify as Christian has fallen below 50 per cent for the first time since record keeping began. (Our fastest-growing religion, off a small base, is Hinduism.) But the most dramatic sign of change is in the declining number of regular church-goers: fewer than 10 per cent of the population now attend church weekly. About 15 per cent attend once or twice a month, and about 25 per cent at Christmas and Easter.

Regardless of your attitude to religion—or to God—there are three big implications of this decline. The first is that many people no longer profess faith in any form of god and as Martin Seligman, the father of positive psychology, has found, faith in 'something beyond ourselves' makes a very significant contribution to our mental health. Second, most people are no longer exposed to regular exhortations from church pulpits to act lovingly, kindly and charitably towards each other, and particularly towards the marginal-ised and disadvantaged: when those lessons are not regularly reinforced, they can easily fade. (Not all Christian churches preach that gospel. Some, like the Pentecostal Hillsong church, preach almost the opposite—that wealth is a sign of God's blessing and so the poor may be regarded as God's rejects.) Third, there are significant social-emotional advantages in belonging to a close-knit faith community with shared values. The *Handbook of Religion and Health*, edited by Harold Koenig and others, drew on a wide range of studies to conclude that religious involvement is positively correlated with wellbeing and life satisfaction, hope and optimism, a clearer sense of meaning and purpose in life, greater social support and less loneliness, lower rates of depression and faster recovery from depression. When loneliness, anxiety and depression loom as public health issues, churchgoers appear to enjoy a protective advantage over non-churchgoers.

At the same time, we should acknowledge that the ferocious and often vicious sectarianism of the past—especially between Catholics and Protestants—was as socially divisive as any of today's wedges. Religion's influence on a culture is benign when it's all about the promotion of kindness and compassion; it's a very different story when the focus is on institutional power and the fostering of prejudice.

* * *

Next up: **our increasing mobility.** Obviously, people are free to move house as often as they like, and almost universal car ownership tells its own story about our love affair with the motor car. But our increasing mobility—in both senses of

21

the word—inevitably contributes to the erosion of social cohesion.

Just like Americans, Australians move house, on average, once every six years. Some people hardly move at all, of course, but that's the national average. So there's a lot of disruption of neighbourhoods, a lot of comings and goings, a lot of adjustments to 'the new people'—or, sometimes, a disinclination to bother with those adjustments. 'You wonder whether it's worth getting to know the new people—they're only renting' is an uncharitable comment I've heard more than once.

Research suggests about half of us don't trust our neighbours, or that we don't feel as if we could call on our neighbours in a crisis. That's a gloomy sign of the problem of social fragmentation: we tend to feel less integrated, less comfortable, less secure in neighbourhoods where we don't feel as if we know our neighbours well enough to trust them, or to rely on them in an emergency. And the levels of reserve are greatest in the most ethnically diverse locations, simply because the sense of 'otherness'—the classic barrier to social connection—is more obvious when there are linguistic, cultural, religious or other gaps to be bridged.

(The COVID-19 pandemic showed many of us that we could, in fact, rely on our neighbours: we simply hadn't got to know them well enough previously to realise that. Crises and catastrophes generally accelerate the process of neighbourhood development.)

The more we move house, the more we have to pass through that period of adjustment when we feel like strangers among strangers. It doesn't require much imagination to see how to deal with this problem—we'll come to that in a moment—but if you don't know your current neighbours, why don't you put this book down for a moment and go and introduce yourself? After all, you don't want to be one of those 'neighbours we can't trust' do you? One of those neighbours we couldn't call on in an emergency? And if you think your neighbours are a bit weird, just try to imagine how you might look to them.

The other big component of our increased mobility is universal car ownership. That belongs on the list because of the way it has so drastically reduced the social benefits of footpath traffic in the life of local neighbourhoods—to say nothing of the isolating effect of driving around in a sealed capsule, usually with no one but yourself on board.

Most of us live in drive-in/drive-out suburbs where we wave at our neighbours' cars as they come and go, assuming the neighbours are in them (though the popularity of tinted windows makes that harder to establish). It's very different from stopping on the footpath for a chat. The growing popularity of electrically operated garage doors further reduces the opportunity for incidental neighbourly contact.

***

When it comes to social trends that reflect a changing way of life, we can't overlook **our relentless busyness**. Have you noticed how proud we all are of being busy, as though there's some virtue in it? It's even changed the way we greet each other: 'How are you going—busy?' As if you must be either busy or useless. Busy or underperforming. Busy or lazy. Busy or dead, perhaps. Even retired people are given to saying, 'I'm so busy I don't know how I ever found time to go to work.'

Why?

One reason is that we actually *are* busier than ever, if you look at the hours we work. (So much for the promise of the digital revolution that was going to usher in the Golden Age of Leisure.) Thanks to our computers and smartphones, many of us feel we are never actually away from work—partly because 'the boss can always reach me', and partly because we too easily become addicted to the messages that keep pouring in, whether we're officially at work or not.

Another reason is that busyness is a great hiding place if you're looking for a socially respectable way of avoiding difficult or demanding social interactions. 'The neighbours are having drinks on Friday night? Sorry—*too busy.*' 'Don't disturb Daddy—he's *busy.*'

A sane person would regard excessive busyness as a health hazard, not only because it tends to increase our personal levels of stress and anxiety but—even more importantly—because it can so easily serve as a barrier to social cohesion. We might try to justify our busyness as a sign of the great contribution we are making to the smooth running of the economic machine, but we might have overlooked our obligation to make a similarly 'great' contribution to the smooth running of the social machine—the neighbourhood, in particular. Being too busy to listen to people who need the support of a sympathetic ear; being too busy to stop for a chat with a needy neighbour or work colleague; being too busy to engage with the concerns of our own children . . . what does this say about our priorities? And what does it say about our commitment to that social-harmony project we were born to engage with?

Beware of busyness: it's the enemy of social cohesion. And therefore, for members of a social species, it's the enemy of mental health, too.

***

Perhaps **the information technology (IT) revolution** should have been top of our list of the Big Seven. What a disruptor it has been! On the one hand it has promised to make us more highly connected—to each other and to all the world's store of information—than we have ever been. And it has delivered on that promise brilliantly. No question. On the other hand, it has made it easier than ever in history for us to stay apart from each other and to settle for fewer of those full-on, face-to-face encounters that not only enrich our social connections but also make a huge contribution to our wellbeing—even to our sanity.

Whether we're talking about email or SMS texting, access to the internet via search engines such as Google, or any of the social media platforms that continue to proliferate, the digital revolution has utterly transformed the way most of us live, work, socialise, gossip and inform (and misinform) ourselves. Increasingly, we use the internet for news, for entertainment, and for something that feels like social interaction but isn't. Interaction mediated through screens is a far cry from the face-to-face variety, and if you've been tempted to blur that distinction in your own thinking, then I might have caught you in the nick of time! (If you already think that a Zoom meeting is pretty much the same as a face-to-face meeting, or that Instagram posts *are* conversations, then I'm already too late.)

25

The crucial ingredient in human interaction is *eye contact*. If you doubt it, think about how awkward it feels if you're trying to have a conversation with someone who refuses to make eye contact with you. (Or consider the close connection many people feel with their dog—partly because dogs, unusually among mammals, are equipped with eye muscles rather like ours that facilitate the direct and steady eye contact their owners respond to so warmly.) You can't make eye contact with someone on a screen, no matter how much you might try to trick your brain into thinking you can. You can't make eye contact with a robot, either, no matter how well designed it might be. Artificial intelligence is, after all, *artificial*—it's an artifice, not the real thing.

Why do you think the heaviest users of social media (young adults aged eighteen to twenty-five) also report the highest levels of loneliness? It's because they are lacking sufficient *true* social connection; they are lacking sufficient eye contact; they are missing too much of the richness and subtlety of face-to-face interaction . . . they are *connected but lonely*.

The issue here is what Dr Michelle Lim—clinical psychologist, loneliness researcher, and founder and chair of Ending Loneliness Together—refers to as **social hunger**. It's a brilliant concept. Think about it for a moment. Social hunger. Just like physical hunger in so many ways. In order to survive— let alone flourish—as human organisms, we all need to eat regularly. Our hunger needs to be satisfied or we suffer. In the short term, that suffering might reveal itself as irritability, impatience or even anger ('hangry'). By contrast, we're more benign, more tolerant, more equable when our physical hunger is satisfied—which is why research on Israeli parole

26

boards' decisions showed they were more lenient after lunch than before. (Bear that in mind if you're ever going before a parole board.)

In precisely the same way as we need to satisfy our physical hunger with regular meals, we need to satisfy our social hunger with regular social contact—the real thing, eye contact and all. If we don't, we're likely to become more irritable, impatient or even angry, without realising where those negative emotions are springing from. You wonder why there's so much abuse, anger, bullying and trolling on social media? There are many reasons—a cowardly anonymity being one of them—but it's partly because many of those abusers have been sacrificing too much face-to-face time in favour of screen time and suffering the ill-effects of social hunger.

Hold everything!

Before we attach too much blame to the digital revolution for its contribution to the increase in social fragmentation, isolation and the rise of individualism, let's pause for a moment and take a look in the rear-vision mirror. Around the middle of the fifteenth century, Johannes Gutenberg in Germany invented the printing press as we know it, though the Chinese and Koreans had invented forms of printing technology many centuries before. Suddenly, in Europe, it was possible to mass-produce the printed word and make books available to the masses. Problem: the masses couldn't read. Thus began one of the slowest but most profound social revolutions in human history: the gradual rise of mass literacy and the decline of the oral culture that had preceded it. In an oral culture, there was no separation between the person and the message. No story—no poem, no song—was fixed by being set down and captured in print. In an oral culture, 'history' is shaped and reshaped in the telling and retelling; instead of stringent obedience to 'the objective facts', orality allows for more subjectivity, more flexibility and a constantly evolving interpretation of 'truth'.

The shift from an oral to a print-based, literate culture was more like an evolution than a revolution. It wasn't until the late nineteenth and early twentieth centuries that school education became compulsory in many countries, including ours. Literacy and numeracy were the foundation skills that lay at the heart of the curriculum (and still do).

Mass literacy meant that most people could read and write (though levels of illiteracy remain stubbornly high in Australia, at around 20–25 per cent: it's a skill not everyone is able to acquire). Wonderful as that undoubtedly is, it had its downside: reading and writing are both solitary, private activities. Print separates the storyteller from the story and so, in acquiring literacy, we were learning to focus on the words in the absence of any relationship with their author.

But print also *mediates* information through the rigid patterns—the relentless linearity—of the medium itself. In English, you learn to read by submitting yourself to the discipline of tackling one word after another, left to right, line after line. And you write the same way; spraying words across a page in a haphazard fashion won't work as a means of verbal communication (though it might produce an intriguing work of art). This doesn't prevent us from saying highly emotional and even passionate things in print—nor does it prevent us from being irrational when we write. But it does mean that when we choose to communicate via the medium of print, we must play by the rules of the medium.

Immersion in the culture of print not only encourages the solitariness of the reader and writer; it conditions us to see the world through the filter of the printed word. We tend to look for—and to admire—linear, logical patterns. In fact, the dangerously misleading myth of Rational Man has been strongly reinforced by the culture of print, and so has the equally dangerous idea that 'the meaning is in the words' when the meaning, in oral communication, is often embedded more in the speech music—tone of voice, rate of speech, pauses, verbal tics—than in the words.

The Canadian philosopher and cultural commentator Marshall McLuhan referred to 'typographic man'—the person whose patterns of thinking and ways of looking at the world have been influenced by a lifetime's submission to the disciplines of the printed word. Such a person might say, 'I'll believe it when I see it in black and white', or refer to 'reading between the lines'. Because print is, in its structure, such a rational medium, you could argue that a print-based culture encourages an unrealistic expectation of rationality in general.

I was a bookworm when I was a kid. I loved nothing better than immersing myself in a book, and was grateful for wet days that allowed me to stay inside and read. I didn't realise that 'bookworm' also implied 'loner', though I knew the most complete enjoyment of a book required solitude. I didn't realise I was being culturally shaped by the medium of print itself—regardless of what content I happened to be reading. I didn't realise I was being swept along by a cultural current that was carrying us towards a more individualistic future. I certainly didn't realise that my devotion to print was conditioning me to adapt to the more socially fragmented society that lay ahead.

For a while, it looked as if television would break the grip of print on our culture, returning us to the audiovisual modes of communication more characteristic of pre-literate, oral societies. Television consumption, at least in the early years of the medium, encouraged *shared experience*—either we sat and watched TV in groups, or we watched something overnight and discussed it with friends and colleagues the next day. TV spawned something of a campfire culture: sitting around the flickering light, hearing the stories of . . . well, Hollywood, mostly. But broadcast TV's cultural dominance is now diminished as the digital media landscape continues to evolve, though talk radio and the burgeoning podcast industry have helped to maintain the oral tradition in the mass-media marketplace.

The digital revolution is not only accelerating the process of social fragmentation by eating into precious face-to-face time; it's also shortening our attention span. In her book *Attention Span*, British informatics professor Gloria Mark reports that office workers using IT now switch their focus every forty-seven seconds. Outside the office, the smartphone is having a similar effect: Mark calls most smartphone users 'woefully distracted'. She reports that university students typically check social media a hundred and eighteen times per day. (Among other signs of our shrinking attention span, she notes that the average shot-length in films is down from twelve seconds in 1930 to under four seconds now.) The digital revolution is making us more sedentary, too: Mark has found that office workers now typically spend 90 per cent of their day sitting at their desks, compared with about one-third of their day pre-email.

**

You might wish to add other items to my seven—such as the misguided move towards more high-density housing (where the emphasis tends to be on privacy and security rather than community), the increasing insecurity of work, the widening gulf between wealth and poverty. But perhaps my basic list is enough to make the point that we are choosing new ways of living that, taken together, increase the risk of fragmentation and, hence, social isolation. And that poses a serious risk for members of a social species. If our emotional security has traditionally relied on the sense of belonging to reasonably stable groups and communities, how will we function in a more fragmented, less cohesive future?

Some answers to that question have already emerged—as they always do when our sense of cohesion and solidarity is under threat. Because we are social beings, our inclination to congregate and connect leads many of us to find new ways of creating and maintaining communities, when more traditional communities have been under threat of fragmentation: witness the rise of book clubs; community choirs; ukelele clubs; community gardens; men's sheds; new political movements (like the so-called 'teals') based on local, grassroots engagement; and the home-church phenomenon as an alternative to more conventional faith communities.

Our essential humanity will always ultimately prevail, but not in some mystical or magical way: it needs each of us to sense the dangers posed by fragmentation and social isolation and then to find ways of averting those dangers in our own life, our own household, our own workplace, our own street.

Imagine Australia as a vast social science laboratory . . .

If we had put our heads together fifty years ago and planned a social science experiment to test the effects of social fragmentation, we might have said, 'Okay, let's devise some ways of shrinking their households for start, so more of them will live alone. Let's bust up more of their marriages and discourage them from having so many kids. Let's secularise the place and disband lots of their faith communities. Let's get them more mobile: make them move house more often, and give them cars so they can drive everywhere, mostly by themselves or sometimes with one or two others. Hey, let's play with their minds so they come to think being perpetually busy is actually a *good* thing. And here's the big one—let's ramp up the technology so we replace a lot of their face-to-face contact with screen-to-screen contact. Let's invent some devices that will have such seductive appeal that people will become addicted to them and will actually prefer using them to spending time with each other. Now, if we do all that, what's our hypothesis? What's our prediction?'

Knowing that we humans belong to a social species; knowing that, like other herd animals, we suffer from being cut off from the herd; knowing that the sense of *belonging* is fundamental to the mental and emotional health of members of our species; knowing that we need lots of interpersonal contact with lots of eye contact *every day* to satisfy our social hunger . . . knowing all that, we would have known exactly what to predict. First would be the emergence of a rampant individualism breeding a narcissistic, Me-centred culture; second, the emergence of a more competitive, less cooperative ethos; and third, a mental health crisis driven by epidemics of loneliness, anxiety and depression.

But this was not an experiment. This was the real thing. We didn't have to predict what might happen; we can observe what actually has happened. And, to repeat an earlier point, no one was telling us to behave in these particular ways. We ourselves, by the choices we have made, have driven the trends that have so radically reshaped our society.

So what has been the result? Can we observe those three main effects we might have predicted?

***

A more narcissistic culture? Witness the declining number of people volunteering to do community service. Witness our shrinking political parties, churches, trade unions and service clubs. Witness the rise of so-called 'identity politics' where the emphasis is on the wants and needs of specific subgroups, based on their ethnicity, gender, sexual orientation, religion or other cultural markers, rather than on the needs of society as a whole. Witness the increasing hostility between the splintering subgroups of churches, political parties and other organisations whose internal schisms are accurately described by Sigmund Freud's reference to 'the narcissism of small differences'.

Witness, above all, the growing emphasis on *personal identity* that has led to an almost obsessive concern with

Me—how I'm *different*, how I'm *unique*, how I'm *special*. As Anne Manne pointed out in *The Life of I*, the pursuit of fame and our obsession with 'making it' in a highly competitive society can also be seen as symptoms of our creeping narcissism. Social media—often used to burnish the image of Brand Me—has become a rich source of fuel for our Me-obsession.

In fact, it looks as if one of the inevitable consequences of social fragmentation—*atomisation* is the sociologists' word—is a form of infantilisation. More and more, we see signs of individuals throwing metaphorical (or actual) tantrums over the fact that they are not receiving the special attention they believe they deserve. An excessive emphasis on personal identity is the equivalent of lying on the floor, drumming your heels and shouting 'Me! Me! Me!' like pre-socialised infants who haven't yet confronted the melancholy truth that they are not the centre of the universe. Yes, belonging to a social species can be a tough gig, and one of the toughest lessons we have to learn is that it's *not* all about me; that fairness and justice will sometimes be better served if I make some concessions to the needs of others; that overemphasising my uniqueness and my claim to special treatment might actually jeopardise social harmony.

The fact that we humans are such a diverse bunch is a source of endless fascination. But a more narcissistic culture, resulting directly from a more fragmented society, has actually encouraged many of us to focus on the ways we're all different (which we are) *at the expense of* our recognition and acceptance of all the myriad ways we are the same. Watch us eat, pray and love. Watch us sneeze, sleep, walk, run and stumble.

Watch us laugh, cry, sing, frown and smile. Watch us follow the dictates of fashion in dress, speech and hair. Watch the behaviour of crowds.

And yet, in spite of our manifold similarities, a Me-centred culture is bound to divide rather than unite us; it's bound to encourage the self-centredness of *difference*. Such a culture is antithetical to our sense of ourselves as members of a community. Instead, it encourages an individualistic exceptionalism that insists on having *my* needs met, *my* rights upheld, *my* preferences respected.

Here's the test of how fragile and misguided our culture of individualism is: it simply evaporates—temporarily, at least—in the face of a crisis or catastrophe of some kind. When a flood sweeps through your town, you won't be worried about anyone's sexual orientation or religious convictions or cultural preferences. You'll simply be lending a hand to anyone in strife; you'll simply be a member of a community pulling together. When a bushfire threatens the houses in your street, your sense of belonging to that community will transcend any concern you might have about people respecting your ethnicity, gender or religion—you'll be too busy holding a hose, or helping some elderly neighbours evacuate their home before it catches alight—and you won't be concerned about the fine nuances of *their* personal identity, either.

***

A more competitive ethos? That's really a by-product of the Me-centred culture. If I rate my identity, my needs, my desires ahead of my sense of myself as a *member* of this family, this neighbourhood, this community, this species, then I will naturally see everyone else in competitive terms. After all, they want the same things I want, so we have to compete for the prize, whatever it may be: money, status, power or simply a bigger share of whatever pie is on offer. Some of us will even resort to a grotesque appropriation of Darwinism and excuse our anti-social behaviour as just another example of the 'survival of the fittest': 'You win or you lose, and I'm going to win.'

You can see the emergence of a more competitive ethos in more ruthless business practices (such as the 2023 exposure of the accounting/consulting firm PwC as having been working against the national interest in the name of profit) and in the commercial marketing strategies—including flash logos—now being adopted by professional people like lawyers, dentists and psychologists who were previously restrained by their codes of practice from indulging in competitive self-promotion.

I recently came across an advertisement in a psychology journal, promoting a service that promised to help clients 'develop qualities that drive human transformation'. The payoff, though, was the significant part of the offer: 'Develop your character to stand out and make an impact—with one simple act of self-improvement every day.' I'm not against self-improvement, of course, but the idea that its goal is to help an individual 'stand out and make an impact'—rather than, say, finding more creative ways of serving others and helping to make the world a better place by promoting social harmony—is just another sign of where a more competitive ethos is likely to lead us.

Towns, cities, states and entire nations have succumbed to the cultural pressure to compete, marketing themselves like commercial brands—complete with slogans—in a contest with each other to win our admiration or our tourist dollars or to encourage us to regard 'nationality' as a significant dimension of a commercial brand's appeal. (How long can Volvo's Swedish heritage survive as a dimension of the brand's appeal, when it is owned by a Chinese firm and most of its cars are now made in China?)

Here's a less obvious manifestation of the competitive culture: the tediously predictable promises of politicians that they will cut taxes—including for the rich—as if that's a way of helping individuals 'get ahead'. (The notorious 'Stage 3 tax cuts' of 2023–24 were, of course, a way of helping the already-wealthy get even further ahead.) In fact, *higher* taxation is the only way to fund adequate provision of services for marginalised and disadvantaged people—part of what 'personal sacrifices for the common good' implies. As the Scandinavian experience has shown, higher taxes increase citizens' sense of engagement with their society and encourage their acceptance of the obligation to contribute to the wellbeing of others.

Through the past twenty-five years, we have seen the competitive culture in a more combative, less collaborative approach to politics, in the increasingly competitive ethos of academia, and in the ugliness of a sporting culture that has been rendered more ruthless by excessive commercialisation and by its integration of heavy gambling promotion. ('What can *I* get out of this?')

The most extreme expression of competitiveness is, of course, war—and even the *talk* of war. This is hardly a new phenomenon, but the rise of individualism, fed by social fragmentation, makes us more likely to see geopolitics in exclusively competitive terms and to engage in war-talk as though war is the natural, inevitable outcome of our competitive urges. Note how the arrival in the White House of that supreme individualist, Donald Trump, signalled a radical shift in the US's stance towards China.

War is the ultimate obscenity—the ugliest bit of evidence that we humans still have some way to go in our evolution towards being truly civilised, wise and clever. The so-called 'just' war is a crazy concept. (Yes, yes: we must defend ourselves against actual invasion, and offer help to other countries who are being invaded and request our support, but Australia has recently been the invader. Think Afghanistan and Iraq: who were we defending there?) War demands of combatants that they suppress their true cooperative, compassionate nature as members of the human species, and their obligation to promote social harmony. No wonder so many soldiers return from active duty in war zones with post-traumatic stress disorder (PTSD). The real wonder is that any of them don't. No wonder we decorate war heroes and thank returning combatants for their service: we have asked them to sacrifice, at least temporarily, some of the noblest aspects of their humanity on our behalf.

***

And what about that third prediction—that, as a result of increased social fragmentation, we would be facing a mental health crisis driven by loneliness, anxiety and depression?

The answer is clear: **social isolation has become our number-one public health issue**, and we are now experiencing loneliness, anxiety and depression in epidemic proportions.

When US social psychologist Julianne Holt-Lunstad boldly declared in 2017 that 'social isolation could be a greater threat to public health than obesity', she put social isolation and loneliness squarely on the political agenda. A greater threat than obesity? In Australia, we are well aware of the health consequences of obesity, including a greater risk of type 2 diabetes and cardiovascular disease. Bad news for the individuals concerned; bad news for the public health system. Now consider social isolation as a *greater* threat to public health than that, and you get the point.

Social isolation erodes our sense of solidarity, community and connectedness, and that sets the scene for rising levels of loneliness. We now recognise social isolation as a risk factor for a variety of diseases: anxiety, depression, hypertension, inflammation, sleep deprivation and vulnerability to addiction, to say nothing of a lower life expectancy. When a herd animal is cut off from the herd—or even when it *feels* itself cut off, excluded, ignored, underappreciated—the consequences can be dire. Based on her paper for the *American Journal of Epidemiology*, Kassandra Alcaraz of the American Cancer Society told Medscape's Pam Harrison that 'social isolation is our most well-established risk factor for poor health and premature death'. There's a good reason why solitary confinement is regarded as the worst punishment we can impose on someone in our criminal justice system.

So what's the scale of the problem in Australia?

Let's start with loneliness. In a national survey of 4026 Australians aged eighteen to ninety-two conducted by Michelle Lim and colleagues for the Ending Loneliness Together network—*State of the Nation Report: Social Connection in*

Australia 2023—it emerged that 32 per cent of Australians feel lonely. That figure rose to 38 per cent for those aged between eighteen and twenty-five, the 'connected but lonely' ones I mentioned earlier. The report also notes that Australians who feel lonely are less physically active, more likely to be addicted to social media, less productive at work, more likely to have chronic disease, and more likely to suffer from depression, social anxiety and a poor sense of wellbeing.

According to the ABS's figures for 2020–22, 21.5 per cent of us—that's 4.3 million people—had a mental disorder lasting for at least twelve months. The most common disorder was anxiety, accounting for 3.4 million people. The symptoms of anxiety and depression are becoming distressingly common among children and adolescents: according to Beyond Blue, roughly 20 per cent of young Australians will have had at least one episode of depression before the age of twenty-five. If present trends persist, about 40 per cent of all Australians will experience a mental disorder in their lifetime.

All those figures are disturbing but not surprising. You could well argue that anxiety, in particular, is an inherent part of human experience. After all, life is mysterious, unpredictable, fragile and fleeting. Uncertainty and ambiguity are our constant companions. Even this planet's ability to sustain us—given our reckless, resource-squandering ways—has become uncertain.

So, yes, we must learn—as humans have always had to learn—to live with some level of anxiety. But the present situation is different. This is not 'normal' anxiety. This is a disease, an epidemic. As are our current rates of depression: this is not about people occasionally feeling sad. This, too, is a mental illness—a disease—that has reached epidemic proportions as a result of the radically different kind of society we have been creating.

There are countless factors that can contribute to, and trigger, anxiety and depression and it would be simplistic to try to capture them in a single explanation. But there is no doubt that, in many cases, loneliness is implicated.

What do we mean by loneliness? It's not just a matter of being alone—some people experience social isolation without feeling lonely, and some people feel lonely in a crowd. Michelle Lim says loneliness can be a feeling of not being 'in tune' with others: it's the *sense* of social isolation, whether you happen to be physically isolated or not. It's always an unpleasant feeling, and sometimes a distressing one, and simply being in the presence of other people might not be enough to address the issue. Sometimes, specific psychotherapeutic support (especially cognitive behavioural therapy) might be required to help the sufferer adjust to a different way of perceiving and interacting with others.

Do we need more psychotherapists?

A cheeky *social* psychologist's answer to that question would be: 'No, we need less social isolation. More face-to-face contact. More stable neighbourhoods and communities. Stronger social connections.' But it is clear that Australia is suffering a chronic shortage of psychotherapists (just like its chronic shortage of medical general practitioners). Waiting lists are too long. Access to a therapist is too difficult, especially in regional areas. A 2023 Budget submission by the Australian Psychological Society noted that only 35 per cent of the demand for mental health services is being met. Pre-COVID, only one clinical psychologist in one hundred reported being unable to take on new clients; by 2022, that figure had jumped to one in three.

Clinical psychologists themselves are suffering from the increased workload generated by the shortage—especially in the context of disasters like COVID, floods and bushfires. A 2023 national study by Emily Macleod and her colleagues at the Australian National University found that one in three clinical psychologists had reported symptoms of depression, while almost half reported low wellbeing and more than a quarter reported burnout. In the words of the president of the Australian Psychological Society, Dr Catriona Davis-McCabe, 'psychologists are crumbling under the pressure of disasters'.

There's no shortage of psychology graduates—psychology is still one of the most popular undergraduate courses, and there are many career paths for non-clinical psychologists—but there's a serious bottleneck at the point where fresh graduates try to get into higher education programs that will qualify them as clinicians. The number of new clinical psychologists entering the profession is a mere 35 per cent of the target in the National Mental Health Service Planning Framework. Combine that with the number of psychologists threatening to leave the profession due to burnout and the situation is clearly dire.

So, yes, we do need more clinical psychologists, just as we need more GPs, more paramedics, more social workers, more nurses (especially in aged care), more emergency workers. But isn't there a risk of focusing exclusively on the need to help people suffering from mental illness—especially those in the grip of our triple epidemics of loneliness, anxiety and depression—while ignoring the causes of the surge in such diseases? To employ a well-worn analogy, if people are falling off a cliff, we obviously need rescue workers at the bottom of the cliff, but we also need to build fences that will stop people falling in the first place. Confronted by an unacceptable road toll, we look for ways to better engineer both vehicles and roads, rather than simply resigning ourselves to the idea that drivers will crash their cars and people will be injured or killed in ever-increasing numbers.

Writing in *The Guardian*, UK clinical psychologist, poet and educator Sanah Ahsan dreams of a world in which we will need *fewer* therapists because we will have addressed at least some of the underlying causes of people's distress. Her hope is for a culture 'where we take the courageous (and sometimes skin-crawling) risk of *turning to each other* in our understandable, messy pain' (my italics). She sees much of the distress in modern Western societies as being a perfectly understandable response to 'structures that are hurting so many of us'.

In an interview with *The Psychologist* about the mental health of children, Professor Robin Banerjee of the University of Sussex refers to the trap of

> thinking our work on mental health has become just a matter of figuring out which kids have problems . . . someone with expertise [can] then 'fix' that child and then they'll be ready to be reintegrated with everyone else. I think that's really a mistake. Because the reality is that those mental health difficulties are not just sitting in that one child's head.

It's the whole system. It's the whole network of relationships
in which that child is embedded. That's what we need to
understand.

In a school setting, for example, Banerjee believes the work
being done with vulnerable or marginalised children needs
to be part of a larger strategy for creating the kind of school
environment that supports everyone.

In other words, the problems of an individual will often be
a reflection of the social setting in which that person is operating, so the most effective 'treatment' will include finding ways
to address problems with that social setting *as well as* dealing
with its effects on the individual. Though the presenting issue
is mental health, the strategies for addressing it might need to
call on the expertise of social, industrial and organisational
psychologists, as well as clinicians.

As usual, context is everything.

In Australia, Michelle Lim identifies a long list of risk
factors for loneliness, including living alone, being single,
lower socioeconomic status, poor attachment styles (often
resulting from an upbringing that discouraged personal
intimacy and connectedness) and a lower level of education.
While Lim asserts that, for some people, 'chronic loneliness
persists regardless of increased social resources', there is no
doubt that revitalised neighbourhoods would go some way
towards reversing the erosion of social cohesion. According to
conventional wisdom, 'all politics is local', and that certainly
applies to the trends that have transformed our society. The
state of the nation starts in the street where we live and in the
choices we each make.

Ultimately, the health of any society (especially its mental health) depends upon the health of its local neighbourhoods: the streets, apartment blocks, suburbs and towns where we actually live; the places where we need to feel as if we belong; the places where we learn to get along with people we didn't choose to live among; the places where feelings of loneliness and social isolation are most likely to overwhelm us if the neighbourhood is not functioning as a community.

This doesn't mean we need our neighbours to be our friends, but it does mean that we all need to take the unique role of neighbour seriously. Recent research conducted by Jasper Muis and his colleagues at the Vrije Universiteit Amsterdam has shown that 'pleasant contact with neighbours' is the key factor in positive ratings of a neighbourhood, and that when people rate their local neighbourhood positively, their sense of *general* social trust also rises.

Melbourne's Scanlon Foundation Research Institute regularly tracks social cohesion and our sense of belonging. Their research has been showing a steady long-term decline in both measures, but that trend was reversed during the first three years of the COVID pandemic, with its attendant lockdowns, mask wearing, physical distancing and other measures designed to encourage us to protect each other's health.

Just like floods and fires and other catastrophes, the pandemic reminded us of what it means to say that we share a common humanity. We rediscovered the importance of the neighbourhood and accepted our responsibility for the wellbeing of neighbours—particularly those at risk of social isolation. We acknowledged the need to make personal sacrifices for the common good. We experienced a surge in the sense of solidarity. There was a renewed willingness to show kindness towards each other. And the Scanlon research reflected that: we felt a stronger sense of social cohesion and a stronger sense of belonging.

Yet the Scanlon report published at the end of 2022, after three years of us living with COVID, suggested that these measures were dipping again, and we seemed at risk of returning to the long-term downward trend. The 2023 Scanlon report confirmed it, with the social cohesion measure falling to its lowest level in the sixteen years since this project began. Anecdotally, there were signs of 'pandemic fatigue' in the community, and a desire to 'put all that behind us', as if the lessons we had learned during the early years of living with the pandemic were now simply to be set aside.

Would we really be that foolish? Would we really be so insensitive to the long-term impact of social fragmentation that we would actually cast aside the lessons that experience—like our experience of fires and floods—had taught us? Would we really want to return to the pre-pandemic culture of increasingly assertive individualism? Would we really choose merely to go with the flow of social change and surrender again to the consequences of those fragmenting social trends as if we had no agency in the matter?

Or will we start the crucial work of rebuilding community, one street at a time? Reflecting on the loss of community in Western societies, the eminent UK economists Paul Collier and John Kay wrote in *Greed is Dead*: 'Soon, we will either be celebrating the value of community or contemplating the awful consequences of its loss.'

Fuelling social fragmentation is like fuelling carbon emissions: what 'trees' will we plant to compensate?

Those seven disruptive social trends are not going to go away. We are not, in the short term, going to reverse them. Households are not going to suddenly stop shrinking—though house prices that are keeping many young buyers out of the market might encourage a gradual return to more multigenerational households: perhaps we'll see more 'granny flats' springing up in more backyards. Divorced couples are not going to reconcile in large numbers, and neither are miserable couples going to resign themselves to their fate the way their grandparents' generation might have in the era when marriage was thought of more as an institution than a relationship ('You've made your bed; now lie in it'). We're not going to flock back to church. We're not going to abandon our smartphones—though, if *we're* smart, we might think about limiting our reliance on them. We're not going to turn our backs on social media, nor are we likely to resist the inroads being made by artificial intelligence into more and more aspects of our lives, from weather forecasting to patient care.

We might not be able to reverse the trends, but if we're more conscious of their impact, mightn't we be able to mitigate their *effects*? Surely it's worth a try.

An analogy: we know we can't reverse the damaging effects of carbon emissions overnight, so we seek ways of compensating—planting more trees, being more attentive to the need for recycling everything we possibly can, gradually replacing dirty energy with clean alternatives, modifying behaviour that recklessly squanders resources or pollutes the world we live in. Perhaps there's a social equivalent.

47

Perhaps there are ways we can modify our choices, moment by moment, by establishing habits of daily life that serve the goal of creating greater social harmony in the household we're part of, in the family we belong to, in the place where we work and *in the street where we live*. Perhaps we ourselves can become more empathic, attentive and respectful listeners as our contribution towards the creation of a culture of listening. Perhaps we can return to our species' core values by adopting kindness as our unflinching, unfailing way of being in the world. If we live in the 'burbs, perhaps we can spend more time in the front yard and less in the back, to facilitate more spontaneous contacts with neighbours.

On a grander scale, we could be rethinking our housing stock and putting more emphasis on medium-density housing, with its built-in encouragement of incidental interactions between neighbours. We could be developing more local rather than regional shopping centres, and finding ways of encouraging more footpath traffic. Smart urban designers and architects are already doing this in many places because they understand the harm that can be done to social cohesion by the creation of urban spaces unsympathetic to casual interpersonal encounters. We could be discouraging excessive car use by creating more attractive, more flexible public transport options (smaller but more frequent buses, for example).

We could be looking for more imaginative ways of encouraging community development—more choirs, dance classes, book clubs, poetry and art classes, adult education groups based in local libraries or underutilised church halls, walking trails and other informal recreational opportunities ... anything that makes it easier for us to engage with local neighbourhoods and communities; anything that encourages us to create more social harmony; anything that promotes the sense of *belonging*.

The pressure to yield to individualism—or even to romanticise it—will not go away, and of course it's true that we humans are independent as well as interdependent beings. Inevitable tensions arise from that duality but, in the end, the sense of our *inter*dependence—our engagement with that shimmering, vibrating web of interconnectedness—must prevail because that's the only thing that will prevent us from descending into the chaos of anarchy. Remember that 'beautiful symmetry of the human condition'? You need the community and the community needs you. That's the glory of being human, but it also defines the burden we must all share.

1

Have another apple, Eve

In the Judeo-Christian creation myth, God warns Adam and Eve against eating from the tree of knowledge, planted at the centre of the garden of Eden. The consequences? 'You will die,' God says. Later, a talking serpent slithers up and assures Eve that, no, she and Adam won't die if they eat from the tree, but they will discover the difference between good and evil and, in that way, become just like God. Eve is attracted by the idea that the fruit will make her wise (the classic error of assuming that knowledge equals wisdom), so she goes ahead and eats it, then offers some to Adam. After eating the fruit, their first blinding insight is to realise that they are stark naked. Second insight: that's a shameful state to be in.

The originators of that myth couldn't have foreseen that another 'tree of knowledge' (the internet) would spring up a few thousand years later, planted in a new Eden called cyberspace, and that it would pose a different challenge: not 'If you eat of the tree of knowledge, you will die', but 'If you overindulge, there might be dire consequences for your social, emotional and moral health'.

Take a bite...

As a result of Allied bombing raids during World War II, 80 per cent of all buildings in Hamburg were destroyed, generating forty million tonnes of rubble.

That's a lot of rubble. And that's also a piece of information which has become, for you, a piece of knowledge. Now you have it, what are you going to do with it? Will you recycle it over morning tea tomorrow, or save it up in case an opportunity arises to demonstrate your grasp of information about the impact of those bombing raids, perhaps when we mark the eightieth anniversary of the end of World War II in 2025? After all, it seems such a graphic piece of information— 80 per cent of buildings destroyed; forty million tonnes of rubble—it would be a pity to waste it. And the figures are so staggering, you might imagine it would be impossible to get them out of your head.

It's possible you will remember that information and you might even find a way to make use of it, but I doubt it. After all, many TV viewers can't recall a single item they saw on the evening news just an hour or two after they saw it, and that information—unlike my raw little sentence about the rubble—is beautifully packaged and professionally presented.

The harsh reality is that most of the information that reaches us each day is neither recalled nor reused. Some bits of it may momentarily distract us because they are quirky or arresting in some way—or because they have a particular relevance to our own situation—but most of it is discarded.

And 'discarded' isn't really the right word, either: that sounds like a deliberate, conscious decision. It's probably closer to the mark to say that most of the information we're exposed to in a day is simply sucked into the black hole of cognitive oblivion. And so it should be.

Yet, this being the Information Age, we struggle gamely to try to get our heads around as much information as possible.

The 'Information Age'?

It's endlessly tempting—and great fun—to attach labels to whatever age we live in. We've had the Age of Enlightenment, the Jazz Age, the Swinging Sixties, then the Selfish Seventies, Anxious Eighties and Nervous Nineties. We've had the Age of Discontinuity, and the Age of Convergence—in everything from the media and politics to gender and 'fusion food'. We've had the Digital Age, the New Age and assorted promises of a Golden Age of this or that.

If you had to choose a label for the current phase of our social and cultural evolution, would it really be as dull as the 'Information Age'? The British academic and author William Davies thinks we have become so obsessed with evoking and recording reactions and 'feedback' from each other—especially via social media posts—that we are living in what he calls 'The Reaction Economy'.

Here's Davies, in the *London Review of Books*, describing his withdrawal from X (then known as Twitter):

When I deleted my Twitter account . . . I was left feeling bereft, as any addict is when their drug is taken away. How was I now supposed to react to the news? And if I had no way of reacting to the news, what did I want from the news?

Am I even interested in the news, if I have no opportunity to react to it? Being in the digital public sphere without any means to react is a bit like being trapped in a shopping mall without any money.

We have certainly become reaction/feedback-crazy but, since our reactions are all supposed to be based on our hastily formed opinions—*I love it! I hate it! I'd give it three and a half stars! It's stupid! It's brilliant! I can't see the point of it! I agree! I disagree!*—I'm inclined to think the most appropriate label for our present era is the Age of Opinion.

In the 2020s, forming hasty opinions seems to be our response to information overload. There is now such a torrent of information engulfing us, and such strong expectations that we should provide feedback—including on practically every purchase we make—we no longer sift and process our experiences as carefully or thoughtfully as we once did. The easy way out is to make snap judgements. In the Age of Opinion, we're *expected* to have an opinion, whether we're equipped to have one or not.

We're also still in our 'postmodern' period in which, thanks to the influence of those two giant figures of the twentieth century, Einstein and Freud—one a scientist, one a storyteller, both of them hypothesisers—we have elevated the concepts of relativity and subjectivity to god-like status, leading to the fashionable claim that *everything's* subjective and *everything's* relative, and from where it's a short step to assert that 'everyone's entitled to their opinion'. Not only are we expected to have opinions about everything from nuclear-powered submarines to the truth about the origins of COVID-19, the current situation in Afghanistan, whether high-speed rail is viable for Australia and who the Americans should choose as their next president—but we expect those opinions to be taken seriously. And we train our children to expect the same.

As a social scientist, I have to admit the possibility that our obsessive tendency to form opinions about everything might have been partly fuelled by the public opinion research industry. Not a day passes without the media releasing the results of the latest survey on anything from voting intentions (no matter how far out from an election) to the issue du jour. And it's not just formal surveys: the mass media have become so enchanted by the concept of the 'vox pop' (from the Latin *vox populi*—the voice of the people) that almost any story will be accompanied by a few snatched comments from hapless individuals stopped in the street, or plucked from a queue for some retailer's discount sale or a rock concert, and asked for their opinion. So we'd better keep topping ourselves up on all these matters in case some wandering researcher or journalist accosts us and demands to know what we think (or, even more alarmingly, what we *feel*) about this or that. Imagine being caught short; imagine being *devoid* of an opinion about the effectiveness of the World Health Organization or the integrity of English soccer or the relative merits of Beyoncé and Taylor Swift. Imagine saying that you're reserving judgement!

The problem is that we are being overwhelmed by the proliferating products of the information revolution—online newspapers from around the world, social media, streaming services, the endless back and forth of texts and emails—plus the assortment of twenty-four-hour news services on traditional radio and TV outlets, to say nothing of 'reality TV' (and I propose to say nothing of it). Where once we lived in a world where we responded primarily to each other, face to face, we now live in a world where many of us respond primarily to *mediated* information. It's not 'reality' so much as representations of reality or messages about reality.

In one of literature's nastiest insults, Somerset Maugham said of Henry James: 'He did not live, he observed life from a window, and too often was inclined to content himself with no more than what his friends told him they saw when they looked out of a window. But what can you know of life unless you have lived it?' Rather weirdly, Maugham might have been foreseeing the impact of the information revolution on our lives: were he alive today, he would most certainly be warning us against the hazards of contenting ourselves with no more than what we see on a screen.

I can hear the howls of protest: 'But these online media *are* part of our reality! An Instagram post is as real as a chat with the woman next door!'

Yes, everything we encounter is 'real', in the sense that it's an observable phenomenon, but if you're having trouble distinguishing between the experience of mediated information and unmediated information, then perhaps it's time for some deep reflection. A good starting point might be the recognition that other people need us *and we need them*. In person. Eyeballing each other. To repeat a point made in 'The Context', we all have an appetite for face-to-face social interaction that includes eye contact, and we suffer 'social hunger' when that appetite is not satisfied. In that sense, we need each other.

The life we *need* to live, if we are to nurture our humanity, is the life lived through our real-time, face-to-face personal relationships. It's no accident that we have created the acronym 'IRL' (in real life) to remind us that there's a great gulf between 'real life' and the mediated, on-screen life that competes so seductively for our attention, and promises us—as the serpent promised Eve—that knowledge will make us wise.

Wise? All this knowledge certainly provides rich fodder for our opinions, and it makes us—like Adam and Eve—ashamed of our nakedness if we don't know what we're expected to know or, worse, if we don't have an opinion about it.

***

What is emerging is something like a series of information clubs whose members can be identified by the range of subjects about which they are suitably informed and on which they can confidently express opinions. If literacy was once the passport to acceptance in educated Australian society, having a confident opinion about whatever slice of 'current affairs' you deem important looks like the emerging alternative.

Who knows where it will all end? I have a vision—a nightmare, really—of 'Trent', the ultimate info-victim, tap-tap-tapping on his keyboard, a bank of screens in front of him, while simultaneously scrolling through the messages on all three of his smartphones, an AirPod stuck in one ear so he can catch the latest episode of his favourite podcast, leaving the other ear free to pick up the audio on his various devices. Trent is a man who knows everything he wants to know. He can tell you what the weather's like in Kansas City right now; he can tell you the result of the latest counting in the presidential election in Chile, and the score in the final of whichever World Cup is being decided. He is right up to date with the flow of texts and emails from his boss in the company he works for—remotely—and he can tell you what 'Susie', an Instagram pal, had for lunch. He knows where to find the most lurid pornography and, if he needed to, he could paddle his digital canoe into the murkiest reaches of the dark web—but he doesn't know where his own kids are, or what they're doing, ever since they insisted that he stop tracking their phones. He'll only realise that his wife has left him when he sees her Facebook post and, after a moment's reflection, he'll probably decide that a virtual-reality woman or an android would be less trouble anyway.

I said it was a nightmare. I know a few info-victims, but they're not in Trent's league. Yet.

I'm no Luddite. I'm as impressed as anyone by the sophistication of information technology and by the ever-expanding range of services available via the internet. In fact, the internet has made the researcher's wildest dreams come true. All that wonderful archival material, now readily accessible. Every article ever published in this or that journal—all there, at the touch of a button. That storehouse of information really is a modern miracle; it's like having the world's libraries sitting on your desk.

Who could deny that the internet has been transformative in many other equally positive ways—from national security to personal pleasure; from its capacity to facilitate global revolutions like #MeToo to its role in bringing far-flung families together or making it possible for people to work remotely when they need to? All true. All wonderful.

Equally astonishing is the fact that, thanks to the pace of innovation, every new device coming onto the market is about to become obsolete because an even smarter version will already be in development.

And yet, as each new wave of the IT revolution washes over us, I'm not sure we're sufficiently alert to the impact that *too much* information—or, at least, too much data—can have on our lives and, in particular, on our relationships. Researchers have been worrying about that for several decades, but their worries (for example, about the brain effects of over-exposure to screen-based information in young children) seem to be drowned in the rising tide of the very technology that concerns them.

Unless we more carefully monitor and assess the impact of the information revolution, I do believe that we will become its victims just as surely as those who were sacrificed as factory fodder became the victims of the Industrial Revolution.

Silly as it may sound, I also believe we should constantly remind ourselves that information technology is 'unnatural'. No matter how sophisticated, brilliant, convenient or effective it may be, our uncritical embrace of it takes us further and further away from the kind of society that best nurtures our human nature and best satisfies our deepest human needs (which do not, by the way, include the need for a constant flow of mediated information).

We have only to look at the motor car, or even the telephone—to say nothing of the printing press—to realise how radically technology can change the way we live and how, even when we are convinced of its value, it may produce unintended effects that we scarcely realise are happening to us. Who knew that our cars would become such a large contributor to the air pollution that now threatens to choke our largest cities to death? Or that traffic accidents would become a major contributor to global death rates, with one person in the world being killed in a car accident every twenty-six seconds? And, in the beginning, did we understand that the telephone, for all its convenience, would make it so easy to stay away from each other, and to have conversations stripped of all the visual messages that make face-to-face interactions so rich and so nuanced? (Phones also create an illusion of great intimacy—that voice in your ear, that audible breathing—which is why, before the digital era, love affairs sometimes moved more quickly on the phone than face-to-face contact, let alone an exchange of love letters, could keep up with.)

Eventually, you'll have noticed, we found a way of combining those two inventions into one: the use of mobile phones while driving has become yet another way of 'staying connected' while increasing the risk of killing or maiming each other.

***

Let's not beat around the bush: as we move through the 2020s, it's becoming obvious that we're devoting too much time to our IT devices. That is *socially* hazardous for us, just as information overload is *psychologically* hazardous, calling on us to process more information than we can possibly absorb. There's a *moral* hazard, as well, and we'll come to that in a moment.

In *Amusing Ourselves to Death,* published in 1985, the American critic and educator Neil Postman wrote, rather prophetically, that 'we live in a world in which the idea of human progress . . . has been replaced by the idea of techno-logical progress in which the aim is not to reduce ignorance, superstition and suffering but to accommodate ourselves to the requirements of new technology'.

Information technology is no exception to the general rule that, in our eagerness to embrace new technology and master it, we can easily find ourselves being enslaved by it. Far from allowing us more time to relax, the new technologies encourage us to do more, to work harder, to run faster . . . and to *know* more. Ironically, while IT is increasing the workload of many people, it is simultaneously putting others out of work.

It is inevitable that the IT revolution will continue to change the way we live, work, socialise . . . and think. This is a true revolution, after all, that's coming at us on a larger scale and at a faster pace than either the Industrial Revolution or the Print Revolution, so we can't expect to be unaffected by it. But that doesn't mean we should allow ourselves to be swallowed or swamped by it.

To ensure that doesn't happen and to protect our social health, there are three temptations I believe we need to resist with great determination: the temptation to let information keep us from each other; the temptation to confuse data transfer with communication; the temptation to believe that because information is 'good', more must be better.

Let's explore the hazards associated with each of those three temptations . . .

The temptation to let information keep us from each other poses a threat to our moral health.
This is the most significant of all the risks posed by the information revolution. Will we become so preoccupied with sending and receiving messages, and so accustomed to interacting with our screen-based devices, that we will allow ourselves to become dangerously isolated from each other?

In 'The Context', I referred to heavy users of social media becoming *connected but lonely*. These are the people who are in thrall to the cascade of information engulfing them, the people who can't bear to be parted from their smartphone—checking it last thing before sleep and first thing upon waking—but who too rarely spend time together, making eye contact and letting the dynamics of human interaction develop between them. It's time to quell our fear of missing out (FOMO) and replace it with FOSI (fear of social isolation), or perhaps even FOLY (fear of losing yourself).

Another reminder: we are herd animals. Our sense of self, and our emotional security, derive primarily from our sense of belonging to social groups—families, friends, neighbours, work colleagues and so on. Our natural habitat is the village (which is why that's become such a trendy word in urban design, in retirement housing, and even in the development of high-rise 'vertical villages').

Evolutionary psychology suggests that one of the key sources of urban anxiety is our increasing remoteness from the natural interconnectedness of the typical hunter-gatherer village. According to that view, the more we cut ourselves off from personal contact (and, incidentally, from contact with the natural world as well), and the more we rely on impersonal technology for transactions and encounters that were previously personal, the more isolated and even alienated we will feel and, in turn, the more restless and anxious we are likely to become.

It would be simplistic to blame information technology alone for the increasing sense of loneliness, social isolation and anxiety all too evident in Australia in the 2020s but, equally, it would be foolish to deny that our obsession with information harvesting makes a significant contribution to the problem.

This is not a new problem. It can be true of reading; it can be true of listening to the radio or watching TV; it can be true of connecting to social media. The issue is whether we are spending so much time in solitary activity—even when it seems to be connecting us—that we are robbing ourselves of sufficient time to be nurturing our relationships within our 'village'.

In *The Moral Sense*, Harvard political scientist James Wilson points to the moral risk associated with any activity that 'cuts the person off from those social relationships on which our moral nature in large part depends'. People engaged in the constant buzz of social media exchanges might not feel socially isolated, and that's the problem: when we're in the thick of it, we don't always appreciate the profound difference between screen-based messaging and face-to-face interaction.

We're not just talking about the need for better time management. Or some vague idea that we should keep in touch, personally, more than we do because that will help satisfy our need for a sense of belonging. That's all true, but the deeper truth is that *our moral sense is a social sense*. Personal relationships are the wellspring of morality: we develop our understanding of right and wrong through the tricky business of negotiating our personal connections with each other. In other words, morality is inherently *relational*. What else could it be? It's not written in the stars. Almost all the things we think of as wrong—from stealing someone's property to physically or psychologically harming a person—are about how we relate to other people. Cheating, lying or exploiting other people are not wrong because some religion says they are; they are wrong because societies can't function harmoniously unless people agree to respect each other's rights, needs and wellbeing. Morality is like a code of practice, arising from our need to find ways of getting along with each other in a spirit of cooperation.

Implication: if we reduce our daily personal contacts with other people below a safe level (remember Michelle Lim's 'social hunger'), then our moral clarity is likely to become blurred. To put it bluntly, the more we sacrifice interpersonal contacts in favour of technology-based connections, the more likely we are to become morally insensitive and even reckless. So another factor potentially contributing to the level of abuse, bullying, trolling and generally antisocial behaviour on social media may be that heavy users are not only socially hungry but morally diminished as well.

I don't want to labour the point, but it's important to acknowledge what we're doing to ourselves when we surrender too much of each day to the seductive charms of mediated information detached from social contact. The process of socialisation—not just as children, but throughout our lives— is fundamental to the process of acquiring what we think of as virtues: things like honesty, integrity, loyalty and, in particular, a respect for the rights of others, a willingness to accept responsibility for the consequences of our own actions and an acknowledgement that personal sacrifices must sometimes be made for the common good.

Two of the most common complaints I heard from participants in my social research program over many years were that 'we seem to be losing our sense of belonging to a community' and 'we seem to be losing our sense of morality—our sense of shared values'. In fact, those are not two complaints at all: they are two sides of the same coin. If we lose our sense of being part of a cohesive, supportive community, it is inevitable that we will gradually lose some of our sense of moral responsibility towards one another. At the most basic level, it's easier to be indifferent or even rude to a stranger than to someone who knows where you live and is likely to see you again tomorrow.

The temptation to confuse data transfer with communication can lead us to believe that machines are better at communication than we are.

The truth is that our IT devices, no matter how dazzlingly quick, efficient and convenient they may be, can only move information around. But human communication is not simply the exchange of information—still less the mere transmission of it. It relies on an interaction between the parties to the process. It's a meeting of minds, not a meshing of machines.

A father is slumped in his chair, scrolling through the messages on his smartphone. His young daughter comes into the room to say goodnight. Why would we be outraged, on the daughter's behalf, if we saw him barely acknowledge her presence and remain glued to the screen? Why is it infuriating when you visit someone and the TV is not only left on but constantly glanced at? Why are we gobsmacked when we see two people dining together in a restaurant, one attending to a smartphone and the other looking bored and ignored?

We react badly to those things because we recognise them as situations in which mediated data is being prioritised over a human encounter. We intuitively grasp the essentially relational aspect of human communication, and we see those situations not only as missed opportunities for personal interaction, but also as an implicit statement to the daughter, the visitor and the dining companion that 'I'd rather give my attention to a device than to you'.

Communication is about the *sharing* of meaning (that's what the *commun–* part of the word is intended to signify, as in words like 'communion' or 'community'). Information, by contrast, is simply a set of symbols we use to try to express those meanings. What a pity we ever coined the term 'mass communication' to describe a process that is really only the mass dissemination of information. Readers and viewers might respond at some level, but there's no personal relationship involved; what happens in that process is not what we normally mean by 'sharing'.

If you fall for the idea that moving information around is the same thing as communication, then you'd naturally be tempted to say that, as machines can obviously move information around more quickly, more accurately and more efficiently than people can, machines must be superior communicators. If you're not careful, you might even find yourself saying things like this chilling quote from the American academic George Miller, in his 1967 essay 'The Human Link in Communication Systems':

> It is quite clear that man is a miserable component in a communication system. He has a narrow bandwidth, a high noise level, is expensive to maintain, and sleeps eight hours out of every twenty-four. Even though we can't eliminate him completely, it is certainly a wise practice to replace him wherever we can ... Our society has already made the first steps towards eliminating human bottlenecks from communication systems, and the years ahead are sure to bring many more.

In case you were hoping that was intended to be ironic, or even satirical, I hate to disappoint you: Miller was dead serious. And so are the people who think we'd be better off if our contact with a bank or retail store happened through a carefully programmed artificial voice that 'knew' how to answer our questions. Or those who think that ChatGPT— the brilliant artificial intelligence system that will answer all your questions and organise information in the form you ask for—will enhance the education process by helping students overcome writer's block, or assist teachers setting exam questions, or by generally cutting down on the sweat of creating original material. Or those who dream of robotic doctors so comprehensively programmed that they can diagnose you and prescribe treatment faster than any GP. And please don't tell me that could be the answer to Australia's GP shortage. Haven't you noticed that the essence of a good relationship with a GP lies in that word 'relationship'? Will a machine know to hold your hand when bad news has to be imparted, or sense that there's something on your mind that you haven't yet divulged in words?

Perhaps we can take heart from German social psychologist Gerd Gigerenzer's 2022 book, *How to Stay Smart in a Smart World*. Drawing on his research at the Max Planck Institute for Human Development, Gigerenzer argues that human intelligence is more powerful than algorithms; that placing too much trust in artificial intelligence (AI) can lead to an unrealistic and dangerous sense of certainty; that it is up to us to shape the kind of digital world we want to live in. That 'dangerous sense of certainty' has already been exposed in our tendency to place uncritical trust in AI like ChatGPT and yet, in the end, *a human being always has to check the accuracy of the output.*

The editors of scholarly journals are already adapting to the new reality and advising potential authors that chatbots like ChatGPT may be used in the writing of academic articles, provided their use is documented and the (human) authors take responsibility for the content. Referring to chatbots as 'automated assistive writing technologies', the editors of the several American Heart Association and American Stroke Association journals have updated their advice to contributors to warn that such technologies 'do not qualify for authorship as they are unable to provide approval or consent for submission'. However, the editors say, 'these tools should be listed in the Acknowledgements'.

In 2023, the vice-president of the World Association of Medical Editors (WAME), Chris Zielinski, co-authored a paper that noted that 'ChatGPT has many limitations, as recognised by its own creators: "ChatGPT sometimes writes plausible-sounding but incorrect or nonsensical answers. Ideally, the model would ask clarifying questions when the user provides an ambiguous query. Instead, our current models usually guess what the user intended."' The WAME paper also noted that 'more alarmingly, ChatGPT may actually be capable of lying intentionally . . . of course, ChatGPT is not sentient and does not "know" it is lying, but its programming enables it to fabricate "facts"'.

Many of the limitations of the first iteration of ChatGPT (such as drawing on outdated material) will have been eliminated as the chatbot is refined and developed, with an exponential increase in the data it draws upon. Similarly, the WAME's advice and recommendations will be regularly updated to keep pace with the technology.

Australian writer Richard King wrote in *The Monthly*: 'Few of us are daft enough to think that ChatGPT is actually thinking. The problem is that anyone using it isn't really thinking either.' That is certainly a key danger—our tendency to over-rely on AI to the point where we don't engage our own critical faculties. In fact, the technology is becoming *so* smart, *so* impressive and *so* convincing, it's tempting to treat it as an extension of your own brain—and therefore almost like your own work.

One of the most popular arguments now emerging in favour of AI's inexorable push into the workplace is that, when AI relieves us of the routine drudgery of our jobs, we'll be free to become more creative. Hmm. That sounds terrific, but what if your job doesn't call for much creativity and can actually be done more efficiently by AI? Are you supposed to accept your redundancy with grace, and shuffle off somewhere to write poetry? AI is just the latest iteration of the technology that was going to 'free' us from the demands of mind-numbing jobs and usher in the Golden Age of Leisure . . . or perhaps the Golden Age of Creativity.

No doubt, in some settings, workers will be liberated by AI and find that they can indeed think more creatively about the meaning and purpose of their role at work—or perhaps hatch clever plots for the sabotage or overthrow of AI. There are bound to be AI Luddites devising ways to do the equivalent of smashing factory machines, just like the original Luddites did. But the modern version of protest will be no more effective than the earlier ones—the work that AI can do faster, more cheaply and more accurately than we can will inevitably come to be done by AI. The question, as ever, is: what *other* work can we humans *uniquely* do?

One thing we can uniquely do, as Gigerenzer reminds us, is check on the accuracy and integrity of the output of AI. Also, more profoundly, we can make careful decisions about where we're happy for AI to take over and where we're not. Part of that decision-making process will—or should—involve us pondering what other kind of work we propose to offer people displaced by AI.

***

Our failure to pay enough attention to the difference between mediated and personal messages helps to explain why so many employees complain that 'there are too many messages and not enough communication' in their organisations. Whenever we fall into the trap of thinking that the dispensing of information can replace the need for face-to-face contact, we're in trouble. Politicians who don't stay in close personal touch with their constituents have no chance of communicating effectively when they make a speech or appear in the media. Preachers who aren't in constant contact with the members of their congregation have no hope of preaching sermons that do more than merely disseminate information.

Commenting on the rise of online dating services, the American psychologist and author Thomas Moore wrote this:

> As a therapist, I've heard this story repeated a dozen times. Two people talk [via the internet] for months and imagine their relationship is deepening. Then they meet in person and—*bam!*—they can't relate. Something has changed. We are not just ethereal presences, or disembodied voices in cyberspace. Our faces and bodies express an enormous amount of data about ourselves that can't be reduced . . . we need souls and bodies to communicate truly. You can't get around this.

Let's all make as much use as we like of technology that moves information around so efficiently. But let's never imagine that—even in the most intimate messages we send—we're doing the same thing we do when we're spending time in each other's presence.

The temptation to believe that information is 'good' can lead us to believe that more must be better.
Information has become so cheap, so plentiful and so accessible, it's as if we are living in the middle of an information

supermarket where most of the goods on offer are free. It's all so seductive that we're tempted to think the mere receiving of information—regardless of its inherent value, or even its veracity—is a worthwhile activity. As with many addictive substances, the more information we consume, the sharper our appetite for it becomes. 'Info-greed' is by no means a new disorder, of course: from our addiction to radio or TV quiz programs, to our enjoyment of board games like Trivial Pursuit—to say nothing of our voracious consumption of non-fiction books—we've long had a fascination with information for its own sake but, thanks to the digital revolution, that fascination has turned, for many of us, into an obsession.

If we create a culture of information dependency, then it's a short step to believing that *any* information is worth having; that information is a valuable commodity in itself, whether or not it is relevant to our lives, and whether or not we have the time, the inclination or the need to interpret it.

If we allow ourselves to be swamped by too many messages, mightn't we risk losing our sense of what's relevant? If we immerse ourselves in a continuous flow of data, mightn't that diminish our capacity to sift and evaluate it? Mightn't there be a risk that we will be *drawn into* the information process to an extent that excludes contemplation of it?

A key part of the seduction happens when we take the entirely unjustified leap from thinking that, since information is good, more must be better; to thinking that the more information we have, the wiser we will become. The American media commentator George Gilder raised some doubts about that when he echoed and embellished T.S. Eliot's famous lines about wisdom and knowledge:

Where is the wisdom we have lost in knowledge?
Where is the knowledge we have lost in information?
Where is the information we have lost in data?

Good questions, all three of them. It's so tempting to turn it all around and believe the opposite, as if there's an inexorable progression from data to information, from information to knowledge, and from knowledge to wisdom. (Let's call it the Adam-and-Eve trap.) It sounds so logical when you put it like that but, as things are turning out, it's probably more accurate to say that our journey towards wisdom may actually be slowed by our dalliances with data.

Isn't the getting of wisdom mainly about acquiring experience—especially the experience of relating to each other—rather than information? Isn't it about living rather than consuming? Isn't it about spending time with each other rather than posting messages mostly designed to promote Brand Me by making me look gorgeous or sound clever?

Once we allow ourselves to become preoccupied with information—even to the point of addiction—the danger exists that we will be using the sheer volume of information as a means of *avoiding* reflective thought. It's as if we're unconsciously saying to ourselves: 'As long as I keep absorbing all this information, I won't have to make any sense of it, or even be particularly concerned about where it came from.'

A related danger is that we might be using information as *an insulation from our personal context*: 'As long as I'm immersed in information, I don't have to confront what is actually going on around me.' (That's actually an old one: men of my father's generation often planted themselves behind a newspaper—preferably a broadsheet—as a way of insulating themselves from the domestic dramas unfolding around them.)

And yet another danger is that we might be using information as a source of *constant stimulation*: 'I'm never bored—there's always something happening online.' (Again, that one's been around for a while: the same thing was often said of TV, and still is by some viewers.) Constant stimulation is, as you would expect, bad for us: we all benefit from time out, quiet time, solitude. We all need to learn how to be still. Constant stimulation is the shortcut to stress and anxiety. Better to be bored, occasionally—or, at least, to simply let your mind wander aimlessly.

Once we become caught on the escalator of the argument that if information is good, more must be better, we may begin to think of information as a commodity to be possessed, just like any other possession we covet. This would simply amount to another manifestation of materialism, another form of greed. Before long, we might start thinking of the amount of information we can access—the number of online news services, the number of social media platforms, the number of streaming services, the number of devices at our disposal—as symbols of our status. There's a consequent risk here that, starting from a young age, we might become even more divided and stratified by information than by other possessions. (For a start, IT devices don't come cheap, so the have-nots will be even more disadvantaged.)

Perhaps we need to remind ourselves that information is not the pathway to wholeness, enlightenment or wisdom, any more than material prosperity is. Information, in itself, sheds no light on the meaning of our life. Indeed, like other possessions, too much information can actually conceal the meaning of our life from us by distracting us from even bothering to contemplate such an idea.

Long before the information revolution, my favourite primary-school teacher, Miss King, knew how easily her pupils could be seduced by the idea that information was just another possession to be flaunted. She was particularly tough on those who were inclined to spout information for information's sake. She called it 'airing your knowledge' and she left us in no doubt that airing your knowledge was no different from any other form of showing off.

***

Can we know too much? That question turns out to be as much about morality as about information. Once we understand that the moral sense is a social sense, we can appreciate afresh the vital importance of nurturing our personal relationships, face to face, and enriching our communal life—especially in the local neighbourhood, which is always the testbed of our commitment to the task of building social harmony. The sense of responsibility towards other members of a community is fundamental to the sense of *belonging* to any kind of community. (Interesting research on the social effect of singing in a choir: people tend to trust those they sing with, even if they don't know much about them beyond the fact that they happen to sing together.)

If we lose our sense of social cohesion and, with it, our sense of shared values, how will we compensate? The standard response is that we'll need more rules and regulations to force people to act *as if* they are morally sensitive. There are some signs of that happening already in our increasingly regulated society . . . but is it what we want? Do we really want a more complicated legislative framework to compensate for a deficient ethical framework?

***

Can we know too much? Perhaps we're finally starting to discern the likely consequences of the information revolution. Perhaps we need to be more diligent in our efforts to keep both the devices and the information in their place, and in teaching our children to do the same.

A good place to start would be to delete terms like 'user-friendly' from our vocabulary. Devices may be easy or difficult to use, but they are neither friendly nor unfriendly. They may be quick, accurate and convenient—and they might even, like Alexa and Siri, appear to be talking to us—but they do not possess human qualities like courage, integrity, fidelity or morality. *They are not like us!* They are not patient, kind, empathic, generous or tolerant, even though robots can be programmed to simulate all those things.

Another protective strategy would be to monitor our—and our children's—screen time more carefully to make sure we're not letting a creeping addiction develop that cuts into the time we need to spend *every day* nurturing our personal relationships. (In 2023, in a possible sign of things to come, TikTok introduced a feature within its app that limits the time young people can spend using the platform.) Meeting online is not the same as meeting face to face. You can't make eye contact with someone on FaceTime or Zoom: you're looking at a screen, not a person. If you already know the person, it's not a bad way to augment your personal connection with them, or to make contact when you can't be together, but you will still need to 'top up' your relationship with face-to-face encounters whenever possible.

We need to keep reminding ourselves that we thrive—socially, emotionally, culturally *and morally*—on our personal interactions with each other: partner to partner, parent to child, teacher to pupil, boss to employee, colleague to colleague, neighbour to neighbour, friend to friend, stranger to stranger. We are at our worst when we are isolated, anonymous and alienated.

The most precious resource we have for coping with life in an unstable, discontinuous, revolutionary world is not information. Our most precious resource is each other. The beginning of wisdom is not to be found in a database, but in the experience of living the life of the human herd and in absorbing the lessons that experience inevitably teaches us about what it means to be human.

Reflections...

- There's nothing wrong with *not* knowing everything—or everything that other people seem to know—or with not having an opinion about everything. More important by far is to know what's happening to the people in your family, your street or apartment block, your workplace: who's at risk of social isolation, who might need an occasional listening ear, who might need a helping hand.

Remember that we are, in our very essence, social beings, not merely the human components in a system of information exchange.

- Are we becoming an angrier society? We might as well admit that the savage lurks in even the most civilised breast. When we loosen our social connections, we increase the risk that the savage will break the leash. We are seeing daily evidence of that on social media, but also some worrying signs of it in communities and individuals. When the sense of belonging has been eroded, the sense of isolation can easily turn into alienation, and that will sometimes be expressed as aggression, anger or even violence—whether verbal or physical.

- Parents are often bullied by their children into giving them what they want—nothing new there. But a child's demand for a sophisticated IT device at too early an age needs to be weighed very carefully not only against the risk of brain effects that are barely understood, but against the risk of slowing down the child's process of socialisation. And that's not just a social risk; it's a moral risk, as well.

2

Fake wisdom

In the Age of Opinion, you can say whatever you like and expect to be taken seriously, as long as you assert your opinion confidently enough and no one in the room has any actual evidence to the contrary. ('As everyone knows ...' or 'I recently read something ...' are favourite rhetorical devices.) In the Age of Opinion, weirdly, there's a suspicion of experts who might actually know what they're talking about—'Why should their opinion carry more weight than mine?'—especially when the internet can provide 'evidence' for practically anything.

If you know where to look, you'll find support for whatever crazy theory you might want to propose—though, given the number of conspiracy theories being floated every day, even the word 'theory' has a bit too much gravitas to be appropriate. There's also a plethora of 'research' available in the mass media and on the internet—some of it rigorous and reliable, some of it decidedly flaky—so you can usually back up an opinion with 'the research says'. In the Age of Opinion, no one is likely to question you too closely about the integrity of the research you're quoting. After all, you're only called on to *express* your opinion, not to justify it.

Easy answers, instant explanations, quick solutions ... there's no shortage of demand for any of that and no time for a more thoughtful, considered approach. In my own field of qualitative social research, I used to insist that no findings be discussed with a client until at least a couple of weeks after all the fieldwork had been completed, so there was sufficient time for rumination, reflection and careful interpretation of the data. Today, clients expect to have so-called 'top-line findings' delivered as soon as the fieldwork is done—or, preferably, to sit behind a two-way mirror so they can observe the data being gathered and draw their own conclusions on the run.

As the world becomes a more uncertain place, with the very survival of our species now in serious question, our appetite for certainty is as strong as ever, or perhaps even stronger. We are so desperate for answers that even uninformed opinions, unsubstantiated theories or reckless generalisations will do.

The problem is that once we've been exposed to that uninformed opinion, unsubstantiated theory or reckless generalisation, we're at serious risk of simply accepting it at face value. If we have no prior knowledge to test it by, and if it sounds plausible, we're likely to take it on board, become attached to it and possibly even be prepared to defend it.

Here's an unfortunate quirk of human psychology: the flakier the proposition we've accepted and the more we lack solid evidence for it, the more likely we are to cling to it.

This is known as the Dunning–Kruger effect, after Justin Kruger and David Dunning, who reported in a 1999 journal article that being ignorant of our own ignorance causes us to overestimate our competence. As Charles Darwin had long ago remarked, 'Ignorance more frequently begets confidence than does knowledge.' And Bertrand Russell was scathing about people whose confidence in their views exceeds their qualifications to hold those views: 'The fundamental cause of the trouble is that in the modern world the stupid are cocksure while the intelligent are full of doubt.'

**

Our attitudes, beliefs, convictions and prejudices are remarkably resilient ('notoriously resistant to change' is a less charitable way of putting it). Once an attitude—or even a piece of information, true or false—takes up residence in our mind, it's very hard to dislodge. Adolf Hitler's arch-propagandist, Joseph Goebbels, understood this when he wrote in his diary that 'experience shows that whoever speaks the first word to the world is always right'. In other words, our minds are highly receptive to *new* information, as long as it doesn't contradict a view we already hold.

Replacing something we 'know' with information that appears to contradict it is a different thing altogether. That's a real challenge for us, even when it's a relatively trivial matter. 'But I'm sure you pronounce your surname Mack-*eye*—I was told that a long time ago,' a man once said to me when he was about to introduce me to speak at a conference. He only mentioned it because someone else had just told him it was

'Mack-*ay*' to rhyme with 'okay'. I assured him that it is indeed pronounced to rhyme with 'hay' (except when I'm in Scotland, where such a pronunciation would simply be mocked), but my words fell on deaf ears. Moments later, clinging to his conviction, he introduced me as 'Hugh Mack-*eye*'. (Better, by far, than the MC who once introduced me as 'Hugh Grant'.)

Or it can be more serious. Having been told that a person you're about to meet is untrustworthy and unreliable, it's very hard to ignore the filter that has thus been imposed on your perceptions of that person. Everything she says and does will raise questions in your mind about her sincerity, her integrity or her real intentions.

If you *know* the world is flat, or that the sun goes around the Earth, it will seem ludicrous for anyone to suggest otherwise. No wonder Copernicus ran into so much trouble! It took nothing less than a scientific revolution to dislodge those ideas from the popular mind.

Intuition is often admired and given credit for perceiving 'truth' in the absence of any other evidence. But intuition can be a trap, too: once you've convinced yourself that something is the case on the basis of nothing more than a hunch, even evidence to the contrary can be dismissed as unconvincing. Early religious upbringing, too, can create certain prejudices, expectations and dispositions that may take a lifetime to modify in the light of personal experience—the idea that 'bad things won't happen to good people', for instance, or that prayer is a way of persuading God to do things to please you . . . make it rain, perhaps, or let your side win a war.

Conventional wisdom can be a bit like that. Things that 'everyone knows' can still be wrong: it's just very hard to convince people of that, once they 'know' what they've been told, or even what they've intuited because 'it's so obvious'.

Let's reflect on a few opinions that have achieved such widespread currency that they amount to conventional wisdom. Unfortunately, that 'wisdom' turns out to be fake. A few lines of argument in this book are unlikely to change many people's minds . . . but let's see how we go.

Fake wisdom: There are distinctive 'Aussie values'.

On 25 April 2006, the Beaconsfield goldmine in Tasmania collapsed. Of the seventeen miners who were underground at the time, fourteen quickly escaped and one, Larry Knight, was killed. The other two, Brant Webb and Todd Russell, were trapped almost one kilometre below the surface. Five days later, contact with them was established and they were finally rescued on 9 May, two weeks after the collapse.

The unfolding drama of the contact, the laborious drilling of a rescue tunnel and the ultimate rescue were widely covered on television—and, incidentally, brought Bill Shorten, then the national secretary of the Australian Workers' Union, to national prominence. A huge media contingent remained at the mine site as preparations for the rescue proceeded, ready to capture the moment when Webb and Russell would emerge.

It was a remarkable rescue that attracted international attention—as have similar rescues, in assorted settings, in many countries. But one of the features of the Beaconsfield saga was the way in which Australian politicians, journalists and other commentators kept insisting that the rescue was a wonderful example of 'Aussie values', 'Aussie courage' and 'mateship' on display, as if Australians would be uniquely concerned about rescuing their trapped miners—unlike, say, Russians or Canadians or Welsh.

Do we imagine that, faced with a crisis like the Beaconsfield mine collapse, people in other countries would have said, 'It looks as if there are a couple of fellows trapped down there. Seems pretty hopeless. Let's call it a day and maybe come back and check the situation in the morning'?

Really? Haven't we seen extraordinary footage of heroic Italians rescuing people from the catastrophic mudslides of 2022 and 2023? Haven't we been moved by the sight of Turks and Syrians struggling against the odds to locate survivors of the 2023 earthquakes? Or Ukrainians desperately search-ing for people in the wreckage of apartment buildings hit by Russian missiles?

Rescuing the victims of a disaster. Caring for the sick and the wounded. Responding to the needs of the disadvantaged and marginalised. Feeding the hungry. Offering a bed to the homeless. These are things that, throughout human history, human beings have done for each other because that's how members of a social species behave when the need arises. Rescuing trapped miners—even going to the most extra-ordinary lengths to do so—is an example of *human nature* on display. These are *human values*, not specifically (and certainly not exclusively) Australian values.

We do ourselves a great disservice when we try to per-petuate the myth that 'Aussie values' are exceptional or even unique, or when we try to appropriate to ourselves the human qualities and values that make this a wonderful species to belong to. Yes, there are other less attractive features of human behaviour—like violence, exploitation, prejudice, neglect of people in need—we might not want to be associated with, and you'll notice we never try to claim them as uniquely ours, even though they are as much in evidence here as elsewhere.

It's a great temptation, when nationalistic zeal is upon us, to make all sorts of outrageous claims about how uniquely good we are. *Our soldiers are the bravest, toughest and most courageous!* No, they're not. Many of them, like many other soldiers, including those we have sometimes regarded as enemies, have been brave and tough, and sometimes courageous. But, as with every other country that has ever fought wars, there are plenty of dark episodes in our military history, including our recent ill-judged military involvement in Iraq and Afghanistan.

Our medical system is the best in the world! No, it isn't. It's extremely good, but so are lots of other country's medical systems. (The Netherlands' system is wonderful. America's is probably the best, if only you could afford to access it.)

We're more passionate about sport than any other nation! No, we're not. Try telling that to English, Argentinian or Spanish soccer fans.

We always punch above our weight! No, we don't. We sometimes do, and we've cracked the formula that says if you put enough money into a particular sport, you'll probably win some medals in international competition. And, like most countries, we've produced some outstanding people who have done outstanding work in science and the arts. But when it comes to human rights, we're hardly a shining example to the world: you wouldn't want to examine our treatment of refugees and asylum-seekers too closely, nor the treatment of our First Nations peoples. And we punch *way below* our weight when it comes to carbon emissions reduction. (We're still selling our coal to other countries and then accusing *them* of polluting.) Nor could we claim to be anywhere near the Scandinavian countries when it comes to social welfare or public housing or a commitment to true equality.

And the famous Aussie 'fair go'? When you examine it closely, that doesn't look too flash, either. Until quite recently, we didn't even give women a fair go, let alone our First Nations peoples.

What are these unique Aussie values, then? Surely we're not going to claim some version of *liberté*, *egalité*, *fraternité*, are we? The French were onto that as long ago as 1789—you may recall they had a revolution about it—and our devotion to the concept of 'mateship' is not only unacceptably blokeish in the twenty-first century but is no more than a rough translation of *fraternité*.

Beware of hubris posing as patriotism! Beware of assuming that our noblest qualities are uniquely ours! Most of the values we claim as cornerstones of our way of life are simply the touchstones of any modern liberal democracy: respect for persons, regardless of age or sex; respect for democracy and its institutions, including the rule of law and the principle of parliamentary representation; the rights to freedom of speech, assembly and religion. All such democracies claim to discourage the exploitation of the weak by the strong, and to abhor prejudice that leads people to make judgements about each other based purely on some category they represent—whether defined by ethnicity, gender, religion, politics or otherwise. All such democracies condemn the oppression and abuse of minorities.

We'd sign up to all those values, wouldn't we? We even manage to adhere to some of them, but we're a bit half-hearted about others. And when we say we aspire to live by those values, we could scarcely claim them as uniquely ours without offending every other liberal democracy on the planet.

What about our allegedly distinctive brand of humour? It's just as derivative as everyone else's. There's actually a very small pool of 'core' jokes that keep being refined and recycled and adapted to suit different contexts and cultures. Even our historical practice of saving our vilest jokes for Indigenous people can be matched by other countries with Indigenous populations. Shame often shows up as humour.

You know that 'quintessentially Aussie' joke about the Texas rancher who visits a cattle station in Far North Queensland? Bragging to the Australian owner about the size of his own ranch, the Texan says, 'It's so big, I can get on my horse on the eastern boundary, ride all day, camp overnight and ride all the next day, and still not reach the western boundary.'

'Yeah,' says the Aussie. 'We used to have a horse like that . . .'

Quintessentially Aussie? Precisely the same joke pops up in Belgium but it's about slow trains, not horses.

Even the suggestion that there's a unique or 'authentic' Australian spirituality looks a bit thin when you examine it. When we examine the concept of 'spirituality' detached from its religious moorings, we're not talking about anything uniquely Australian:

- the sense of our interconnectedness with all creatures and with the earth that sustains us

- the need for kindness and compassion in all our dealings
- the urge to create myths and metaphors and tell stories that express our deepest yearnings, and that capture our most appealing visions, dreams and beliefs about the world and how to live in it
- the need to honour our ancestors and respect their heritage
- the value of quiet contemplation and deep meditation upon the meaning and purpose of our lives.

You can find those themes everywhere from the Aboriginal Dreaming to Christianity, from Hinduism to Buddhism and from Baha'i to Humanism or SBNRs (spiritual but not religious). Different practices, different myths, different words, but essentially the same yearning for meanings that will help us make sense of our life in this world, and perhaps even in some unimaginable world to come.

***

To say that our values are not distinctively our own is not to denigrate them. On the contrary, we should draw comfort and even inspiration from knowing that our culture has so much in common with others, that our foundational values are shared with like-minded societies around the world, and that our spirituality taps into universal themes.

'Aussie values' are distinctive is not only fake wisdom. Clinging to the idea of Australian exceptionalism might actually weaken us by blinding us to the larger truth about the common humanity we share with people of every colour,

creed and culture. It might also blind us to the truth about ourselves, including our shortcomings.

When you consider the diversity of the Australian population and the many cultures we now incorporate into our national ethos, any references to 'Aussie values' seem glib. Even references to 'Indigenous and non-Indigenous culture' seem absurd—as if there were just one of each—when we know there are, and have always been, many distinct First Nations with their own language and their unique cultural beliefs and practices.

We are arguably the world's most successful multicultural society, with people having come here from about 200 different birthplaces around the world and half of our present population either having been born overseas or having at least one overseas-born parent. It would simply be foolish to try and synthesise all that diversity into some recognisably distinct 'Aussie values'. But some people continue to try, even to the point of declaring some things 'un-Australian', though that term generally means nothing more than 'unacceptable in a civilised society'.

No—our values are not distinctly or uniquely ours. They, like our culture, reflect our complex interdependence with all those cultures that continue to shape our socio-cultural evolution.

Fake wisdom: Humans thrive on stability.

In Australia in the 2020s—a time of constant change and the threat of more upheavals to come—it's tempting to yearn for stability. How often do you hear it: 'I don't want to move because the kids would have to change schools and that would be too disruptive.' Or, 'We're all so resistant to change, aren't we? Why can't things stay the same!' Or, 'Uh-oh, we have a new CEO. Here we go again—it'll be yet another reorganisation. More chaos.'

Here's one of the great paradoxes of the human psyche: we want to be left in our comfort zone and yet we thrive on the experience of being taken out of it. We do tend to resist change—and our highly filtered, self-protective view of the world helps protect us from changing our *minds* about things—yet too much stability turns out to be bad for us. What we humans *actually* thrive on is instability—and just as well, given the inherent uncertainty and unpredictability of life.

It's a weird piece of fake wisdom, this one. It's as though we dream of achieving the very condition that would be least productive, least stimulating and least satisfying for us. The calm, untroubled state we claim to want is likely to lead to feelings of restlessness, anxiety and, ultimately, boredom— unless you happen to be a monk or a mystic who has withdrawn from the fray to devote your life to prayer and meditation.

Even the much-vaunted *peace of mind* we all crave—with some justification—can easily be misrepresented. It doesn't refer to a detached, antisocial state of being 'left in peace', undisturbed by too much disruption, too many challenges or too many people making too many demands on us. (We're humans, remember: our gig *entails* people making demands on us.) Peace of mind is a highly desirable psychological/ spiritual state that can not only coexist with the demands of normal human life, but is actually one of the most precious resources we need for dealing with life's uncertainties. A clear sense of our life's meaning and purpose, for example, can help sustain us through all kinds of upheavals along the way.

If we are to flourish, we need to change. And not just to change, but to be open to the prospect of constant change. It can easily feel like the opposite, and yet we know how desolate it sounds when someone says *nothing ever happens to me*. As noted in 'The Context' my book *What Makes Us Tick* identified the desire for something to happen as one of the ten psychological desires that drive us.

That's why it's a paradox: we seem to want two apparently incompatible things at once: constancy and change.

The big name in this field is Jerome Kagan, a professor of psychology at Harvard, who died in 2021. Kagan introduced the idea of 'nodes of uncertainty' in human development, claiming (with strong evidence) that learning to deal with the unfamiliar is such a huge part of our cognitive and social development that it is more influential than the libidinous factors described by Freud in shaping our personalities. Kagan asserts that children are most powerfully influenced by the puzzles that confront them, demanding to be solved.

Kagan's views have been supported by neuroscientists such as Professor Mark Johnson, associate director of the Centre for Brain and Cognitive Development at Birkbeck College in the University of London. Johnson notes that as children develop, they help to further their own development by actively seeking out *novel* information from their environments. In other words, we have an innate urge to expose ourselves to the shock of the new.

From our earliest years, it's the strange, the new, the surprising—the discrepancies and uncertainties—that most intrigue us and have the biggest effect on the development of our personality. And throughout our lives, it's the unusual events, both pleasant and unpleasant, that we tend to remember most vividly. We note exceptions. We focus on the unusual. We're intrigued by the unexpected.

And we often exaggerate our account of things to make them sound more exciting or dramatic or unusual than they were. The car crash we *nearly* had; the bout of flu that *nearly* put us in hospital; the storm that *nearly* wiped out our street. Traumatic events in our lives are often recounted with a kind of relish—as if we can't tell the story often enough, because it's a reminder that *something was happening to us*. In a sense, we felt more fully alive because we were dealing with a challenge.

No one welcomes disasters—fires, floods, droughts, pandemics, depressions, wars—yet the almost universal human response to crises and catastrophes is that they bring out the best in us; they remind us of what it means to be human. We don't need to be told to be kind to each other when the going gets tough; we are naturally kind. We don't need to be told to make personal sacrifices for the common good when a fire or flood has swept through our town; we just do it.

Here's an extreme case: I recently met a retired American academic who had worked in London in the early 1950s. He told me he was initially shocked, and then intrigued, by the number of Londoners who said to him, 'You know, we really miss the war.' When he looked incredulous, they added,

'Oh, of course we don't miss the bombs, the death, the destruction, the terror of it. What we miss is the solidarity.'

Even the worst cases of instability have their positive side: they shake us from the complacency that stability can induce. If we were slipping into a self-absorbed state, more concerned with our own comfort and pleasure than the needs of our neighbours, a crisis would soon knock that out of us.

Perhaps we were ill-equipped to cope with the demands made on us by the COVID epidemic—lockdowns, masks, keeping our distance from each other, working from home, home-schooling the kids, abandoning travel plans—because life had been *too* stable in the lead-up to the pandemic. Twenty-eight years of uninterrupted economic growth, and the assurance that it would continue, may have lulled us into a self-absorbed torpor. Perhaps that's why our patience ran thin so quickly; perhaps that's why some people protested at the need for any sacrifice—even the 'sacrifice' of having to receive a potentially life-saving vaccination.

My parents' generation, by contrast, had lived through World War I, the Spanish flu, the Great Depression and World War II. Members of their generation often looked back and were grateful for hardships and privations that had clarified their values and ordered their priorities: 'It was the making of us.' They had no experience of sustained stability, nor any reason to expect it.

I still love this passage from P.G. Wodehouse's *Summer Lightning*, the gentle irony disguising a serious truth about us all—that we are only made strong by having to deal with the vicissitudes of life:

When some outstanding disaster happens to the ordinary man, it finds him prepared. Years of missing the eight-forty-five, taking the dog for a run on rainy nights, endeavouring to abate smoky chimneys, and coming down to breakfast and discovering that they have burned the bacon again, have given his soul a protective hardness, so that by the time his wife's relatives arrive for a long visit, he is ready for them.

Given the facts, why do we cling to this fantasy that what we thrive on is stability and certainty? Obviously, there are times when we feel we've had quite enough drama for the time being, thank you—times when we do wish for a little calm before the next storm, when we'd like to be able to report that everything is 'steady as she goes', precisely because we know those periods are the exceptions. It's more normal to be dealing with challenges and setbacks—in the family, at work, with our health, among our friends. Instability is the stuff of life.

Not entirely, though. Most people in a loving relationship would prefer that it went on as it is, without the threat of inconstancy. Most of us yearn to be securely loved, rather than having to live with the uncertainty of unresolved tensions or half-hearted commitments.

A stable, loving, committed relationship is like a shelter in a storm. A safe place. When so much going on around us seems to point to instability—from relationship crises among friends and family, to the threats posed by climate change— we cherish that one piece of stability all the more.

***

Here's another sign of the stability paradox: adventure holidays. If your life is not providing you with enough uncertainty and unpredictability, you might care for a bit of skydiving, paraskiing or jet boating. White-water rafting, anyone? The adrenaline rush associated with 'adventure' is a proven refresher. Even the thrill of a rollercoaster ride at a theme park is actively sought by people who know they will be energised by the experience of something that feels like danger.

We all know that vigorous cardiovascular exercise—its own form of disruption—strengthens the heart and the blood vessels that supply the brain and helps people feel mentally sharper. Gentler pursuits like walking or cycling have obvious physical benefits as well, but they carry an additional advantage—they expose us to new situations, a changing scene and the possibility of unplanned conversations. Personal encounters of all kinds—talking, interacting, engaging—are a critical source of brain stimulation, and we know that the brain can retain its plasticity well into old age if it is being regularly and sufficiently stimulated. Too much stability is bad for your brain!

Why do we like card games, board games, crosswords and puzzles so much? Because of the emotional arousal associated with being at the mercy of the unknown and having to meet the challenges posed by the game. Why do people get so worked up over sporting contests? Because, even as spectators, they thrive on their sense of engagement with the action, the challenge, the excitement . . . and the unpredictability of the outcome. (Notice how the crowds tend to stay away from a sporting fixture whose outcome they regard as a foregone conclusion.)

In those ways, we're much the same as we were when we were young—bored by the familiar and the predictable, constantly seeking new worlds to conquer, deliberately exposing ourselves to uncertainty.

More dramatically, some people deliberately resign from a job that's going well, just to try their hand at something new. Others leave a well-paid job and pull the children out of school to take an extended overseas trip, or tow a caravan around Australia on the grounds that 'you don't want to die wondering'.

Even more dramatically, here's what Margaret Thatcher, the British prime minister who waged war with Argentina over control of the Falkland Islands, told a Scottish Conservative Party conference in 1982: 'It is exciting to have a real crisis on your hands, when you have spent half your political life dealing with humdrum issues like the environment.' Ouch.

To stay sharp, we need things to happen. We need unexpected events—surprises, even emergencies—to crash into our lives and disturb our complacency. We derive very little benefit from following the same routine, day after dreary day: even negative disruptions—illness, failure, retrenchment, disappointment, disaster, loss—teach us far more about ourselves (and about what it means to be human) than we can ever learn from breezing through the easy stuff.

Next time you find yourself wishing for a quiet life, be grateful that yours isn't.

Fake wisdom: The mass media are more powerful than we are.

I once toyed with an idea for a short story to be called 'The Television Bug', about an evil genius who was developing a weird kind of virus that could be transmitted via TV broadcasts, thus infecting entire viewing audiences.

The idea was that these viruses would somehow carry with them the essence of the messages embedded in the program content. When they were transmitted via commercials, viewers would fall in helplessly with the advertisers' recommended courses of action. Thanks to these bugs, political broadcasts would have a previously undreamed-of power to persuade. When the bugs were transmitted during programs showing violence and mayhem, the population would be roused to correspondingly aggressive, antisocial behaviour. If they were transmitted via porn movies . . . well, you get the idea. (If I'd been as smart as Richard Dawkins, I might have called them tele-memes.)

In fact, it wasn't such a radical idea. It was simply an extension of a widespread belief that mass media are more powerful than we are.

It's a strange thing, this idea that *mediated* information—that is, information that reaches us indirectly, via some medium or other—has some magical power that direct, person-to-person messages lack. Yet it runs deep in our culture and always has, ever since we started drawing pictures on cave walls or writing stories and poems on papyrus scrolls. It's as though placing a message in the context of a medium—*any* medium—imbues it with the power of that medium and makes it seem more significant than the things we simply say to each other.

'I'll wait until I see it in writing,' we say, assuming that a written message has more validity than a spoken one. 'I know he loves me—he sent me a text that said so' is only a minor variation on the traditional punch packed by a love letter.

In a moment, we'll consider what Canadian philosopher Marshall McLuhan might have meant when he so famously suggested that 'the medium is the message'. For now, we could certainly say (rather more prosaically) that the medium—*any* medium—seems to amplify the perceived significance of the messages it carries. A message delivered on TV is more likely to be taken seriously than the very same message delivered across the breakfast table. A meal photographed and posted on Snapchat becomes somehow more significant than the one sitting in front of you on your plate. Indeed, photos—in any setting—are another example of the phenomenon: you knew your sister had a new baby because she told you on the phone, but now you see the photo . . . and, wow, there it is. (This is partly a function of the fact that the eye beats the ear, every time.)

Actually, my favourite media story concerns a baby photo. A mother is walking her baby in a pram when a passer-by stops her and says, 'What a beautiful baby!' The mother replies, 'That's nothing—you should see her photo.' A curious extension of that same idea is now occurring in the offices of plastic surgeons who have to deal with people requesting surgery that will make them look like the airbrushed and photoshopped images of themselves they have posted on social media. (The phenomenon has come to be known in the profession as 'Snapchat dysmorphia'.)

***

Before we venture any further into the realm of social media, let's focus on this idea that *mass* media hold some special power over us . . .

People who feel disgruntled about the state of contemporary society are always on the lookout for a scapegoat: it might be the decline of 'traditional values', the lack of visionary leadership or the impact of neoliberal economics. Over the decades of conducting hundreds of research projects exploring Australians' attitudes, beliefs, dreams and nightmares, the most consistent focus for such blame has been 'the media'.

I've lost count of the number of times I've heard people say, 'Television has made us a more violent society' (though we're actually becoming *less* violent), or 'Don't you think the media are teaching our children an undesirable set of values?' (though media content can't compete with parental example or peer-group pressure when it comes to influences on children's values), or 'The Murdoch press has a huge influence on elections' (even though there have been many occasions, including the 2022 federal election, where the Murdoch press backed the wrong horse). Newspaper editorials may gravely advise their readers how to vote at elections, but readers will please themselves, based on their own experience, their own expectations and their own dreams.

Yet the temptation to overestimate the effects of the mass media on our attitudes and behaviour is very strong. It's a view the media themselves would like to encourage, of course: they'd like you to think they're powerful, so you will take their content more seriously. And they'd like their advertisers to think the same thing. It goes without saying—given all we know about attitude formation—that the mass media can play a very important (even powerful) role in *reinforcing* attitudes that already exist. Indeed, rather like going to church, that's the whole point of reading particular newspapers, listening to particular radio presenters or watching particular TV current affairs shows: we want to hear the day's news, sure, but even more, we love to have our existing convictions strengthened, our existing worldview confirmed and our existing values burnished.

It's all in the eye of the beholder, of course. In the week when Jacinda Ardern resigned as New Zealand's prime minister, I was shown *The Australian*'s coverage and thought it read like a parody of extreme right-wing journalism. In fact, I fleetingly wondered whether I was seeing a mocked-up hoax rather than the real thing. Others I discussed it with simply regarded it as an entirely realistic, justifiable condemnation of a naive and ineffective leader who couldn't lead.

Which of us was right? As with every other form of human communication, there's a basic 'law' operating: it's not what the message does to the audience but what the audience does with the message that determines the outcome. If you enjoy watching Sky News's 'After Dark' programming, that might be because you can immerse yourself in the warm bath of familiar prejudice, or because you enjoy being outraged by hearing views you furiously disagree with, or perhaps because you occasionally want to check up on what 'the other side' is up to. Whatever your motivation for tuning in, the least likely outcome is that your existing attitudes will be changed.

***

One of the most cited books in the history of mass-media research is Joseph Klapper's *The Effects of Mass Communication*, published in 1960—one of a spate of books published in the 1960s that revolutionised our understanding of the process and effects of mass communication. It made the persuasive point that *audiences do things with television programs*, rather than television programs doing things to audiences. The overwhelming message of those early researchers was that the TV audience is active, not passive, in its approach to mass media, and that the media tend to play a reinforcing rather than a converting role. Reinforcement is an effect, of course, but it's not the effect so many people feared back then, or that many people still fear today.

Interactive online games are a very different matter: the recurring theme of parents of kids who have become addicted to video games is that 'they are like different people—they go into the zone—they're rude to me and they get really angry when you tell them to stop'. But, generally speaking, TV itself has never been like that in its effect on viewers, young or old, because it's not interactive. However involved we may be, we're still observers, not participants.

How easy it is to believe—and yet how wrong—that watching a particular kind of TV program, such as crime drama, will shape our attitudes and behaviour in ways that mimic the program content. Whether it's crime or politics, the word 'brainwashing' is often used. But there's an important caveat that suggests we're more aware of our ability to filter and interpret media content than we might care to admit: most of the concerns about brainwashing, and about the political effects of media bias, are assumed to apply to 'other people'—people more naive than me, people less informed than me, people more gullible than me.

TV has been part of Australian life for almost seventy years. By now, surely, we should be wary of the idea that televised messages have some irresistible power over us. Where are those magic advertising campaigns that were going to convert us all into brand-obedient automatons? Where are those televangelists who were going to stimulate a religious revival by harnessing the power of the media? Where are the famous examples of election campaigns that swayed the electorate to vote against its better judgement? They don't exist.

It would be absurd to suggest that watching TV or reading newspapers or listening to radio has no effect on us at all. If we read or see or hear something in the media that we have no way of testing against our own experience, we'll naturally be inclined to accept that it's true, assuming we trust the source. But picking up information from the media is a relatively trivial 'effect' if that information has no particular relevance to the way we live. Media content is often, perhaps mostly, mere fodder for subsequent idle chatter. 'I heard a thing on the radio this morning about censorship in Indonesia', or 'I saw a really interesting panel discussion about global warming—I think it's already out of control. You should have seen this woman's earrings, though. I found it hard to take her seriously', or 'I cried through most of *Home and Away* last night. I felt really sorry for Kirby'.

It's important to distinguish between program content effects and the effects of exposure to the medium itself. 'The medium is the message' is now a mere cliché, but when the phrase was first used in the 1960s by Marshall McLuhan, it shook the media research community by alerting us to the fact that the most *significant* effects of the mass media on people's lives were unrelated to program content, but were a function of the character of the media themselves.

We've already discussed the effects of the switch from an oral culture to a print culture. The same kind of analysis can be made for the switch from print to an audiovisual culture dominated by television.

In fact, the primary effect of the media lies simply in the time we devote to media consumption that might have been devoted to other things, such as talking to each other. Writing in *The New York Times*, economist and author Jonathan Rothwell cites research that shows a slight but steady decline in IQ among heavy consumers of television, apparently associated with the decline in reading and social interaction—both regarded as potential IQ boosters.

There are some educational programs that are deemed capable of boosting IQ measurements (about which I'm personally sceptical, by the way), and the introduction of TV to some parts of India was historically associated with inspiring a greater push for equality among women. But the overall impression to emerge from the most recent research only confirms what media research has been saying for more than sixty years: we use the mass media to serve our own ends, and the media's effects are less to do with the content of the programs we watch and more to do with the nature and extent of our relationship with each medium ... and with what we are *not* doing (such as talking to someone) when we are watching TV, for example.

Apart from the self-evident uses of the media for 'information and entertainment', and for the gratifications associated with reinforcement of existing attitudes and prejudices and the pleasure of identifying with particular characters in particular programs, many people use the media to keep them company. Radio does that best of all by creating the illusion that someone is talking directly to us. But many TV viewers—especially those who live alone—treat the television as a companion, and report that they talk to the screen, or simply leave the TV on as a comforting 'presence' in the house. Strong emotional bonds can develop between viewers and particular presenters—'Oh, we love Laura'—but many viewers describe their TV itself as if it's a kind of 'perfect person' with whom they can have the ideal relationship. It's reliably there, often amusing or stimulating, sometimes serious and informative, but never offended if you fall asleep in front of it or shout back at it.

We also use the mass media as a pastime—literally a way of passing the time—where our demands are very modest: keep me mildly entertained, stimulated, distracted or tranquillised when I have nothing better to do.

***

The 'fake wisdom' on this issue—that we are somehow the victims of mass-media power—deeply concerns me not only because it happens to be wrong, but also because it represents an abdication of the responsibility we all bear for the way we choose to spend our time, and the way we monitor our children's time usage. Imagine if it were true that the mass media are more powerful than we are; imagine being driven this way or that by the things we watch on TV, listen to on the radio or read in newspapers and magazines. The truth is that *we* are in control here: we ourselves make the choices to watch or not watch, to listen or not listen, to read or not read. And then we either ignore what we've seen or heard because it doesn't relate to us or, if it does seem relevant, we interpret it *in our own way.*

To repeat the central message: the media we fear for their awesome power are, in general, powerful only in their ability to please us by reinforcing what we already believe. In his heyday on Sydney radio station 2GB, broadcaster Alan Jones 'ruled the airwaves' ... which meant that he had the highest-rating program in Sydney's crowded radio market, peaking at about 17 per cent of the available morning radio audience. Which meant that more than 80 per cent of Sydney radio listeners never tuned into his show.

Powerful? Jones's political influence was formidable but, as far as his audience was concerned, it's a safe bet that he was preaching to the converted and the converted loved being preached to (as the converted always do). Ben Fordham, who now occupies Jones's former slot, attracts a similar-sized audience, which suggests that's about the size of the audience who are looking for that kind of content.

When it comes to the mass media, the *real* power lies with the audience, in our ability to switch off, literally or meta-phorically, and in our ability to interpret what we see and hear to suit ourselves. In his *London Review of Books* review of Prince Harry's autobiography, *Spare,* Andrew O'Hagan wrote that 'The press is only as powerful as Harry allows it to be: it's his monster, and he gives it oxygen.' Correct. And that applies to all of us.

Fake wisdom: Social media can satisfy our need to belong.

In 'The Context', I described social isolation as our number-one public health issue, because 25 per cent of Australian adults have reported feeling lonely most of the time and because of all the negative health consequences that flow from loneliness. I also mentioned that the loneliest age group in our society are those aged eighteen to twenty-five, who also happen to be the heaviest users of social media.

Happen to be? That makes it sound like mere coincidence. In fact, it's no accident that the heaviest users of social media would feel the loneliest. After all, they have chosen to trade off so much social interaction time in favour of digital, screen-based exchanges that it's not at all surprising they would experience Michelle Lim's 'social hunger'—whether they realise it or not.

That piece of information alone should be enough to convince you that online connections are so profoundly different from face-to-face connections that it's actually absurd—though very clever of the IT industry that has spawned them—for online platforms to be described as 'social' media. *Antisocial* might be closer to the mark. Or perhaps *subsocial* or *quasi-social*. Labels like those would at least remind us that what we're doing when we connect via Facebook, X (formerly Twitter), Snapchat, Instagram, TikTok or any other online media platform is not what we normally mean by 'social', and we do ourselves a massive disservice when we attempt to use one as a substitute for the other.

Don't get me wrong. I fully grasp the value of online platforms. They are wonderful 'message boards' for family members and friends who can't manage regular face-to-face meetings, allowing them to stay in touch with each other's activities—complete with photographic evidence of everything from a new baby to a delicious meal. And, within friendship circles, such media can be a very neat way of exchanging quips and comments on the day's events, gossip or any other bits of information that don't warrant a face-to-face meeting or a phone call—perhaps because the circle is too far-flung to make such encounters feasible.

Better than nothing? Sure. Brilliant at maintaining a sense of connection with people you know and want to stay connected with? No question.

But do these media satisfy our need to belong, or to be heard, as folk wisdom is now so fond of claiming? Are the dozens or hundreds of social media 'friends' actually *friends*? As Melbourne oncologist Ranjana Srivastava wrote in the *New England Journal of Medicine*: 'Our social networks may appear to be larger these days, but they're increasingly virtual and fragile. Facebook friends seldom appear at the bedside with magazines or flowers. Twitter is no match for real conversation.'

Are online groups really like face-to-face groups? Two words should be enough to dispel that idea: *eye contact*. If it's present, then we're in a situation where our need to belong and our need to feel as if we are being heard have some chance of being satisfied. If it's absent, there is simply no chance at all. It might *feel* like 'belonging'; we might *feel* as if we're being heard in the same way as if we were face to face with the

107

other person. But that's a dangerous delusion. If we indulge it, IT can lead us into that sad state of being 'connected but lonely' . . . and we probably won't even realise it's happening to us, because there's so much activity, so many exchanges, so much traffic on that little screen. Surely, with all that going on, I'm satisfying my need to belong? I *feel* as if I'm accepted here—in fact (as some social media users say), 'I feel more accepted here than I do in my own family.' While that may well be literally true for those users, the challenge, ultimately, is to find a place of acceptance and belonging 'IRL' rather than via a screen-based device.

There's something of the self-fulfilling prophecy here: the more time we spend on quasi–social media platforms, the more 'at home' we will feel there, scarcely noticing that the whole thing is so artificial—two-dimensional, for a start—that it is simply incapable of satisfying our deep human need for face-to-face interactions based on eye contact. (Ask any neuro-scientist; ask any clinical psychologist.) Social connections via eye contact make a crucial contribution to our mental and emotional health.

Again, I emphasise that I'm not opposed to 'social media'. Again, I emphasise that I fully grasp the valuable role they can play in our lives. All I'm saying is that they need to be kept in perspective; they need to be kept in their place.

Writing for *The New York Times* in 1998, years before Facebook or Twitter (now X) took off—though there were already a few early social media sites around, but at a time when email had become an established part of life—American novelist Richard Ford said this:

I don't have E-mail. I'm not on the Internet. I don't have
a cell phone or call waiting or even a beeper. And I'm not
proud of it, since my fear, I guess, is that if someone wants
to find me using all or any of these means, but can't find me,
they will conclude that, for technical reasons, I don't exist
any more.

(Even as I type Ford's words into my computer, it's urging
me to conflate 'any more' into 'anymore', which would be
grammatically incorrect in this context and so I'll resist that
digital nudge.)

Ford was not alone back then in wondering whether he
didn't exist if he didn't have email. Today, in spite of its many
attractions and advantages—its speed, efficiency, convenience
and encouragement of more informal communication—many
users are wondering whether email is a kind of electronic quick-
sand that will suck us down and eventually smother us. That's
certainly a feeling I have when I return from a break away
from email—on holiday, for instance, or during an extended
period of uninterrupted writing—to find hundreds of emails
banked up, needing to be sorted and, in a tiny minority of
cases, responded to. The strong preference for SMS texts over
email, particularly among younger users, suggests that texts
and instant voice messaging feel like the logical 'next step',
being even faster and more informal than email.

But Ford's broader point is still valid today, in the context
of burgeoning social media: are we going to fall for the trap of
thinking that if we're not on Facebook, X, Snapchat or Instagram, we don't really exist? Are we so desperate to be 'in touch'
that we have actually confused data exchange with personal

relationships? Are we so afraid of 'missing out' that we're prepared to sacrifice time we might spend with family, friends or neighbours in favour of watching that screen, just in case something pops up that we 'need' to know? Have we become so subservient to online culture that we prefer watching total strangers' short videos on TikTok to hearing our friends or neighbours telling us what happened to them yesterday?

You've seen it happen at a family gathering, or with a group of friends over coffee: one or two of those present are surreptitiously—or, increasingly, quite openly—scrolling through messages on their smartphones, perhaps smiling or frowning, perhaps even dashing off a quick response and then, eyes glazed, smiling vaguely as they try to look as if they're still connected to the here-and-now, flesh-and-blood, three-dimensional group around them.

And we're so familiar with the phone-victim phenomenon in restaurants, it's become a trope of contemporary life.

There are people whose lives and careers have been badly damaged by the attacks on them on social media. Question: why do they even look at what's being said about them? Why would you want to read something that's slanderous, poisonous and calculated to erode your self-confidence, especially when it's anonymous? Social media—except when you're dealing with people actually, personally known to you—is, after all, the ultimate coward's castle. It's where bitter, angry, frustrated, disappointed, prejudiced, confused and lonely ('socially hungry') people can lash out and say whatever they like about anything or anyone without fear of repercussions. No accountability. No means of redress for the harm they cause. It's a safe haven for malefactors.

People may say—people *do* say—that it's essential to their work to know what people are saying about them . . . or saying about anything. Some believe it's vital to stay in touch with 'what's trending on Twitter', as if that's a kind of finger-on-the-pulse exercise. In fact, it couldn't be further removed from the rigorous procedures of valid public opinion research—which is where you go if you *really* want to know what people are thinking.

But enough of that. I'm not on social media and I expect to make it to my grave without being exposed to the abuse that may well be lurking out there in cyberspace. People occasionally used to write me nasty letters written on paper, most of them anonymous. At least the digital revolution has put a stop to that.

***

When social media are kept in their place: *good*. When social media are such a big feature of your daily schedule that you can't imagine a day without them: *hazardous*. When social media are eating into time that might otherwise be spent nurturing your personal relationships: *bad*.

If you delude yourself into believing that your social media connections are just like your face-to-face connections, you may well be at risk of ending up in the 'connected but lonely' category.

If you find yourself complaining that you're too busy and that one of the demands on your time is the weight of social media posts, think again. As with the mass media, so with social media: all the power lies with us. It is in our power to switch off—even for days at a time—and it is certainly in our power to filter what we expose ourselves to, and to monitor the time we (and our kids) are spending in that other world.

It's a tough discipline, for ourselves and our children, to switch off or even to cut down, because we're up against the smartest industry in human history. It's an industry that designs its products to draw us in and keep us there. Those products reward us for staying. They pander to our interests and reinforce our prejudices like nothing else on earth does. They are *designed* to get us addicted. The infamous 'social media echo chamber' actually works. Switching off can feel like . . . abandonment.

If you need guidance—and some practical tips—to help you move social media (and IT more generally) from master to servant in your life, Kristy Goodwin's 2023 book *Dear Digital, We Need to Talk* is a good place to start. And let's not forget the Grand Human Project in which we are all supposed to be engaged. Building social harmony. Maintaining social cohesion. Responding to people's need of us, of our *presence*.

You have family connections to nurture. If you're a parent, you have kids who need you to hang out with them—not for a bit of carefully scheduled 'quality time' but just . . . time. You have friends who need to see you, who need the comfort and reassurance of regular eye contact with you. You have work colleagues who want to feel as if you take them seriously enough to listen patiently and attentively to them. You have neighbours who would like to know you well enough to be sure they could call on you in a crisis, or even for a cup of tea if they're feeling a bit lonely.

Now ... when all that's done (*and* you've worked, slept and eaten), how much time is left in a day? By all means, devote some of it to social media use, but don't ever assume that what you're doing online is in the same league as those things that really do satisfy the deep human yearning for a sense of belonging.

In an interview for *The Saturday Paper*, Lally Katz, one of our most prolific playwrights, succinctly captured the difference between being connected online and being connected to the community you're actually living in: 'I left social media because it was causing me so much anxiety. It also made me lose my own life. We are constantly seeing these other lives and saying, I should be there, I should be doing that. When really, all we need to do is look at what is around us.'

***

It is 'fake wisdom' to suggest that our need for a sense of belonging can be satisfied on social media. In the case of children and adolescents, however, that 'wisdom' is not only fake but dangerous.

There's mounting concern among experts in the field about children engaging with social media before they are mature enough to understand and avoid some of its pitfalls—including the possibility of online bullying and abuse. In 2023, the US surgeon general, Dr Vivek Murthy, expressed the opinion that, in the light of all the information available to him, 'thirteen is too early ... the skewed and often distorted environment of social media often does a disservice to many of those children'.

That strongly echoes the views of US psychologist and adolescence researcher Jean Twenge, perhaps the greatest authority on the impact of the new technologies on immature minds. Twenge says, unequivocally, that she would not give a smartphone to anyone under the age of fourteen and, even then, she would advise parents to install an app that limits an adolescent's use to ninety minutes per day. Twenge's research has led her to conclude that 'the more time teens spend looking at screens, the more likely they are to report symptoms of depression'. (*Connected but lonely*, again?)

Fake wisdom: To change people's behaviour, you must first change their minds.

In the Age of Opinion, when we attach so much importance to 'what people think', this has become such a popular assertion that I hesitate even to challenge it. But challenge it I must, because . . . it's wrong. Or, at least, it's wrong far more often than it's right. But you can see where the 'wisdom' comes from. Sigmund Freud told us that 'the thought is father to the deed' (which doesn't help to explain 'thoughtless' behaviour, be it the recklessness of passion or the mindlessness of hooliganism, nor the many thoughts—especially those involving conscious intentions or resolutions—that never make it into action). It's a short step from that fake wisdom to the conviction that, if we see some behaviour we want to change—drink driving, for instance, or children who leave their dirty clothes strewn all over their bedroom floor—we must first work on the 'thought that is father to such deeds' or, in other words, the attitudes we assume have given rise to that behaviour. Surely, we say to ourselves, if we can persuade people to change their *minds* about drinking and driving, or using the bedroom floor as a wardrobe-cum-washing basket, then, in a direct causal leap from mind to action, they will stop doing it. *Easy!*

Our own experience should have taught us that it doesn't work like that, but the conventional wisdom seems so plausible that we cling to it. (Ahoy, Dunning–Kruger!)

Commercial marketing people fall for the same trap. 'We have to change the consumer's attitude,' they say, when in fact what they really want to change is consumer behaviour and they are deluding themselves about how best to do it—using 'persuasive' advertising, for example, rather than dropping the price or improving the product's performance.

To get to the nub of the issue, let's first ask ourselves this: what makes people behave the way they do? The short answer is that they respond to the influences of the social and physical environment in which they're operating, which includes everything from parental example to urban design, and from workplace design to the weather. Yes, there are genetic dispositions, there are sometimes powerful 'inner voices' that drive us and there are bodily needs that drive us, too. But, overwhelmingly, our patterns of behaviour are shaped by our social and physical environment—from infancy onward.

In the case of that commercial example I mentioned, we're far more likely to be influenced by direct marketplace pressures on our behaviour—things like price, availability and the performance of the product—than indirect appeals to 'the mind' via advertising.

Underneath all that lies another simple truth about human behaviour: we tend to take the line of least resistance. If it's

115

easier to drop your dirty clothes on the floor than take them to the laundry basket, and you can get away with it, that's a pretty powerful motivator to keep on doing it. If you're happy with the product you're using, why change?

Think about the process of attitude formation. Mostly it's about us learning from our personal experience: what happens to us forms our attitudes and beliefs. Sometimes, 'what happens to us' includes what people say to us—especially if they are people in authority and/or people we admire—but where our own experience can be used to test the validity, or the appeal, of something we're being told, the lessons from that experience will prevail.

That's another way of saying 'behaviour causes attitudes', which is far closer to the truth than 'attitudes cause behaviour'. Our environment shapes our behaviour; behaviour creates 'experience'; experience, in turn, leads us to form opinions, attitudes and beliefs about the way the world works.

Some examples. The advent of the contraceptive pill changed attitudes towards sex and parenthood. The development of the morning-after pill changed attitudes towards abortion and, indeed, blurred the distinction between contraception and abortion. New technologies (ranging from the printing press to the internal combustion engine, from personal computers to smartphones, from ATMs to robots in factories) create new experiences that change attitudes to information, travel, work, leisure, money and shopping. The fast-food revolution changes our eating patterns and, inevitably, our attitudes to cooking, eating and nutrition are affected. Increasing life expectancy—along with myriad other factors—changes the way young people approach marriage and parenthood (including the choice of the 'right time' to have children). A change in the price of things can change our purchasing behaviour and, in the process, our attitudes. The impact of price rises on cigarette sales has been one of the most effective ways of reducing the incidence of smoking and, in the housing market, if you simply can't afford to buy a house, you might well come to believe that there are all sorts of advantages to renting.

This is one reason why the various forms of cognitive behavioural therapy have become such a popular branch of psychotherapy. Because these therapies focus on behaviour change, rather than trying to address the antecedents of the problem behaviour, they can often produce positive and rapid results, especially in changing addictive or compulsive behaviour, or behaviour associated with PTSD.

***

It would be wrong to be too black and white about this. The attitude–behaviour link obviously carries two-way traffic, but the greatest volume of traffic by far is travelling from behaviour/experience *to* attitudes, not the other way around. To complete the picture, it's fair to say that experience shapes our attitudes and those attitudes, in turn, may well influence our future behaviour. Attitudes are a key part of the process of learning from experience, but they are not usually the starting point.

People typically (but not always) express attitudes that seem consistent with their behaviour, so it's tempting to say, 'Ah, that person behaved like that because of the attitudes they hold.' Tempting, but simplistic. Even when we acknowledge the subtlety and complexity of the attitude–behaviour link, the evidence strongly points to a different conclusion: that person holds those attitudes because of their patterns of previous behaviour—their personal experience.

Not everyone enjoys the comfort of attitudes and behaviour that 'line up'. But saying one thing and doing another, or behaving in a way that's inconsistent with your beliefs, is a pretty uncomfortable state to be in. The pioneering American psychologist Leon Festinger made a serious study of the relationship between attitudes and behaviour, focusing particular attention on the emotional problem created for us when our attitudes and behaviour are out of kilter. When we think one way but act in another, we experience what Festinger called 'cognitive dissonance'—a fancy way of saying 'mental disharmony'.

Our natural reaction to the experience of cognitive dissonance is to look for ways of closing the gap between the inconsistent attitude and behaviour. The big question for Festinger was: how will we do it?

If you really believe that attitudes are the cause of behaviour, then the logical answer to that question is that people will modify their behaviour to align it more closely to the attitudes they profess to hold. In practice, Festinger found, the more likely response is that we will shift our attitudes to line up with our pattern of behaviour.

You can see that process in action on a national scale when you ponder the effects of the changes that have been reshaping Australian society over the past fifty years. When a society becomes more fragmented and less cohesive, our behaviour changes: we become more individualistic, more competitive, more materialistic. And then, in turn, our attitudes and values begin to shift: we become more narcissistic, less empathic, more obsessed with individual entitlements and questions of *personal* identity.

But let's look at the process at the level of the individual. Suppose you're a basically honest person who believes in truth-telling as far as possible. Your attitude, learned from your own experiences through childhood and adolescence, and into adulthood, is that 'it pays to tell the truth'. Now suppose you take a job with a public relations firm and find yourself working for a client who needs you to 'spin' a series of media releases to make it seem as if her company is more public spirited and socially responsible than you know it to be. You turn out to be rather good at creating the media releases the client wants, and you attract high praise from both your client and your employer. In fact, before long, your services are in increasing demand from other clients of the firm who want to harness your ability to put the most positive spin on awkward situations.

A couple of friends who have known you well over many years take you to task for the job you're now doing. Without any hesitation, you find yourself justifying the idea that these are well-meaning people you represent. They are doing their best in difficult circumstances and are trying to make up for the mistakes of the past. And, in any case, no one is all bad: even companies that might have damaged the environment can be sorry for what they've done and donate huge sums of money to worthy causes . . .

Your friends are aghast but all that's happened is what usually happens: your attitudes have gradually shifted to line up with your new patterns of behaviour. And you probably *do* experience these new clients as pleasant, sincere, well-meaning people in your personal dealings with them. When your friends describe some of your media releases as dishonest, you're outraged. 'You simply don't understand the big picture,' you say, 'or the way these things work.'

People who experience religious conversion often do so in response to changes in their circumstances that lead them to perceive religious messages in a new light. Their attitudes have changed because their experience of the world has changed, perhaps because of bereavement, or retrenchment, or a life-threatening illness ... or perhaps because they've fallen in love with a person of strong religious faith.

The popular saying that 'travel broadens the mind' captures the same idea: exposure to new and different experiences—especially those that enable us to experience other cultures—has an illuminating effect on our own attitudes, often expanding our minds in new directions. A friend has described the effect on her parents of their first overseas trip, taken late in life: from having previously been rather straitlaced, judgemental people, they became far more tolerant, cheerful and easy to live with.

Racial prejudice, similarly, can be broken down by the experience of getting to know someone from a previously despised ethnic group—though prejudices can be so strong that, even in such a situation, people may say, 'Oh, *he's* a good bloke, but I still don't trust the rest of them.'

It's an inexorably predictable process: we cling to our existing attitudes until *something happens* that disrupts previous patterns of behaviour and threatens us with cognitive dissonance if we don't change our tune.

New *information*, on its own, has far less chance of changing us than new experience does, simply because it's so easy for us to filter, distort and misinterpret the new information in ways that allow us to remain comfortable with our framework of existing attitudes and beliefs.

***

Once we understand where our patterns of behaviour come from, we know where to look for clues about how to *change* people's behaviour. So let's go back to those two examples I mentioned: drink driving and messy kids.

For years, governments around the world have grappled with the problem of drink driving. Millions—billions— of dollars have been spent in media campaigns designed to change drivers' attitudes by warning them of the dangers of drinking and driving. These have ranged from attempts at rational argument, showing how even one drink can adversely affect your reaction time, to graphic pictures of the carnage caused by drink driving, to explicit abuse of offenders, as in a Victorian campaign that declared: 'If you drink then drive, you're a bloody idiot.'

Many such campaigns can rightfully claim to have changed attitudes, at least as far as attitude measurement is possible. But 'changed attitudes' can be an almost meaningless concept unless the change has been wrought by some change in people's actual experience. It's easy enough to *say*, 'Oh, yes, drink driving is dangerous and we shouldn't do it', but still feel there are circumstances in which it's justified or simply unavoidable—or even, as a research respondent once said to me: 'I reckon a couple of drinks actually sharpen me up a bit.'

All this can happen with no significant change in drivers' behaviour. Surely it's not *attitudes* we want to change, it's behaviour.

How? The most effective intervention in the drink-driving environment has been the introduction of random breath testing. Not as effective as a device that would make it impossible to start a car if your blood-alcohol reading is over the limit, but still pretty good. And it's changed driving *behaviour* in a way no previous 'attitude-change' campaigns have ever managed.

The coda to the story is that, inevitably, attitudes towards drink driving have changed quite radically in the wake of widespread behaviour change.

You want drivers to slow down? Install speed humps and chicanes. You want fewer crashes? Make cars and roads safer. Change the systems, change the driving environment and watch driver behaviour change.

And the kids' dirty clothes on the bedroom floor? The solution is certainly not to nag—surely experience has taught us the futility of nagging. The solution is to look at the environment in which the behaviour is occurring and see how we can change that. A *system* change. How about the exasperated parent saying: 'New arrangement as from today. I don't pick up any clothes from the floor, and I don't wash anything that isn't in the laundry basket. If it's not in the basket, it doesn't get washed. That's the system.'

The first time a particular item of clothing is expected to have been washed, there'll be cries of protest: 'But you *knew* I needed my sports uniform for Thursday. I can't wear it looking like this.'

Answer: 'Not my problem. I wash what's in the laundry basket. If it wasn't in the basket it wasn't washed.' No need to nag; just change the system. Change the environment and watch the behaviour change in response. Not overnight, but inevitably.

Here's my favourite domestic example. In spite of being reminded many times, a boy fails to wipe his feet whenever he enters the back door of his home, and often trails mud into the house. 'He's got a poor attitude,' says his irritated father.

Maybe; maybe not. His attitude is irrelevant. It's his behaviour that annoys his parents.

Solution: Lock the back door when the boy is outside. (A significant change in the environment.) When he tries to come in, the parent asks, 'Have you wiped your feet? When you've wiped your feet, I'll open the door.'

It won't change behaviour miraculously in one go. But do it four or five times and the new system will have registered. The habit will be established.

Loud protest from parents: 'Who's got time to go locking the door four or five times? Why can't he just do as he's told? I've told him often enough.'

Response: Locking the door and asking the question a few times will take far less time and effort than endless nagging and unpleasant altercations. Short-term inconvenience, yes, but a lowering of the frustration level for all concerned and a reasonable prospect of success. And never a mention of attitudes.

Every manager knows that the layout of an office and the nature of the office systems will have a direct effect on the work practices and productivity of the people who work there. Illumination levels, noise, territorial spaces, privacy, access to windows, visual distractions . . . all such factors influence the way we behave, and changes in them can produce dramatic improvements or deterioration in the quality of the work being done. In turn, *attitudes* to the organisation, and to work itself, may also change.

This is not to say there's no role for messages in the process of changing people's behaviour. We need to discuss the changes we want, and explain any system changes we're making, and then we need to offer positive reinforcement of the changed behaviour, most easily through praise.

Back to the marketing example. If you want to change consumer behaviour in response to your brand, improve the product, give away samples, do in-store demonstrations, drop the price, improve the display, change the pack . . . *do* things that alter the environment in which consumers behave. Then use your advertising campaign to reinforce the new attitudes that flow from those new experiences.

Next time you hear someone say, 'I think we've got an attitude problem', try replying, 'Isn't it a behaviour problem we've got?' That will refocus the conversation.

Don't plead with people to change; make change easy and attractive by tweaking the environment they operate in.

Fake wisdom: We should 'maintain the rage'.
The most bizarre moment in the lead-up to the 2023 referendum on the Indigenous Voice to parliament came when former Liberal prime minister John Howard, advocating a 'No' vote, asserted that we should 'maintain the rage'. It was never made clear what particular rage he was talking about, or against whom it should be directed. But he said it as if he believed 'maintaining the rage' was a good thing to do—even the *right* thing to do.

That phrase—'maintain the rage'—was born in the aftermath of the 1975 dismissal of the Whitlam Labor government by the governor-general. The subsequent election campaign run by the Labor Party called on voters who were angry about the dismissal to 'maintain the rage' all the way to polling day. (As it turned out, they didn't: the electorate endorsed the governor-general's action by electing the 'caretaker' government led by Malcolm Fraser.)

The idea that we should 'maintain the rage' has taken hold, more widely, as if there's some value—even some virtue—in staying angry; as if letting go of our anger would somehow be a sign of weakness; as if the outrage we felt at the time we were offended would lose some of its force if we let our passions cool into a more considered response.

Political rage is one thing; personal rage is another. Yes, revolutionaries—like the early women's libbers—are often motivated by their anger over injustice, oppression or inequality, but that is a rather different emotion from the anger we feel towards each other personally. Being consumed by *personal* anger—like being consumed by hate—is a corrosive state that is more likely to inhibit our capacity for effective action than

125

to enhance it. Doing something 'in a rage' rarely ends well for any of us.

I know that what I am about to suggest sounds like a tough call. It *is* a tough call. Yet the most liberating, healing, therapeutic thing we can do for ourselves when we have been wronged or offended by someone is . . . *forgive them*. Research (by Loren Toussaint and Everett Worthington) shows that to be true, but so does common sense. Isn't it obvious? Until we forgive, we are condemned to remain victims.

Naturally, it's easier to forgive when someone has offered us an apology. But even if no apology is forthcoming, even if the perpetrator seems to have 'got away with it', even if it feels as if the perpetrator doesn't even understand that you have been hurt or offended . . . forgiveness is still the best way to resolve the situation. For a start, it will defuse the self-destructive effects of rage.

This is not to suggest for a moment that when we have been hurt, offended or abused, we should 'forgive and forget'. That's unrealistic, unhealthy and unhelpful. Forgiveness has far more potency when we forgive *and remember*. We will not try to pretend that nothing happened but we will go on, knowing that it *did* happen *and* that we have chosen to forgive the person responsible—perhaps warning them that it mustn't happen again.

Nor am I suggesting that perpetrators of criminal behaviour shouldn't be charged with the offences they have committed. Justice must be done. Crimes must be punished. And people who have been involved, for example, in sub-criminal sexual exploitation or harassment or abuse of any kind must be called out—loudly and unambiguously—by their victims, their employers and whoever else has been adversely affected by their behaviour.

People who have wronged or offended should be given the opportunity to apologise and to offer whatever reparation might be appropriate. But even if they don't apologise—perhaps *especially* if they don't apologise—then you yourself have the power to release yourself from the coils of victimhood; you yourself have the power to set yourself free from the corrosive effect of simmering rage and resentment; you yourself—and only you—have the power to shake off that most ruinous, self-destructive of all human temptations: the temptation to exact revenge. It might taste sweet in the short term but, in the end, revenge means you have lowered yourself to the same level as the one who wronged or offended you. It's like wrestling someone in moral mud. It demeans you. It diminishes you. It's undignified, ignoble and unworthy of your best self.

Oh, but it *is* tempting! How delicious it seems in prospect, to make that person pay for what he's done to me. Yet, if I yield to the impulse to take revenge, I will have lost my position of moral strength. I, too, will have behaved badly. I will have compounded the original offence by committing another.

Better, by far, to follow the example of those who have known that the *only* way to rise above the sense of victimhood and the *only* way to break the cycle of enmity is to be true to those 'better angels of our nature' that Abraham Lincoln so eloquently described. As Marcus Aurelius put it in his *Meditations*, 'The best revenge is to be unlike [the person] who performed the injury.'

127

Many people find—sometimes to their own surprise—that once they *cease* 'maintaining the rage', they can find the moral, emotional and spiritual resources to forgive all kinds of wrongs committed against them. Some of the most spectacular examples of forgiveness make the news—like the Abdallah family in Western Sydney who, in 2020, forgave the drunk driver who lost control of the car he was driving and killed three of their children and their niece. Or the Amish community in Nickel Mines, Pennsylvania, who forgave the shooter who killed five teenage girls in the local school in 2006. And while we're considering dramatic examples of the healing power of forgiveness, we must acknowledge the inspirational case of Nelson Mandela, who forgave those who had held him captive for twenty-seven years and went on to become the first black president of South Africa.

Forgiveness is a choice. To choose *not* to forgive is to choose to remain a victim, as if we are determined to hang on to the offence as a way of defining ourselves by constantly refuelling our rage or bitterness: 'Look how badly I've been treated!' But would you ever really want to be defined by your victimhood rather than your nobility? To be defined by your capacity to stay angry rather than your capacity to forgive and get on with your life? Our failure to forgive locks us into that role.

We can't talk about forgiveness without also mentioning humility—the 'queen of virtues', according to French philosopher Simone Weil. To forgive requires humility—the very same quality we need if we are to apologise sincerely. Humility is the sweetest and noblest of all human qualities because it acknowledges our oneness with the frailty of humankind. Even when you've been assaulted, abused, harassed or exploited by other people acting out of malevolence, foolishness or recklessness—or any other form of human frailty—your forgiveness says, in effect, 'You hurt or offended me, but I forgive you because, although we may be frail in different ways, I have my frailties, too.'

Forgiveness is how we take back control. It's a decisive, positive action that helps to heal both the forgiver and the forgiven. By example, it teaches the perpetrator a powerful lesson about the human capacity for dignity, respect, kindness and compassion. Forgiveness is the way we rise above victimhood, and there is no other way to do it.

'Maintain the rage'? Not if you want to bring out the best in yourself.

Fake wisdom: Pork-barrelling buys votes.

To wrap up, I have to share with you this delicious example of fake wisdom from the field of federal politics. You know what pork-barrelling is, right? It's an American expression but, as former NSW premier Gladys Berejiklian described it: 'All governments and all oppositions make commitments to the community in order to curry favour.' That might be the intention of so-called pork-barrelling, but is the conventional wisdom justified?

According to research conducted by the Australian National University's distinguished professor of political science Ian McAllister and federal MP Andrew Leigh, this is 'fake wisdom', too. McAllister and Leigh analysed voting figures for the 2019 federal election, in the wake of a major 'sports rorts' scandal involving the National Party senator Bridget McKenzie and her decision to award a disproportionate number of grants to upgrade sporting facilities in marginal electorates being targeted by the Coalition.

It was widely regarded as a scandal at the time and the process was heavily criticised by the Australian National Audit Office. But did the strategy work? According to McAllister and Leigh, it did not. There was no sign of an increased Coalition vote in those electorates targeted by McKenzie. The researchers speculate that voters' low opinion of politicians—'people in government look after themselves'— might mean that pork-barrelling is simply regarded as normal, as Berejiklian suggested, rather than 'special treatment'. Voters are not mugs—we know when we're being treated cynically. So flagrant 'vote buying' is likely to be a turn-off or, at the very least, a non-event.

And yet, true to the Dunning–Kruger effect, McAllister and Leigh report that in their straw poll of politicians, the overwhelming majority still believe pork-barrelling works.

Reflections ...
- I hope the last few paragraphs of the section on social media and belonging didn't sound preachy. My heart bleeds for people who are trapped in the coils of social media and can't see—can't even imagine—a way out. All I can do is remind us (myself included) of our responsibility to be *present* to each other. Our devices are seductive enough to trick us into thinking we're present, even when we're very clearly absent.
- 'Fake wisdom' is appealing because it has such a plausible ring to it. It sounds sensible. Or perhaps it sounds

appealingly outrageous—like a conspiracy theory that admits you to some secret inside knowledge of how the world *really* works. But we need to guard against accepting propositions that might actually affect the way we live without checking to see if there's any solid evidence to support them. Let's be sure we're not one of those people in whom 'ignorance begets confidence'.

- I'd be the first to admit that making reckless generalisations can be fun. As a researcher, I have often made generalisations, though I hope they were never as reckless as those made by armchair social commentators who have never spent any time closely and sympathetically studying—and listening to—the people whose behaviour they claim to understand. Being opinionated (even outrageously so) among friends has always been part of the currency of social life. But being unjustifiably opinionated in the public marketplace of ideas is a dangerous game. 'Fake wisdom' is always at risk of being exposed by the evidence.

- After all this fake wisdom, now might be a good moment to reflect on the real thing. When we consult the wisdom of the elders—the ancient wisdom of different cultures, different religions, different philosophical traditions—we find a recurring central theme. It's not about the pursuit of happiness, wealth, power or status, but it points to one simple proposition: *We should treat others as we ourselves would want to be treated.* No wonder it's come to be known as the Golden Rule.

3

Are we ready for true gender equality?

There is no doubt that, by the time second-wave feminism found its voice in the early 1970s, we were way overdue for a gender revolution. Until then, we had been a society in which it was simply taken for granted—even by many women—that women were destined to be second-class citizens: the legal system said it, the financial services market said it, the workplace said it and the cultural context certainly said it. Until then, Australian women had been conditioned to accept that they were living in a society dominated and controlled by men and that, in most cases, they would acquire a kind of second-hand identity from the men they would marry.

It sounds absurd today, but there was a time when a married woman took her husband's initials as well as his surname: my mother was 'Mrs J.C. Mackay' (my father's initials), not 'M.E. Mackay' (her own initials), as if her identity were all about being the wife of Mr J.C. (no wonder we came up with 'Ms'!). There was also a time when a married woman needed her husband's permission to get a passport to leave the country, but a married man didn't need his wife's permission. Women in the public service had to resign from permanent positions once they married, since permanent positions were reserved for 'breadwinners'. Older unmarried men were referred to as 'bachelors' but older unmarried women were typically given the more pejorative label 'old maids'. No father ever wondered if he was letting his kids down by taking a paid job, but plenty of pre-revolutionary mothers did. Women were deemed unsuitable for all kinds of jobs because of the inconvenience of menstruation and childbirth. Women were banned from the public bars of hotels: if they were lucky, there might be a 'ladies lounge' out the back.

That was the world of my own childhood and young adulthood, and it pains me to recount all this stuff. On a brighter note, I recall the utter gender blindness of the teacher of our co-ed class in Years 5 and 6. Never a hint of gender bias in either direction; gender was simply not an issue. There was never a suggestion of different treatment for girls or boys (except that boys learned to play the flute and girls the recorder—but that was school policy, not our teacher's idea). We were treated in every way as equals—a positive experience that made me wonder why my parents then sent me to a single-sex secondary school, staffed entirely by male teachers, where girls were considered decidedly 'other'.

When I was first in the workforce, and for some years afterwards, women received lower wages for doing the same work as men, simply because they were women. And their superannuation benefits (if any) were correspondingly lower, too. Sexual harassment, sexual exploitation, sexual violence . . .

these were the darkest manifestations of a culture that taught boys and young men that females were essentially inferior beings, to be treated more like property than like equals who are entitled to all the same rights and opportunities—especially in education and employment—as males.

The Australian National University's Michelle Ryan has described the problem as 'the deeply entrenched systems of gender inequality that structure our organisations and structure society more broadly'. Ryan wrote that in 2023, pointing out that those structural inequalities have still not been sufficiently addressed.

It's not only the 'deeply entrenched systems' but the deeply ingrained stereotypes that have inhibited the final push towards universal acceptance of gender equality. UK researchers Paul Hutchings and Katie Sullivan were reporting as recently as 2023 that, in their study of the concept of 'a real man', women tended to describe a real man as 'someone who was loyal and supporting of their family, sharing responsibilities with childcare and chores', while men typically referred to 'playing sport, going to the gym, drinking, and aggression'. The researchers were careful to point out that male participants were not saying that these were behaviours they themselves carried out, but how they felt they were *expected* to behave to be perceived as a 'real man'.

The problem is that such stereotypes were transmitted to generations of young children over a long period. In one of my research projects in the 1980s—a mere forty years ago—a mother described her young son playing with a group of girls and saying, 'I'll go first—I've got a penis.' (The girls' response was not reported.) Such behaviour started young because it was strongly reinforced by the culture—including the religious culture where, even today, male supremacism is so deeply embedded in the theology, the hierarchical structures and the practices of some churches that, for them, the ordination of women to the priesthood remains inconceivable.

As the early signs of a gender revolution emerged, Australian men were notoriously slow to catch on . . . and so were some women. In 1989, I was reporting that many mothers were feeling uncomfortable about their own daughters becoming *too* liberated, and about their sons feeling intimidated by the rising generation of feisty young women: 'I find myself reacting badly to all these girls who ring my son up. I keep feeling that *he* should be doing the ringing up.' Even in the 1990s, it was a commonplace that women *washed* the dirty dishes, but men merely *helped* with the washing up—as if it were taken for granted that it was really her job; he was simply helping her get it done.

Same for housework more generally: women who had paid employment often complained that as they tried to induct their husbands into the arcane mysteries of domestic work, they were up against a hero mentality. One woman, I recall, described her pleasure when her husband spontaneously vacuumed the carpet in anticipation of some friends coming for dinner. But her pleasure turned to incredulity when the friends duly arrived and, as they came through the front door, her husband drew their attention to the clean state of the carpet and—*guess what?*—mentioned that he was responsible.

Another respondent described an incident where her husband had announced to her that he'd pegged out the clothes, clearly expecting a pat on the back or a round of applause.

'Well done,' his wife responded. 'I've been pegging the clothes out for a long time, and I don't recall anyone ever commenting on it. How come it's such a big deal when you do it? By the way, you haven't pegged the socks in pairs.'

These were mildly amusing signs of tectonic shifts taking place in our culture, as the messages of the women's movement gradually penetrated the thinking of men who hadn't realised the need for a revolution, didn't appreciate that 'equal opportunity' meant what it said, and were yet to discover that 'power sharing' meant the days of male supremacism were numbered.

Some men capitulated in ways women found pathetic rather than heroic: the so-called SNAG (Sensitive New Age Guy) came and went rather quickly, because he lacked the capacity for robust debate of gender issues that women wanted; he seemed preoccupied with wanting to *feel* like a woman ('I wish I could bear children, too.'). The metrosexual similarly came and went in a cloud of aftershave. Largely a figment of the imagination of a New York advertising executive (female, as it happens), the metrosexual was supposed to be a more enlightened male response to feminism than the SNAG, but there were only ever about six confirmed sightings of Australian metrosexuals.

What women were waiting for was men who were both comfortable with their own masculinity and serious about the idea of equality with women. It was neither a cave-in nor a caveman that women wanted: what they wanted was a radically different kind of man. In a 2003 research report, I dubbed him the 'the New Bloke' and, thirty years after the revolution began, he began to arrive on the scene in serious numbers (though, in my 2007 book *Advance Australia . . .Where?*, I was still only able to describe him as an emerging subspecies).

The New Bloke—typically heterosexual—was no wimp but he was no male chauvinist, either. He was—and still is—as interested in having a good time as any bloke ever was, but the big difference is that he *knows* women are equal and he knows what that means. He accepts that a serious relationship with a woman involves taking her identity and her needs as seriously as his, and that the woman's agenda is just as important as the man's. (Some of his best mates are women, by the way.)

These more sensitive and enlightened (and mostly younger) males were genuinely liberated from the shackles of male supremacism. Often posing as traditional larrikins, they wouldn't want you to know they were helping to reshape the world in favour of true equality, but that was their agenda. They wanted us all to lighten up, and to accept that the only pathway to healthy relationships between the sexes lay in an acceptance of genuine equality. Any other way of operating struck them as being unfair, unsustainable and just plain silly.

That was a genuine new wave of equality-based masculinity and that first wave of New Blokes has now reached middle age. They are notable for their unselfconscious commitment to equality in parenting and household chores, as well as an open-minded approach to their own earning capacity relative to that of their wife or partner. The example they have set for their sons is radically different from the example set for them by their own fathers.

Meanwhile, even though this was the turn of the twenty-first century, there were still plenty of (mostly older) men who were engaging in 'mock sensitivity', praising women's newfound sense of independence while appropriating it in a very old-fashioned way by declaring how much more interesting and attractive *to them* 'the wife' had become now she was going out to work every day. One woman told me that her husband had enthusiastically supported her decision to undertake a university degree by correspondence but, after she became puzzled by the lack of any response to the assignments she was sending in, discovered that when he had offered to mail them for her, he had actually been putting them in the bin.

Men in high places were not exempt from such hypocrisy. You could hear their sighs of self-satisfaction at how actively they were promoting women, as though this had been something they had spontaneously chosen to do and should therefore be praised for—not unlike the husband who pegged out the clothes. I once sat on a board with a man who vigorously advocated the appointment of a certain woman to the board. She proved an excellent choice and began raising serious questions about the organisation's finances—the area of her advocate's particular responsibility. He was unimpressed: 'She's just a jumped-up housewife with too much time on her hands,' he complained privately to the (male) board chair.

Some men were simply angered by the prospect of any change to the status quo. Sexual violence was the ugliest expression of their rage and confusion. We've come a long way since those dark days (though still not far enough), and the fully evolved New Bloke might not yet be in the majority. But, looking back, could anyone doubt that a revolution was needed—and that it would need to be nothing less than a strident, assertive and even aggressive movement that would expose the evils of male-supremacist attitudes and behaviour? No one, surely, except those unreconstructed male supremacists.

Misogyny: a symptom of male self-loathing

The male neurosis we call 'misogyny' has been with us for a long time. The first description of the phenomenon—like so many of our cultural stories—came from the realms of ancient Greek mythology. And, like so much other Greek mythology, it was the product of a shamelessly male-supremacist culture in which women were regarded as inferior to men and were treated harshly in order to maintain their subservient status. As the English classicist Mary Beard has noted: 'The more you oppress, the more you're preoccupied by those you oppress.'

Now that we are coming to understand more about the psychology of gender, a curiously paradoxical aspect of misogyny emerges. Although women are its explicit focus, misogyny may not actually be rooted in men's hatred of women at all: more likely, it's about those men's hatred of themselves. It's a safe bet that domination of others is always about personal insecurity. Here's what the misogynist may really be saying: 'I am disgusted by, or ashamed of, or disappointed in some aspect of my own masculinity but I can't deal with my self-loathing, so I project it onto women.'

There will be many causes of that loathing, shame or disappointment, and they will vary from case to case, but it's safe to assume that there are at least four primary drivers of misogyny—two of them psychological and two of them the product of contemporary culture.

140

The first, and perhaps the most basic driver, arises from the fact that we are all located on a gender continuum: if men didn't have a 'feminine side' and women a 'masculine side', what underdeveloped creatures we would be, and how incapable of understanding each other! But, for some men, this is such a challenging or even repugnant concept, they may deny or repress their own 'feminine side', and be embarrassed about it, mystified by it or even ashamed of it. This is fairly and squarely a man's issue, but if he lacks the insight or the emotional equipment to deal with it, then he may simply attack or belittle women as a way of distancing himself from that aspect of his own nature. To re-phrase that quote from Mary Beard: 'The more you repress, the more you're preoccupied by what you repress'—a recurring theme in psychology.

A second potential psychological driver of misogyny is 'loveless sex': the tendency of some men to regard sex as a mere vehicle for release of sexual tension—effectively using any available woman as a slightly more interesting alternative to masturbation. Of course, particularly among young people—and particularly during sexually permissive periods of our social evolution—it would be unrealistic to assume that all sexual behaviour is driven by romantic love, or implies a commitment to spend a lifetime with this person and to produce children with them. Consensual, recreational sex is a common feature of youth culture in many societies, including ours. But where a man experiences no feelings of affection or respect towards a woman he is having sex with, a common outcome is that, post-coitus, he despises himself and projects that negative response onto the woman concerned—or, indeed, onto all women. ('Projection'—denying our own faults and frailties by

141

identifying and criticising them in others—is a great place to hide from the truth about ourselves.) So women become mere objects to exploit, and possessions to use and discard.

Wherever it may have come from, the attitude that 'women are for fucking' is likely to be strongly correlated with misogyny. In her 1971 classic *The Female Eunuch*, Germaine Greer drew on the account of one young man to portray the consequences of loveless, exploitative sex among groups of young men in the English industrial towns of that era— though Greer made the unwarranted assumption that the self-loathing of those young men, projected onto the women they exploited, was a sign of some universal male hatred of women. (The good news is that many men actually love the women they are with, and respect women generally.)

And then there are the drivers of misogyny that arise from this particular moment in our sociocultural development. In Australia in the 2020s, one of those factors is undoubtedly the 'hangover effect' from the gender revolution, described in the previous section of this chapter. Male supremacism is a very comfortable cocoon for men who are culturally insensitive and morally blind. Talk of 'gender equality' sounds dangerous to such men, and they are likely to feel bewildered and defensive about the very concept of power-sharing since it implies—obviously—a loss of automatic power for men, everywhere from the boardroom to the bedroom.

Another contemporary factor arises from the online world, where easy access to pornography that portrays women as mere sex objects is bound to reinforce any hint of misogynistic feelings in men—especially young men with little or no personal experience of romantic love or even of sex.

In 'The Context', I referred to our reliance on groups of all kinds to nurture and sustain us to give us the sense of 'belonging' that is so fundamental to our mental and emotional health. And then, in chapter 2, I referred to the inability of online groups, gathering on social media, to replicate the 'real thing' (person-to-person, face-to-face contact with others, incorporating that all-important eye contact). But, in the contemporary world, where social isolation has become our number-one public health issue, many people do resort to online groups to create their sense of community, no matter how superficial, spurious or dangerous that may be. Not surprisingly, people who are socially isolated—especially if they are also feeling lonely, anxious, depressed and/or underappreciated—are likely to be attracted to online groups that welcome them and seem to comprise people who feel the way they do. Hence, as part of this process, we have seen the rise of online groups such as 'incels'—involuntary celibates—that encourage and reinforce misogyny among men who may have been rejected or disappointed by women. Similarly, MRAs (Men's Rights Activists) encourage the belief that, in the wake of feminism, men are being victimised and disadvantaged relative to women

Sometimes, no doubt, misogyny does not arise from any of those four factors, but is just another tediously predictable prejudice that, like most prejudices, is based on fear of 'otherness'. For some men, women are simply mysterious creatures who seem unapproachable, incomprehensible and, ultimately, 'other'. And otherness—whether based on gender, ethnicity, religion or any other aspect of a person's identity—is not something we're good at handling: we tend to fear it and then convert our fear into hostility.

Even 'simple' misogyny can be more complicated than other prejudices, because it sometimes hides behind an ugly mask of deception. Just like that malevolent husband who openly supported his wife's academic ambition and secretly sabotaged her work, many men express their fear of women— or their loathing of themselves—by appearing to put women on a pedestal, claiming that 'equality' would reduce them to a lesser position in the male mind. And some men are so fixated on women as sex objects that they can't untangle their sexual predations from their smug supremacism, posing as 'lovers' of women while using them as mere vehicles for sexual gratification and then secretly despising their own behaviour. ('How would you feel if someone treated your mother or sister like that?' is a question they'd be too ashamed to face.)

Is Australia any worse than comparable societies when it comes to the lingering effects of male supremacism expressed as misogyny? Impossible to know but, anecdotally, many women believe the raffish blokeishness of Aussie male culture has been an effective disguise for misogyny. Yet females in many other societies have been victimised by misogyny, especially the cowardly, anonymous expressions of it on social media—the kind of thing that wore down leaders like New Zealand's Jacinda Ardern and Scotland's Nicola Sturgeon.

Julia Gillard, who was on the receiving end of far-from-anonymous misogyny during her turbulent period as Australian prime minister, called it out in the federal parliament in her famous 'misogyny speech' of 2012. But as she herself later wrote, in *Women and Leadership*, it would have been more effective if a male politician had said the things she said, and said them much earlier than she had. Gillard's point is that when the message of true equality comes from men, it is likely to be taken more seriously by misogynists—though some of them might need extended psychotherapy to cure their condition.

Misogyny is obviously a problem for women, but it is a problem that only men can fix. When you look at that list of potential drivers of misogyny, you realise that none of this has anything to do with who women are or what women do or what women want. Misogyny is not usually a male response to women's behaviour; it is more commonly a male response to men's own behaviour.

Preparing for the final push

Male supremacism is bad, wrong, ugly and stupid. As its long history in Western culture has demonstrated, it's also unfair and unjust because it deprives women of the opportunity to reach their full potential. It institutionalises inequality. If we are going to be able to give ourselves any credit for being even a little more enlightened than our forebears were about gender issues, then any vestige of male supremacism must be consigned to outer darkness.

As part of the process of ridding our social structures of such flagrant inequality, we need to declare peace in the gender wars—apart from those light-hearted moments when it's fun for women to roll their eyes and say 'Men!', or for men to roll theirs and say 'Women!' *Vive la difference* . . . of course! Equality doesn't mean we aspire to be all the same—either within gender categories or between them. Some women have different interests and competencies from some men, just as there is a huge range of interests and competencies *within* gender groups. And, obviously, we're not biologically the same. But when it comes to rights, needs, entitlements, status, roles and responsibilities, we are undeniably equal. Any other view of the world makes no sense at all.

If the gender revolution is to mean anything, it must surely mean that, thanks largely to the sustained work of some inspirational pioneering women, we are finally going to commit ourselves to gender egalitarianism. We are going to acknowledge that men and women—and all other gender categories—are equal partners in the continuing Grand Human Project of building social harmony. If we can't build and maintain harmony across the gender spectrum—putting an end to rivalry, hostility, bitterness, prejudice and suspicion—then the entire project is doomed.

We are at a delicate point in this process—a point at which we need to remind ourselves that any hint of female supremacism, sometimes disguised as 'correcting the imbalances of the past'—would be just as bad, wrong, ugly and stupid as male supremacism. It would be equally unfair and unjust. At any sign of it we should shout in a loud voice: 'Stop! We're just repeating the same error. In fact, we're *compounding* the error.' For example, a writer friend was recently told by a literary agent in the UK that the fine quality of his work was irrelevant: he had no chance of getting it published because he is an older white male. It was clear to him which part of that description was actually the heart of his problem.

I was distressed not only to hear that such a prejudice would be made so explicit, but also puzzled by my friend's reaction: he thought it was fair enough. He accepted that 'men have had it their own way for long enough' and he was prepared for his work—regardless of its quality—to be sacrificed as part of an appropriate correction for the male-supremacist sins of the past.

I disagree. It would not be a correction; it would be an overcorrection. It would imply that women can do no better than men have done when it comes to sorting out the real meaning and the practical implications of equality.

When a prominent female gender activist passed on to me a scurrilous claim made by another woman about a man we both knew, I expressed my strong disagreement with what had been said, because I knew the claim was false. 'I'll believe *her*,' the activist said to me, 'because she's a woman.' My opinion was rendered worthless by my gender—exactly the complaint women have been making for a very long time. That's not a correction of injustice; it's a perpetuation of it.

Another example: a few years ago, I sat with a group of people engaged by a media organisation to come up with a list of the most influential people in Australia at that time. (A weird thing to be doing, I agree.) Early in the voting process, a woman in the group announced that she would only be voting for women.

I recently visited an all-girls school where I saw a sign on the wall of a classroom: *Who rules the world? Girls!* Same old. Same old. Can't enlightened females do better than unenlightened males used to do? Is this where the women's movement is going to land—in the same tired old place where too many men have stood for too long? Hasn't the whole *point* of the gender revolution been to right the inarguable wrongs of the past, not by repeating them but by showing us a *third way*, a better way, a more enlightened way of righting them?

This is not to deny that, early in the revolution, 'affirmative action' was a perfectly legitimate circuit breaker. Indeed, it was a necessary strategy for redressing the shocking imbalances, inequalities and injustices of the male-supremacist culture. Not by asserting female supremacism, but simply by demonstrating what 'fairness' and 'equality' could look like in practice.

The very phrase 'affirmative action' now sounds almost as quaint as 'women's liberation', though the concept has recently been given the more prosaic moniker 'quotas'. They, too, have been a very good idea, not as a permanent solution, but as a temporary—and highly effective—intervention in such areas as appointment to boards and preselection of MPs.

In federal politics, preselection quotas have worked brilliantly for the Labor Party. The Liberals, by contrast, have thus far rejected the very idea of quotas, though it was fleetingly floated after the 2022 federal election in which ten sitting Liberals lost their seats to so-called 'teal independents', all of whom were women.

The time has come for such a serious commitment to gender equality that, after fifty years of revolution, it should no longer strike us as a debatable issue. All of us who believe in gender equality must now simply live *as if* that's the only world we understand. Take off our battledress. Throw away our rhetorical weapons. Time for peace. Time for a more compassionate, mutually respectful approach. Time for reconciliation. Even in the most pragmatic terms, it's time to acknowledge that attacking each other's attitudes not only produces defence but usually reinforces the very attitudes we're trying to change.

We need to become gender-blind in politics, in employment, in academia, in the arts, in religion and in the culture more broadly. Don't publish that book because it's by a woman and it's time for women to 'have their turn'; publish it because it's a bloody good book. Don't award this year's prize (for anything) to a woman on the grounds that we have to 'redress the balance'—that's the old, outmoded 'affirmative action' line. All these years later, what an insult to a female winner it would be if she were to learn that the judges had imposed a pro-female (or, perhaps, anti-male) bias on themselves. No: award the prize to whoever is most deserving of it.

We also need to become more gender-blind in language. We've come a long way, but we still say 'actress', 'hostess' and 'waitress' (to say nothing of the execrable 'waitperson') when 'actor', 'host' and 'waiter' will work in precisely the same way as gender-neutral words like 'director, 'politician', 'priest', 'poet', 'plumber' or 'writer' (we've never said 'writress' and we certainly don't say 'writeperson'). Drop the gender tags, unless there's some special reason why you need to add 'female' or 'male' to the label.

Perhaps (dare I say it?) it might even be time to move on from the specificity of 'feminism' to adopt a descriptor that fully embraces the spirit and messages of feminism but places them in the context of an even grander and more inclusive vision: *gender equality*. If what we really want—what we're finally ready for—is true gender equality, then let's declare it by adopting a gender-neutral label. Let's call ourselves, unequivocally, 'gender egalitarians'.

Eva Cox, an ardent and perceptive advocate for women's rights, declared in a 2018 speech that 'feminism has failed and needs a radical rethink'. Feminism has not failed, but perhaps it has stalled. Perhaps the time has come to acknowledge that 'feminism', as a label, has done all the revolutionary work it can do. If that's the case, wouldn't it make sense for all of us who are committed to the spirit of feminism to regroup, rethink and come up with a new strategy to close the remaining gender gap? The goal doesn't change, but we increase our chances of achieving it if we adopt a fresh approach.

If, on the other hand, we simply go on doing and saying the same things we've always said and done, the danger exists that our message will sound more adversarial than egalitarian, more competitive than cooperative, and more about women than about all of us. It's far harder to recruit recalcitrant males to the cause of feminism than it is to convince them of the fairness and justice of gender equality. It is also hard for people of fluid or non-binary gender identities to believe they are included in the agenda of those marching under the banner of feminism, whereas 'gender equality' acknowledges and enfolds us all.

If I say, 'I'm proposing this because I'm a feminist', the response is likely to be different from the response I'd receive if I said, 'I'm proposing this because I believe in gender equality'. Same idea, same goal, different strategy.

Another danger of persisting with the old label is that the internecine struggles between those who interpret 'feminism' in different ways—comparable to the bitter conflicts between religious denominations—will continue to create confusion, even among women. For example, the slogans and ideological positions of radical Marxist feminists, who see the oppression of women as being tied to the gendered structures of

150

capitalism, run the risk of becoming counterproductive when they appear to denigrate equally passionate liberal feminists who are focused on eliminating gender inequality by promoting equal opportunities for women and men within existing economic structures.

The price revolutionaries often have to pay is that they will receive less credit than they deserve from the people who subsequently benefit from their relentless, revolutionary toil. Younger women might sometimes acknowledge the pioneering work done by their mothers and grandmothers but they will typically refuse to be too impressed: some of them express incredulity that women could ever have put up with being second-class citizens. They urge the militants to 'move on'. They refuse to conform to the particular meanings of 'liberation' that had currency thirty or forty or fifty years ago, 'before we were even born'. (They would simply be baffled by Germaine Greer's assertion in *The Female Eunuch* that you're not truly emancipated if you're sickened by the idea of tasting your own menstrual blood.) Liberation, for them, means both 'free to choose' and 'free to change'. What they are embracing is the idea of true gender equality based on mutual respect, not mutual suspicion.

The recent appearance near Old Parliament House in Canberra of statues of Dame Enid Lyons and Dame Dorothy Tangney, the first female member of the House of Representatives and the first female senator respectively, has been widely acclaimed and generally recognised as long overdue. Those statues are a symbol of the need to recognise the role of women in our history more fairly, more generously and more accurately than was the case in the bad old days.

The 'feminist critique' will always have its place in academic historical analysis, but when so much careful work has been done to bring us to the threshold of true gender egalitarianism, clinging to the label 'feminist' runs the risk of sounding as if we don't want the war to end. As if it's likely to be more productive to maintain a competitive stance rather than a cooperative one. As if we've got to keep *fighting*—a bit like that lone soldier of the Japanese army, Teruo Nakamura, who kept fighting World War II in the jungle of Morotai for twenty-nine years after peace had been declared. Is that the role any of us want for ourselves?

If you're seriously committed to gender equality—if you're keen to stamp out any sign of gender bias or prejudice, let alone supremacism—then you're a true egalitarian. Even better, you're a harmony-builder and a peacemaker. Welcome to the future! This is not about 'women having their turn'. This is about all of us laying down our arms and embracing each other as equals, about acknowledging and respecting each other's differences—just as we acknowledge and respect differences within genders—but always in the context of our *common* life, our *common* purpose, our *common* humanity. Because that's the point: in the end, we're all human—different but equal. If we were to show positive or negative bias towards any person on the basis of their gender, that would be sexism. It would be unfair and unjust. And stupid. And wrong. And all those other things I said before.

Gender diversity

Part of the revolutionary challenge, for many men *and* women, lies in coming to terms with the increasingly overt manifestations of what is now broadly known as queer culture, which can refer to sexual orientation or gender identity. Just when people might have been congratulating themselves on their more enlightened attitude to equality between men and women, they have come to realise that 'gender equality' is a more complex, more nuanced concept than they might previously have imagined. *Gendy neuch* has already entered the language as slang for 'gender neutral'.

One of the many ugly manifestations of male supremacism was the toxic culture that encouraged relentless teasing of boys and young men whose sense of gender was at serious odds with that culture, either because they were homosexual, confused about their gender identity or, in some of the most painful cases, gripped by the conviction that they were actually trapped in a body of the wrong sex. Homophobia is far from dead, but at least it is no longer blithely accepted, or even sanctioned, as part of the culture, in the way it once was.

The term *gender dysphoria* has only entered common usage in the past few years, but the phenomenon is as old as humanity. It refers to the condition where someone is convinced that the gender they identify with doesn't match the sex characteristics they were born with. Gender dysphoria occurs in both biological males and females, though until recently it was more common among males than females. Those of us who have never experienced the condition might find it almost impossible to imagine what it must feel like. We might also find it hard to appreciate the pain of those who face mockery, resistance or rejection as a result of their experience of dysphoria.

In a 2023 interview, Chris Harkien (not his real name), a transgender male, spoke of the pain of being a biological girl who suffered from gender dysphoria from the age of about three, when he 'knew' he was really a boy. He experienced shame at being forced to wear girls' clothing and to have a girl's name. Fully expecting his body to become masculine at puberty, he was shocked when it didn't, and reported feeling nausea and revulsion at its female form. The persistent and severe depression, anxiety, shame, self-harm and a constant struggle against suicidality all dropped away when he decided to transition: 'It was then possible to build genuine relationships based on who I am rather than trying to hide myself continually. My constant fear of being exposed evaporated.'

It was always true, but only now strikes us in a vivid way, that a gender revolution would entail the need for a more sympathetic and inclusive attitude to people declaring themselves lesbian, gay, bisexual, transgender, intersexual, pansexual, non-binary, asexual—either permanently, or, sometimes, during an experimental phase of their personal development. Indeed, our growing acceptance of the idea that we are all located on a gender continuum, and that 'gender' may be a more fluid concept than we once thought, demonstrates that we have indeed been experiencing a revolution.

At first, the revolutionary focus was on equal rights for women, but now that message is firmly lodged in the nation's psyche (even though more progress obviously needs to be made to achieve true equality in practice) we realise that gender equality is a broader concept than that. The voices of transgender and non-binary people, for example, have already been raised in protest about the sometimes-simplistic nature of calls for women's rights: 'Equal rights for women, sure, *but what about equal rights for us?*' By which they mean:

what about equal rights for people with non-cisgender identities who have felt excluded from the conversation? (If you're not up with 'cisgender', it simply means people whose gender identity matches the sexual identity assigned to them at birth.)

***

The growing use of the pronoun 'they' to apply to a non-binary or gender-fluid individual does not come easily to people who think of that as an exclusively plural pronoun—although we are already quite comfortable with 'them' and 'they' as a singular pronoun in sentences like 'If someone asks for your help, you should give it to them', or 'There's someone at the door—see what they want'. Unlike the French with their subtle use of *tu* and *vous*, we already use 'you' for the second-person singular *and* plural, so we could conceivably apply the same rule for the third person.

Or perhaps we could borrow the non-gender-specific *ta* from Mandarin. Or we could come up with an entirely new non-binary pronoun that makes more grammatical sense than 'they'. The Swedes have simply taken *hon* and *han*—their third-person singular female and male pronouns—and refashioned them as the non-binary *hen*.

But we don't have to decide any of this in a formal way. We don't have a language academy like the French; we prefer to let our language evolve organically. Over time, usage will determine the fate of 'they' or the birth of a new, gender-free pronoun; the human equivalent of 'it'.

In passing, we may note that the mid-2020s obsession with personal pronouns is partly a serious move by people who believe they have had to wrestle for too long with gender issues and now want recognition for having resolved them. But it's also partly a reaction to the state of the world: when the planet itself threatens to become uninhabitable, ecosystems are failing in response to species extinction, society is fragmenting and many of the biggest social problems that confront us—homelessness, poverty, domestic violence, political corruption—seem beyond our control, it's natural to look for things we *can* control. And so the focus narrows and we concentrate maximum attention on such questions as individual personal identity and . . . pronouns.

Difficulties arise in many families when gender adjustments have to be made. Some heterosexual relationships survive, at least as friendships, when one partner declares that she or he is, for example, lesbian, gay or bisexual and forms a same-sex relationship, or transitions to another gender. But some don't and, especially when children are involved, this can be as fraught with tension and difficulty as any divorce might be. Even less-complicated gender-based scenarios can pose a challenge for families, friends and colleagues. In one case, a man whose wife had died and who subsequently revealed that he was really a woman at heart changed his identity, including his name. His/her work colleagues struggled to adapt to referring to their long-term male boss, now wearing women's clothing, as 'she', and calling her by her new name, though they eventually managed it. Her children, of course, continued to call her 'Dad'.

Some parents report feelings of great distress when one of their children decides that their birth gender no longer feels right to them—or perhaps never did. Such parents are not only likely to be emotionally destabilised by the prospect of having to adjust to a gender transition but also by concern for their children's physical and mental wellbeing on the journey through a radical and potentially non-reversible process. 'What if he wants to change back later?' some parents are asking, in response to stories they've heard about surgical transitions that were later regretted. Another specific concern is the lack of safety data about the long-term effect of female hormones on males, or male hormones on females.

Although different jurisdictions have different laws about the assignment of gender identity, the Family Court has ruled that a child under the age of eighteen cannot be given so-called 'puberty blockers' unless there is a medical diagnosis of gender dysphoria, both parents have given their consent and the treatment is provided by a specialist multidisciplinary team. Diagnosis of gender dysphoria is generally based on a deep sense of alienation from one's body starting in early childhood, rather than a sense of sex–gender disjunction acquired during adolescence which may turn out, in some cases, to be a temporary symptom of broader issues. In other cases, late-developing gender issues may turn out to be permanent and resolvable only through gender reassignment—hormonal and/or surgical.

When I recently addressed the staff of a girls' school on the subject of kindness, the only questions put to me after my talk related to the challenge of dealing with the growing number of girls who were wanting to reassign their gender, or at least be open to that possibility. (Tricky, in a girls-only school.)

Is it suddenly 'fashionable' to play with gender identity, then? A kinder—and more likely—explanation is that our attitudes have become more sympathetic to the full range of gender identities, and we have developed a deeper appreciation of the complexity and potential fluidity of the sense of gender. People feel more comfortable about expressing gender doubts and preferences than they previously did. And isn't it healthier for people to be either choosing to identify with a different gender, or experimenting—even temporarily—with other gender possibilities, rather than feeling privately confused or even ashamed of their feelings?

The danger here is that a person adopting a non-obvious gender identity will feel that this is the most significant thing you need to know about them—or, more broadly, that gender identity is the most significant thing we all need to know about each other. A person's gender identity is certainly an *interesting* thing to know, especially if there are romantic possibilities lurking in your mind. You will need to know you're not going to make a fool of yourself by showing sexual interest in a person whose sexual identity excludes the possibility of partnering with a person like you.

While gender identity is obviously a critical part of our private sense of self, it is far from being the most important aspect of personal identity. Identity is, primarily, a social and relational concept. It's about how we *identify* each other in the world. My own identity, for example, starts with my name, Hugh, and includes being a son, a brother, a husband, a father, a grandfather, a friend, a colleague, a neighbour, a member of a choir, a patient, a customer and so on. All these *relational* aspects make the biggest contribution to my overall identity— since identity is, in the end, not only about the way we *feel*, but also about the way we are perceived and characterised by others. We might choose to share some internal, unseen, private aspects of our sense of self with others, so they become part of our public identity, or we might not. Our gender, our religious faith (or lack of it), our political convictions, our cultural tastes and preferences, our ethnic heritage . . . it's up to us to decide whether or not these and other aspects of our private sense of self should become 'labels' by which we are known to others.

While we're in the post-revolutionary process of downplaying differences between men and women, let's extend that same process to include people at every point on the gender spectrum. Let's not make a huge thing of our differences—gender or otherwise. Let's remember, always, that we are one; that none of our differences—whether based on ethnicity, politics, religion, cultural tastes and preferences, or gender—are nearly as significant as the humanity we share. And let none of us assume that our particular gender represents a superior life form. Vocal minorities and silent majorities both need to be careful that they are not, by their sound or their silence, contributing to social tension and promoting discord rather than harmony.

MeTooFar?

As with the need for a revolutionary women's movement to redress the injustices and inequities of the past, so there was a crying need for a movement that would expose sexual harassment, abuse and exploitation—especially in the workplace. Given our long cultural history of male supremacism, it's easy to see how women have been intimidated—'frozen' is a word they often use—when subjected to unwanted sexual attention amounting to abuse or even assault from males, especially those in positions of authority over them.

The MeToo movement began before the term 'hashtag' existed. It was started in 2006 in the US by Tarana Burke, an African American woman whose initial focus was on the sexual abuse of black women by white men—that toxic blend of white supremacism and male supremacism. But, over time, her campaign resonated far more widely than that and was finally turbocharged by the internet. Women's long-suppressed rage about sexual exploitation in all kinds of settings—whether motivated by racist, sexist or class-based prejudices, or arising from power imbalances—gradually broadened the focus of MeToo.

The Hollywood 'casting couch' was infamous: it was based on the assumption that granting sexual favours to a movie producer or director would increase a woman's chances of landing a role in a movie. It took the courage of women to call out such behaviour in the case of Harvey Weinstein, the co-founder of entertainment company Miramax, and their accusations ultimately led to his trial and conviction on multiple charges of rape and sexual assault. (It should be noted that, decades earlier, Marilyn Monroe had called out the same kind of behaviour in the article 'Wolves I Have Known' she wrote for *Motion Picture and Television Magazine* in 1953, after she lost a contract with Columbia Pictures for rejecting a sexual overture from the co-founder and president of Columbia, Harry Cohn.)

Burke's initiative brought the movement into being, but the publicity surrounding the Weinstein case emboldened women all over the world to start shouting 'me too!' as they charged men in powerful positions with having sexually exploited them in various ways.

As with the Women's Movement, the #MeToo movement has been a very necessary correction to the male-supremacist culture that has protected predatory males and allowed them to get away with sexual abuse or assault, whether criminal, offensive or merely inappropriate. Now, at last, women—especially young women—have growing confidence in the idea that if they are on the receiving end of uninvited and unwelcome sexual behaviour, their complaints are likely to be taken seriously.

The great benefit of this revolutionary push is that it exposes the ugly reality of sexual exploitation, in the workplace and elsewhere, and it shatters the cone of silence that had previously surrounded it. Though too many women, in too many settings, still feel powerless to protect themselves from harassment, serious progress is being made. In the age of #MeToo, women are being encouraged to reject the (always-repugnant) idea that they should be expected to put up with sexual misbehaviour as the price of working in a particular industry or for a particular organisation, or attending a particular church, or belonging to a particular family.

#MeToo has not yet brought sexual predation to an end; it has not yet restrained all those in a position of authority from sexually harassing, assaulting and abusing people who work—or want to work—for them. And, as Jennifer Robinson and Keina Yoshida point out in *How Many More Women?*, too many rich and powerful men try to deflect public accusations of sexual assault by suing their victims for defamation. But #MeToo has encouraged people to speak up, to report criminal behaviour and to adopt an attitude of zero tolerance towards any sexually motivated improprieties.

Obviously, that's all been a very good thing. The #MeToo movement has been heroic in its aims and positive in its impact.

As with all new forms of enlightenment, however, there are risks of unintended consequences and the possibility of harm if the revolution is not sensitively managed. Even #MeToo might go too far.

One risk is that we might elevate victimhood to such a superior status that it appears, especially to impressionable young people, as a desirable state. We don't want to reach the situation, surely, where someone can stand up and say, 'I'm an abuse victim' and be applauded not only for their courage in speaking up but also for the fact of *being* a victim—or, in contemporary parlance, a 'survivor' who refuses to be victimised. (By the way, I wonder if 'survivor' is a term that needs to be used rather more sparingly, lest it downplay the experience of people who have actually survived near-death experiences such as a serious illness, being wounded in military combat, a plane crash or a fall from a cliff. I'm not sure that 'survivor' is the appropriate term for a person who has experienced sexual harassment, though it obviously applies to survivors of rape—one of the most vile and contemptible crimes in the chamber of human horrors.)

To create a 'culture of victimhood' would be utterly counterproductive. Writing for the online journal *Quillette*, American psychotherapist Lisa Marchiano tells the story of a twelve-year-old girl, the daughter of a client, whose seventh-grade teacher began the school year by having students share their preferred pronouns. Immediately afterwards, this girl began identifying as gender-fluid and, according to her mother, became preoccupied with her new status as a member of an oppressed minority. As Marchiano writes, 'though the teacher undoubtedly meant to communicate tolerance and acceptance, she inadvertently created an inducement to victimhood'.

Marchiano also notes that a new moral culture of victimhood is emerging on college campuses, where being a victim 'raises one's standing and confers virtue, in part because it mobilizes protection and support', which is obviously a positive outcome. Less positive, Marchiano says, are the effects of a victimhood culture that rewards us for feeling aggrieved, helpless and weak. 'It encourages us to experience ourselves as being at the mercy of external forces beyond our control . . . it can also foster a sense of helplessness with negative implications for mental health.'

US academic and writer Geoff Shullenberger—echoing the work of French philosopher René Girard—believes the rise of 'victim power' is a symptom of the erosion of respect for other sources of authority and legitimacy in Western society. Shullenberger focuses mainly on the US, but the same might be said of the UK and many other Western democracies, including Australia. (The 2023 Royal Commission into the Robodebt scandal was a recent reminder of some of the ways governments can lose the respect of those they govern, especially when they seem to have been corrupted by their own power.) His disturbing point is that in a situation where democratic institutions and processes are losing respect— too adversarial, too corrupt, too divisive, too unresponsive to the electorate—people seeking power may harness the widespread sympathy and concern for victims (not only of sexual abuse, but also of police brutality or any other form of victimhood) to gain political, economic or cultural power for themselves.

In our culture—especially our religious culture—we have a long history of turning victims into martyrs and martyrs into saints. But the more immediate personal issue is whether we are running the risk of overplaying the very idea of (other people's) victimhood, as a way of hiding from our own guilt and shame about having ignored or denied the problem of sexual harassment and abuse for so long. The real challenge, now, is to re-educate men while also finding better ways of encouraging and empowering young women, in particular, to be more confident in speaking up when they need to, and to *avoid* situations that might potentially position them as victims. Thanks to #MeToo, big steps have already been taken in this direction.

In today's more enlightened commitment to true equality, a male tradie whistling at a woman as she passes a building site has become unacceptable. Though he might well have meant it as a lighthearted compliment, the risk, now, is that it will be interpreted as a signal that 'men make the rules', 'men own the space' and 'men set the tone'. Those implied messages can be both distressing and deeply offensive to a woman.

Even in the mid-2020s, men can still be heard expressing confusion about what is and isn't acceptable to do and say in the presence of women. In some cases, these are men who are genuinely struggling to come to terms with the full import of gender equality. While their intentions are good, their attitudes and behaviour may still be being influenced by the weight of habits formed by their upbringing and the potent examples of their own fathers and grandfathers, for whom they may feel lingering affection and respect. Their journey towards full appreciation of gender equality will be assisted by more good examples of how to live the post-revolutionary life, more peer pressure on them from other men, more encouragement from the women in their life and less adversarialism . . . all those things will contribute to the final stages of male adaptation. This was never a 'men's movement', after all. Women did all the hard pioneering work: men have only had to acknowledge that the women were right to rebel, and then modify their own behaviour to fit the new environment.

In other cases, though, men's claim to be confused about how to act towards women sounds rather like a disingenuous copout. Have they not been paying attention? Have they not noticed that there has actually been a revolution? Have they not heard its resounding core message to men that *all* women, in *all* circumstances, must be treated with the respect due to equals? There's a simple rule that flows from that message: Before you do or say anything to a woman, ask yourself: 'Is this respectful? Will this be well received? Or am I falling into the old trap of acting as if men own the game?'

What might once have been regarded (by men) as 'a bit of harmless groping' was never harmless and should never have been regarded as harmless, precisely because it implies the very lack of respect for women that lies at the heart of male-supremacist culture.

Every situation is unique, and power imbalances can still cause some women to feel so intimidated that they 'freeze' rather than speak up. Of course we should be encouraging women to call out bad behaviour, *every time*, but we should also be doing far more to educate men about issues like consent and respect—to say nothing of the need for kindness and consideration in their behaviour towards women. All of us—women and men—need to ensure that there is zero tolerance of sexual harassment and abuse in the culture of our workplaces, families or friendship groups.

The principle involved could hardly be clearer: all persons, regardless of gender, in every situation, must be treated respectfully, and no deviation from that principle is acceptable. Overindulgence in alcohol doesn't excuse deviations; office Christmas parties don't excuse deviations; laughter doesn't excuse deviations. 'It was just a bit of fun' is no excuse for abusive or disrespectful behaviour.

And yet even a movement as well intentioned as #MeToo needs to play its part in ensuring that, in all cases of a man being charged with a sexual crime, justice is done. There is a risk that our determination to bring the long history of predatory male behaviour to an end may take a quasi-puritan turn and that people will be inclined to brush aside the fundamental legal principle of 'presumed innocent until proven guilty' in the case of criminal charges of sexual assault brought against a man. Unfortunately, there are documented cases of false rape accusations, and letting the law run its course remains central to our system of justice. People accused of serious sexual assault will continue to be charged, tried and found either guilty or innocent; let the rest of us reserve judgement until such matters are settled in court.

At the same time, we know that courts are not infallible; any system in which 'the best barrister wins' is inherently flawed. And there are times when those close to an alleged victim of sexual assault simply find it inconceivable that her accusations could be false—regardless of the legal verdict. Nevertheless, in any case of 'her word against his', we must not fall into the trap of automatically assuming that 'her word' will always be right, simply because 'men have had it their own way for too long'—any more than we should fall into the old trap of assuming that the woman is lying or 'making trouble'.

#MeToo has led to a long-overdue public conversation about consent in relation to sexual behaviour. True gender equality obviously requires a mutually respectful gender culture—and that, in turn, demands that the need for consent must be taken seriously by any parties to a sexual encounter. Yet, even here, some men have completely missed the point. Commenting on the (male) expectation that 'liberated' women will now behave just like men when it comes to dating and sex—including being more reckless than they really want to be—some young women say that it can now seem 'uncool' to withhold consent, and that feelings of vulnerability can seem shameful. (We still have some way to go.)

**

Revolutions are never neat and tidy. Outcomes are never entirely predictable.

Did Betty Friedan, Kate Millett, Germaine Greer or, indeed, Simone de Beauvoir ever imagine or intend that the women's movement would spawn a gender revolution that would go way beyond the question of equal rights for women and men, and wake us up to the complexity and fluidity of the gender spectrum itself?

I doubt whether they saw all that coming, but that's the world we now live in.

We also live in a world where much work still needs to be done to eliminate violence against women, to eradicate misogyny, and to convince the remaining male chauvinists/supremacists to understand, appreciate and accept that the significant changes wrought by the gender revolution are irrevocably embedded in the culture. Turning the clock back is not an option: not in a single workplace, not at a single social event, not in a single household, not in a single relationship.

Footnote: 'Cancel culture'

There's an unfortunate human tendency for revolutionaries to crow over their achievements and then to intimidate those who they believe have been vanquished. In that way, it's easy for positive social change to be undermined by the behaviour of the very people who have helped bring it about. The shift from passionate revolutionary to punitive puritan can be a very short journey, as people who see their position as not merely correct but *pure* try to insist on everyone conforming to their interpretation of 'enlightenment'.

The contemporary cultural phenomenon known as 'cancel culture' is not confined to gender issues, but many of its toughest and angriest manifestations are being directed at people—men and women—who are judged to have been insensitive or insufficiently enlightened in their gender attitudes.

'Cancel culture' is the latest manifestation of an ancient tendency among people with a self-righteous, puritanical disposition to believe that those whose attitudes or behaviour deviate from some gold standard of purity should not merely be exposed or condemned, but ostracised boycotted and shunned. It's the witch-hunt mentality, the vigilante mentality, the fundamentalist mentality—a deliberately divisive movement that prioritises 'righteous' (even if misguided) anger over any attempt to understand the influences and conventions that shape human attitudes and behaviour.

There's a perfectly natural—and less extreme—tendency to weigh information about the flaws and shortcomings in the lives of people whose work we admire against the quality and enduring significance of their work. Sometimes, we might be quite condemnatory of, for example, a scientist's or a philosopher's private life, while still acknowledging the value of their contribution to our knowledge or understanding of the world. But we usually stop short of letting our reservations about people's politics or gender attitudes lead to a comprehensive rejection of their work.

'Cancel culture' is different. It goes much further than reappraisal by insisting that a person whose attitudes or behaviour offend against current mores should be wiped from the record; obliterated—as if they had never existed. It also tends to ignore the fact that most of us are a combination of noble and dark impulses . . . and that people can change. (John Newton, the author of the hymn 'Amazing Grace', was once a vile slave trader.)

The problem about such a zealous campaign is that each successful cancellation stimulates the appetite to go further. Some people, fired with puritanical zeal, advocate such things as pulling down statues of people they no longer admire or approve of, silencing people who say things they don't agree with, campaigning against commercial brands whose proprietors or marketers are perceived to have offended against the new cultural norms in some way, 'cleansing' or even banning books no longer considered appropriate. And yet, to 'cancel' the past is to rob us of the opportunity to learn from the mistakes of the past and to see how far we've come. And to 'cancel' dissident voices in the present is to rob us of the benefits of healthy debate that might actually illuminate our own understanding of an issue—even if only by giving us fresh grounds for believing that we were right all along!

Should notoriously misogynistic—or even chauvinistic—artists, scientists, philosophers and writers of the past have their work destroyed or suppressed because their gender-based values don't line up with ours? Should we ignore or downplay the work of Albert Einstein, for instance, because he apparently treated his wife extremely shabbily—once writing to a friend that he regarded her as an employee he couldn't fire, and ultimately driving her to a nervous breakdown? Should we burn the novels of Graham Greene or the philosophical works of Bertrand Russell because they were both incorrigible philanderers—now regarded as a sure sign of exploitation of women? Should we evict Socrates from the pantheon of Western philosophy because he explicitly regarded women as inferior to men, and no better than slaves? Should we eschew the works of Richard Wagner because he was a sexist, a womaniser and a 'wife stealer' or perhaps because his music became so strongly associated with the Third Reich?

Where will we draw the line if we are hellbent on cancelling manifestations of a culture, or of personal behaviour, we no longer approve of? Pop stars, TV shows, commercial brands, entrepreneurs, journalists, novelists . . . the family next door? Are we seriously going to police their every word to ensure they are conforming to our particular view of gender—or religion, or politics, or . . .?

If we are to declare peace in the gender wars, if we are to commit ourselves to a new spirit of cooperation in the work of building a more harmonious, creative, tolerant and productive society, then we'll need to be less concerned about trying to 'cancel' people, and more concerned with encouraging each other to create the kind of world people will admire—and be grateful for—fifty or a hundred years from now.

Whenever we feel ourselves fired with cancellation zeal, we would do well to acknowledge that our present state of cultural evolution—including our supreme confidence in our own virtue—may well be subjected to revision in the future, perhaps even to ridicule. Let each era recognise its heroes— or, at least, the women and men who attracted positive attention at the time—and let those of us from a subsequent era ponder and learn from such adulation, especially when we see it as misplaced. Let each era read its own books and see its own movies, and let those who come afterwards look back at them from the perspective of their own 'enlightenment'. How else will we learn about social evolution and moral relativism?

We might also do well to ponder the advice given by Buddha: 'Do not be a judge of others . . . Those who judge others only harm themselves.' That advice was echoed by Jesus of Nazareth, in his famous Sermon on the Mount: 'Do not judge, so that you may not be judged.' In today's climate, we might express such an injunction like this: 'Do not be too keen to cancel others, or you might be cancelled yourself.'

A little humility might encourage us to devote less energy to cancellation of people—present or past—we don't approve of, and more to the promotion of social harmony. Let Marcus Aurelius have the last word: 'If you are pained by external things, it is not they that disturb you, but your own judgement of them. And it is in your power to wipe out that judgement now.'

Reflections . . .

- We are living in an exciting period of post-revolutionary adjustment to the new enlightenment about gender. As we come to terms with greater gender fluidity and diversity than many of us have previously encountered, the key word is *equality*. Other key words, as ever, are *kindness*, *compassion* and *empathy*. And now, more than ever, we need to learn *acceptance*, too. People who choose to live differently from us are still part of us. (Remember that shimmering web!) We need to stay humble about all this. Getting arrogant and antsy about something as deeply personal as gender identity is bound to be counterproductive.

- The 'dangerous period' I've referred to several times is only dangerous if we are intransigent in the views we hold about gender identities, and gender roles and responsibilities. Revolutions always kick up dust that can obscure our view of the world for a while. Let's be patient as the dust settles. And let's acknowledge that things will never be perfect. Huge progress has been made and the necessary remaining steps will best be taken in a spirit of sympathetic cooperation and mutual respect between people at all points on the gender spectrum. Beware of being too zealous, lest we fall into the trap of simplistic overreach and overcorrection—a sure pathway to more conflict and confrontation.

- My only fear about the gender revolution is that, because we are in the midst of a highly individualistic phase of our sociocultural evolution, we might be inclined to place too much emphasis on personal identity—and *gender identity* in particular—as a basis for asserting the differences between us. That would create the risk of losing sight of the deepest truth of all: regardless of our position on the gender spectrum, or how hard we've fought to gain recognition for it, we all share a common humanity. The best outcome of the gender revolution would be for our wholehearted embrace of our common humanity to lead us into new depths of tolerance, sensitivity and appreciation of all our nuances of difference. After all, it's easier to accommodate (and even celebrate) those nuances when we feel ourselves secure within the bonds of our oneness. We are not merely 'one' with those who are like us; oneness means what it says. It includes all of us.

- How do you think we'll be viewed by those who look back at us from the perspective of, say, 2075—assuming our species has survived that long? (I won't be around, but you might.) What aspect of today's gender culture do you think they might want to 'cancel'? I predict they'll shake their heads at our obsession with pronouns; at our failure to treat persons as persons, irrespective of gender;

173

and at our reluctance to accept that, when it comes to gender, we are spread across a very broad spectrum. And they'll probably have trouble grasping the point of single-sex schools (which will by then have become largely obsolete), unless it was to perpetuate an unhelpful cultural gulf between male and female, based on definitions of gender so narrow that such schools became uncomfortable places for young people experiencing gender fluidity. But perhaps in another fifty years or so, they'll praise our belated attempts to become true egalitarians.

- PS: Here's another ugly prejudice that needs to be called out . . .

Now we're finally tackling sexism (and racism) with some vigour, it's time to turn our attention to another offensive 'ism': *ageism*. Time to embrace generational equality as enthusiastically as we are now embracing gender equality. Research conducted by Alexis Polidoras and others at Newgate Research for COTA Australia in April 2023 revealed that 35 per cent of older Australians (aged fifty plus) report having been victims of age discrimination, including 24 per cent who report workplace discrimination on the basis of age. For those aged sixty to sixty-nine, 42 per cent have experienced age discrimination, including 31 per cent who have experienced it in the workplace. Like all prejudices, ageism sometimes tries to pass itself off as a joke: referring to COVID as the 'Boomer remover' was often thought to be witty rather than deeply offensive to older people. In a similar vein, we talk about 'the ageing population' as if that's a worry—a looming burden on our society and our economy.

The truth is that today's older Australians are healthier, fitter, better educated, more engaged and more willing to contribute to society than any comparable age cohort in the past. Quite apart from those who are remaining in paid work for longer than any previous generation, almost half are doing unpaid work—mostly in the form of volunteering—and many are the beneficiaries of our compulsory superannuation scheme. Though some of them (like some younger people) need pensions, public housing and extra health care, older Australians, generally speaking, are not a burden but a precious resource of experience, wisdom and energy.

4

Poverty is everyone's problem

'Poverty' can be a startling, even shocking, word to use in contemporary Australian society. It throws out an unwelcome challenge to our longstanding myth of egalitarianism, and to the idea that ours is the land of opportunity for all, the land of the 'fair go'. Surely, we say, this is the kind of place where anyone with a decent education, hard work and a bit of luck can succeed. In the words of a recent prime minister, Scott Morrison, 'If you have a go, you'll get a go.' (Dismal implication: if you're not getting a fair go, it's presumably your own fault for not having a go.)

The very idea of poverty contradicts the popular view that, if we're not exactly classless, then at least we're a broadly middle-class society—sure, there are a few wealthy people at the top of the heap, and a few people struggling at the bottom, but most of us are getting on okay. Embracing a fiction like that means we're practically obliged to deny the existence of any significant poverty or, at least, to claim that poverty in

Australia shouldn't be compared with poverty in other places: 'There's no such thing as *real* poverty in Australia—not like parts of Africa or Asia. You can't live in a house and drive a car and call yourself poor.' (Oh, yeah? Read on.)

Another favourite way of avoiding the issue of poverty in Australia is to quote the ancient Latin proverb, 'Not he who has little, but he who wishes for more, is poor.' There you go; that puts it into perspective: *it's all in the mind.* That allows you to say that poverty is not really about the lack of money or possessions—it's really about some people foolishly and unrealistically aspiring to get what they don't have. 'If only poor people would stop wanting more, it would cease to be a problem for them.' Very neat. Very smug.

If you still feel a bit awkward about the topic, you can argue about the definition of poverty. What do we mean by poor? Where should we draw the line? How many poor people are there, really? Aren't we exaggerating the problem even by calling it poverty—a bit of inequality, maybe, but full-blown *poverty*? In *Australia*? Nah.

In fact, more than three million Australians are poor. The 2023 figure was 3.3 million, to be more precise. And, yes, we do need to define what we mean by 'poor' in order to comprehend a figure like that. Obviously, poverty is a relative term. Obviously, poverty means different things in different places. Obviously, poverty is somewhat subjective: some people might feel poor and others, in similar circumstances, might not. A useful definition of poverty could run something like this: a person who can't afford to participate in their society in what most people would consider a normal way can be classified as poor.

In a society like ours, 'normal' means that you're not often troubled by the thought of having to do without something you need because you can't afford it. If you're a parent, it means you can afford to feed your kids nutritious food and give them breakfast before they leave for school each day. You can afford to pay for their school uniforms and excursions. You can afford to have an occasional meal out, or take an annual holiday away from home. You can afford to go to the dentist, pay your electricity and gas bills without too much strain, and if you have a car you can get it regularly serviced. It means you can afford to keep a pet, feed it properly and take it to the vet when it's sick. It means you can afford to buy occasional non-essentials.

'Poverty' means such things are simply out of reach—including, too often, good nutrition. A few years ago, a UNICEF study found that 16 per cent of dependent children in Australia lack reliable access to safe and nutritious food. At the time, I struggled to come to terms with that figure, but when you realise that 20 per cent of Australian households are trying to get by on an average income of around $24,000 per year—that's the *average* figure, which means many are struggling to get by on far less than that—you realise that, once housing and other fixed costs are met, food insecurity remains a significant problem for millions of Australians. To put it bluntly, poor people often experience hunger. Some schools now provide breakfast for children who would other-wise have to go without.

As for things the rest of us might regard as little luxuries—new shoes for fashion rather than practical reasons, an occasional treat for the kids, a new shirt because you liked the look of it, an impulsive weekend away somewhere, upgrading your smartphone? Such things are laughably remote from people living below the poverty line. As is 'the examined life': when Socrates so heartlessly said that 'the unexamined life is not worth living', he was referring to the elite of Athens (not to anyone as inferior as women or slaves, for example). An 'examined life' is not a priority for someone struggling to pay the rent, or someone who needs help to fill out a form at Centrelink. If you're living below the poverty line, 'keeping your head above water' is your main concern.

The 'poverty line'? That's a more objective way of approaching the definition of poverty. In Australia, we generally accept the poverty line as being set at an income level that's 50 per cent of the median income of all wage and salary earners. According to the Australian Council of Social Service (ACOSS), the poverty line in 2022 was set at $489 per week for a single adult. So you'd be regarded as poor if you earned *less than* that figure. *Less than.* If you were unemployed and on JobSeeker, the most you could receive would be about $485 per week. If you were on the age pension, the maximum you could receive is about $500 per week. While you're pondering those figures, also think about the cost of housing, food and groceries, transport, electricity and gas bills.

It might help to put all this into perspective if we were to talk about the inequality of wealth and income in Australia, rather than simply focusing on poverty. It's a tricky area, and there is a great deal of disagreement among economists about how these figures should be calculated. But let's think broadly about the relativities.

Try this: a joint study by ACOSS and the University of New South Wales concluded that the top 20 per cent of Australian households are almost *one hundred times richer* than the bottom 20 per cent.

Or this: according to *The Australian Financial Review*, our top fifty CEOs had an average annual income of $6.18 million in 2022, almost one hundred times more than the average annual income of $65,000 for all wage earners.

Or this: David Richardson and Matt Grudnoff of the Australia Institute report that, between 2009 and 2019, the top 10 per cent of income earners received 93 per cent of income *growth*.

Or this: the top 20 per cent of Australian households own more than 60 per cent of Australia's wealth. The bottom 20 per cent (that's the same number of households) own just 4 per cent. That leaves the famous Australian middle class—60 per cent of households—owning the remaining 36 per cent.

Need I go on?

It's not much consolation, but perhaps worth mentioning that inequality is far worse in the US: the top 20 per cent of Americans own 86 per cent of the country's wealth, leaving just 14 per cent to be distributed among the other 80 per cent of the population. Eminent Australian economist Roger Wilkins and colleagues have noted that Australia is 'more equal' then both the US and France, but also that Australia has become steadily more unequal over the past thirty years.

The main point to emerge from the merest glance at these figures is that the gap between the top and bottom of the economic heap in Australia is *wider than it has ever been*. It's not only that the rich are getting richer and further out of

181

sight of the poor; it's also that both groups are growing, and the vaunted Aussie middle class is shrinking.

So let's go to the heart of the matter . . .

Why are so many Australians poor?

There's a long list of factors contributing to poverty, and it's hard to see what the poor could have done about any of them, whether they've 'had a go' or not.

Let's start with **the family you were born into and the place where you live.** Single-parent households are over-represented among poor households and, yes, postcode is a chillingly accurate predictor of poverty.

Australia's shocking drift towards greater **educational inequality** means that what was once regarded as the surest pathway out of poverty and disadvantage—a good education—is now increasingly denied to children who live in poorer parts of the country and have access only to under-resourced public schools. We are now handing more than $16 billion of public money to private schools, every year. Many of those schools are already wealthy but cheerfully accept the additional largesse. In return, are they accountable for how they spend all this public money? No. Do they offer to share their libraries and sporting facilities with nearby public schools, or lend them their school buses to take children from those schools on excursions? Just ask them.

Who's surprised that the gap in educational performance between the richest and poorest Australian schools is among the highest of the world's wealthiest countries, or that it's steadily widening? Overall standards of school education keep falling, dragged down by the poorest schools. Poorer schools inevitably have more trouble attracting outstanding teachers, and almost no possibility of including the all-important subject of music in their curriculum. (Why mention music? Perhaps because, as Shakespeare put it in *The Merchant of Venice*: 'The man that hath no music in himself/Nor is not moved with concord of sweet sounds/Is fit for treasons, stratagems and spoils.' Or, more pragmatically, because of the strong evidence linking music education—including both performance and composition—to performance in other subjects.)

Until we tackle the scandal of inequality in school funding, we have no hope of restoring our public education system to the high standard it once enjoyed, where you received a world-class education at your local public school because that's where all the public money available for education was spent. *All* of it.

Unemployment and underemployment are obvious contributors to poverty. An increasingly casualised, part-time workforce edges more people towards the poverty line. In 2023, we were celebrating the fact that unemployment had fallen to its lowest level for many years, though it was predicted to rise steadily through 2024. In any case, we need to remember that, in Australia, you count as employed if you have at least *one hour* of paid employment per week. So the real issue is *under*employment—that is, people who want more work than is available. That figure remains stubbornly high, with more than one million Australian workers being underemployed.

Although we are starting to address the issue of poverty among **people with a disability,** including a long-overdue push to help them into employment, it has long been the conventional wisdom that 'poverty is disability's close companion'. And the same goes for the carers of people with a disability.

The high cost of **housing** has led to the concept of 'after-housing poverty', where low-income earners spend so much of their income on housing (either in mortgage payments or rent) that they effectively live below the poverty line, even though they may be decently housed. More than ten years ago, the Reserve Bank was warning that the cost of housing was being driven up by investors forcing first-home buyers out of the market. Which was a polite way of saying that the wealthy were making life harder for the poor.

At its most extreme, the housing problem manifests itself as homelessness. More than 120,000 Australians, tonight, have nowhere to call home—some because their homes were lost in a fire or flood, some because they've left an unsafe domestic setting and haven't yet found a permanent alternative, but most because they are caught in a poverty trap.

There are many other factors associated with a higher risk of poverty: being an Aboriginal or Torres Strait Islander, a recent immigrant, a refugee, a person seeking asylum, a person with chronic health problems. Age and gender are also relevant, with young people more likely than older people to be underemployed, and older divorced or widowed women at particular risk of falling below the poverty line.

Another risk factor we rarely mention—either through embarrassment or ignorance—is **intelligence**. Which is not to suggest for a moment that all people living in poverty have more limited cognitive capacity than others, nor that all wealthier people are brighter than all poorer people. That's obviously untrue. But it would be insensitive and lacking in compassion not to acknowledge that limited cognitive ability will be a significant factor contributing to unwise decisions (both life choices and financial decisions) and reduced opportunities for work.

Clearly, intelligence is a matter of genetics (though education helps us make the most of what we have), so it is particularly cruel for people endowed with above-average cognitive capacity to denigrate those who are less well endowed. Equally cruel would be a failure to acknowledge low IQ as a factor not only in the incidence of poverty, but in the operation of society more generally. It is a central theme of this book that we all share a common humanity regardless of our multitudinous individual differences, and that each of us bears responsibility to care for those who need our help.

You're reading this book, so you might find it almost impossible to imagine what it must be like for the roughly 20 per cent of the population who have trouble reading— even to read a bus timetable, or the instructions on the medication that's been prescribed for them. Not all those people have limited cognitive capacity: some may experience dyslexia or other learning disorders; some may be from non-English-speaking backgrounds; some may have been deprived of sufficient learning opportunities to master literacy. But if you think of yourself as 'smart', you might be inclined to think that people who, for whatever reason, appear less smart than you are inferior in some way. Would you dare to think that about people who happen to be taller or shorter than you? About people who happen to have blue eyes rather than brown? People whose skin colour happens to be different from yours? Genetic inheritance is one of the things over which we have no control, so it would be both foolish and cruel if we were to discount the difficulties faced by people in our midst who happen to have inherited limited cognitive capacity.

***

We could go on with that list, because there is a huge range of factors—personal, societal, circumstantial, genetic, accidental—that contribute to the incidence of poverty. But always the nagging question: in an affluent society like ours—by some measures, the world's richest country—how do we let such factors lead to poverty? And why do we let the poor *stay* poor?

If inequality is the real issue, perhaps we've been asking the wrong question. Instead of 'why are so many Australians poor?', perhaps we should be asking this one:

Why are so many Australians rich?
That might look like a silly question to ask in a culture that seems to worship wealth, to confuse 'wealth' with 'worth', to admire the rich simply for being rich and to encourage young people to seek wealth as a life goal in itself. In a culture that has largely surrendered to the blandishments of materialism, you'd expect a wealth class not only to emerge but to burgeon. And so it has.

How did they do it? As with poverty, many factors drive the acquisition of wealth and high on the list is **the accident of birth**—the family you're born into, and the place where they happen to live. As with poverty, so with wealth: your genetic inheritance, including your cognitive capacity, will play a huge role in determining the trajectory of your life. And the kind of education your family chooses for you will also play a big part in shaping your goals and motivations.

If you're raised in a culture of affluence and ambition, with success typically defined in material terms, you're probably going to end up rich when compared with the bulk of society.

Given that sort of background and heritage, it's easy to identify some of the factors that drive and facilitate the acquisition of wealth.

Many wealthy people will tell you that the secret of their wealth is no secret at all: **hard work and perseverance**. And there's no doubt that, when wealth is the goal, many people will work very hard indeed to achieve it. Others, of course, may also work extremely hard—as teachers, nurses, paramedics, police officers, manual workers, cleaners or anyone on a fixed income—but never acquire wealth. So there's more to it than hard work.

Starting—or inheriting—a successful business obviously helps, and some wealthy people are only *incidentally* wealthy because they've operated a particular enterprise that turned out to be more profitable than they had expected: a mining company, a media empire, a trucking firm, a chain of retailers, a fashion business, an IT start-up. Many enterprises fail, but the successful ones tend to reward their founders and those who inherit the business very handsomely indeed. By the way, 'successful business' is probably the right term to apply to the highest paid medical specialists, too (though not to hard-working and grievously underpaid GPs).

Sorry to mention it, but **greed** can't be discounted as a motivation for the acquisition of great wealth. When you look

187

at people at the top of the economic heap, it's sometimes hard to resist asking the question, 'How much is enough?' If you had ten million, did you need twenty? If you had one hundred million, did you need two hundred? At what point did you stop working to make yourself and your family comfortable enough to lead a worthwhile life and pay your dues to society, and start working merely to amass more wealth, with no particular thought about its purpose? Greed is like that: it leads us to think that having more of what we already have—wealth, power, possessions—will make us feel better. If you fell for the idea that money can buy happiness, then you presumably think that overflowing coffers will lead you to be overflowing with joy. Really? Just ask the lawyers who help rich families sort out their money squabbles. (On the other hand, 'enough' money can certainly help lift people out of the misery of poverty.)

Prioritising **'making money'** as the primary focus of your work—or even thinking of that as being the essential purpose of your work—can certainly make you rich, though it may well erode the sense of your life as having any nobler meaning and purpose. (As we transition from a manufacturing to a transactional economy, it turns out that moving other people's money around is a very good way of making money.) In fact, making money appears not to be too hard if you're single-minded or lucky enough, if you're born in the right place at the right time, and if you go to the right school and mix with the right people. What can be hard, later in life, is deciding what it was all *for*.

The assumption that **wealth equals power** drives some people to acquire vast wealth, even if that involves the exploitation of others in order to achieve their goal. (On the evidence, the assumption that 'wealth equals power' seems pretty safe, at least in an economic sense.)

Overestimating your value to an organisation can help to make you rich while exacerbating inequality, especially when senior executives judge themselves to be, say, a hundred times more valuable to the organisation than most other employees. Laughable as it sounds today, there was once a convention in the more civilised, more egalitarian corporate culture of the past that a chief executive should receive no more than ten times the average salary paid to all employees.

And then there are the lurks, the dodges, the schemes that enable wealthy people to increase their wealth via **tax avoidance**. Many of them prefer the more genteel term 'tax minimisation', and insist that it's only sensible to pay the least amount of personal income tax you can possibly get away with. But is it?

You meet a wealthy man. He seems warm, charming, sincere and generally well intentioned. And then you find he has a large amount of money salted away in offshore bank accounts—in the Cayman Islands, say—for the sole purpose of minimising the tax he would otherwise have to pay in Australia. Ponder that strategy for a moment: this is a person who has amassed serious wealth working in Australia, who then seeks ways of minimising the income tax he pays into Australia's coffers.

We've heard too many ugly stories of fabulously wealthy people who brag about the small amount of income tax they pay, as if to say, 'I want all the benefits that making money in Australia has brought me, and I want to continue to enjoy living here, but I'm buggered if I'm going to pay any more tax than I can get away with.' In one infamous case, a mega-rich person publicly declared that *he* would decide what to do with his money rather than 'giving it to the government' (i.e. the community).

When you hear wealthy people talking about 'giving something back' via philanthropy, it's hard to avoid the impression that they must have 'taken' a great deal if they now feel some moral pressure to give some of it back.

***

One significant difference between wealth and poverty is that wealthy people are usually able to make choices about what they will do and how they will do it; poor people, hemmed in by circumstance, are generally not free to make such choices.

Wealthy people usually strive to become wealthy, whereas the poor never set out to be poor. So, by implication, the rich seek inequality because they seek an ever-larger share of the available economic pie—often without consciously appreciating what they're doing, and sometimes claiming that they are actually helping to increase the pie for everyone to share. That claim is based on the infamous 'trickle-down effect'— where increasing wealth at the top is supposed to benefit people all the way down to the bottom. The US economist John Kenneth Galbraith described this using the 'horse-and-sparrow' metaphor: 'If you feed the horse enough oats, some will pass through to the road for the sparrows.' In Australia, the 'trickle-down' theory has been disproven by events: growth in wealth at the top has coexisted with growth in the number of people living in poverty, and with a widening gap between the two.

But let's not focus too much attention on the rich. Let's confront a rather painful possibility that implicates many more of us in the problem:

Are we, by our own actions, helping to institutionalise poverty?

We help to widen the gap between rich and poor—and to ensure that the poor stay poor—whenever, as employers, we ask our employees to work regular overtime (whether paid or unpaid), thereby creating fewer jobs.

We do it whenever, as well-paid home owners, we do all our own domestic chores instead of employing someone else to do them. (The counterargument that this will create a 'servant class' overlooks the historical fact that many industries—from education to fashion to food production—began by people deciding to outsource things they used to do for themselves.)

We do it whenever, as governments, we offer property investors incentives (such as negative gearing) that push up house prices and squeeze the poor out of the market.

We do it whenever we offer tax cuts to the rich that inevitably reduce the resources available to address the needs of the poor.

We do it whenever we introduce disincentives to employment, like payroll tax, that encourage employers to trim their workforce.

We do it whenever, as taxpayers, we try to avoid paying the tax appropriate to our income, given that income tax is the most efficient way of redistributing wealth to meet the needs

191

of the poor. It is a valid criticism of the way our society runs that so many charities have sprung up to relieve the suffering of the poor: in a kinder, more compassionate society, that would be a non-negotiable target for government spending, not something that relies on private charity. And, by the way, the 'needs of the poor' have nothing to do with what we think the poor might *deserve*. In a truly civilised, egalitarian society, we have only to establish that a need exists to have defined an entitlement. The poor are entitled to our support because they are poor. Period.

We help to institutionalise poverty whenever we encourage governments to use public money to swell the coffers of non-public schools. (Which is not to argue against the existence of private schools, but only to suggest that any group or institution that wishes to establish a school outside the public system should not be entitled to receive public funds.)

We help to institutionalise poverty whenever we allow ourselves to think that prosperity is our *right*—or even our good luck—and the poverty of those at the bottom of the heap is inevitable, unavoidable . . . and bad luck for them.

***

Former US president John F. Kennedy once said: 'If a free society cannot save the many who are poor, it cannot save the few who are rich.' Save the rich from what? From becoming corrupted by their wealth? From becoming arrogant about the position in society their wealth has bought them? (Some wit remarked that Elon Musk should be tried for 'crimes against humility'.) From becoming insulated by their wealth from an awareness of what life is like for those on the margins?

Yes, all of those things.

There is nothing wrong with wealth, but everything is wrong with greed, selfishness, and insensitivity to the needs of those around us who are less well off than we are. The poor and otherwise disadvantaged are an integral part of who we are as a society; each of them is *one of us*.

There is nothing wrong with a big pay packet, but everything is wrong with an obsessive desire to pay less than your fair share of tax. There is nothing wrong with enjoying material comforts, but everything is wrong with a preoccupation with material possessions. As the British philosopher Bertrand Russell put it: 'it is preoccupation with possessions, more than anything else, that prevents [people] from living freely and nobly'. To which we might add that our preoccupation with *our* wealth, *our* prosperity, *our* material comfort and the indulgence of *our* children—unless it is tempered by charity, compassion and generosity towards those in need—will ensure that the poor stay poor, that the egalitarian dream fades away, and that Australia becomes a harsher, more rigidly stratified society.

Is that what we want?

If not, we must find more creative and equitable ways of distributing the available work, and we must also find more compassionate and generous ways of supporting those who can't find enough work to get them above the poverty line. And we must find a way of dealing more fairly with those who simply lack the capacity to earn an income, whether through disability, disadvantage, misfortune, or a lack of the competencies—including cognitive competencies—required to perform paid work.

Do we want to make the marginalised and disadvantaged feel ashamed of themselves? Do we want to humiliate the poor? Or are we prepared to say, 'They are part of us. We must bring them with us, regardless of the cost to ourselves.' As the US philosopher John Rawls expressed it in *A Theory of Justice*: 'social and economic inequalities, for example inequalities of wealth and authority, are just only if they result in compensating benefits for everyone, and in particular for the least advantaged members of society'. Echoing Rawls in a recent speech to the Australian Council of Human Rights Agencies, former premier of Western Australia Geoff Gallop argues that 'we've had a long period in which economic freedom has been prioritised over social equality. Fairness has been the inevitable loser, followed by a growth in distrust of mainstream governments whether left or right.'

If some government is finally brave enough to tell us what it would cost to create a genuinely egalitarian society, and what that would mean for the radical reform of our taxation system, we must be courageous—and generous—enough to say, 'Let's do it!'

To let the poor—all 3.3 million of them—stay poor and therefore disadvantaged would be to abandon not only the ideal of egalitarianism, but to cast doubt on our understanding of what it means to be civilised and, indeed, on our understanding of what it means to be human.

Reflections . . .

- History tells us that inequality ultimately breeds revolution. We're not anywhere near that stage yet—and let's hope we never approach the situation of pre-revolutionary France, or even of contemporary America. But we need to be clear about the direction we're travelling in and to be sure that's where we want to go. We still indulge ourselves in the myth of the land of the 'fair go', even of the egalitarian society. But we're a long way from that. We're already so stratified by wealth and income inequality that it looks rather as if we're prepared to settle for becoming another one of those boringly predictable, highly institutionalised three-tiered societies. Are we willing to settle for that? *Are we?* If we try hard enough, we can insulate ourselves from what's happening below us on the socioeconomic heap, but that only makes us complicit in the remorseless process of stratification.

- I mentioned radical taxation reform. As long as we're in the grip of neoliberalism, that's not going to happen. And it will never happen until both sides of politics agree that it should. But societies change and evolve. We had a small glimpse into what radical reform could look like during the COVID-19 pandemic. Under a conservative government, robust income support measures temporarily lifted about half a million people out of poverty. If we really dream of a more equitable, more compassionate, more egalitarian Australia, we will eventually have to rethink the nature of the link between taxation, social justice and personal morality. And we might have to demand that politicians wash their mouths out every time they say 'tax cuts'.

5

The Boomers' Legacy

What a ride the Baby Boomers have had!

The products of our highest birth rate since 1921, they were the beneficiaries of a post-war economic boom that ushered in an era of unprecedented prosperity. They became, up to that point in our history, our most highly educated generation, setting a pro-education example that subsequent generations have enthusiastically followed. They also established new records for international travel, for home ownership and for divorce. In their middle years, they were buffeted by the highest unemployment rate since the Great Depression. They had to contend with an often baffling information technology revolution that their children and grandchildren took in their stride. And they were the generation that took up the cry for women's rights and fought hard to make it happen. Time after time, in so many ways, it has fallen to the Boomers to be social pioneers.

The members of the Boomer generation were born in the fifteen years after the end of World War II, 1946–61. (That rather conveniently fits the fifteen-year span that demographers typically use to define a 'generation'.) In 2024, the year of this book's publication, the oldest of them are turning seventy-eight and the youngest sixty-three.

At the peak of the boom in Australia, the birth rate reached 3.6 babies per woman. That meant the Boomers, relative to total population, had a bigger footprint, a louder voice and more economic muscle than either their parents' or their children's generation. The birth rate has been in steady decline since the end of the boom and, at 1.6 babies per woman, has now reached its lowest point in our recorded history.

For reasons we are about to explore, the Boomers were dubbed the 'Me Generation' by their parents and other observers of this feisty, rebellious, hard-to-ignore cohort. They themselves, later in life, often characterised themselves as the 'stress' generation as they set new records for the use of tranquilliser and anti-depressant medication. Along the way, they've also been known as the 'denim' generation (forever young, though it's stretch denim these days), the 'sandwich' generation (when they were simultaneously caring for elderly parents *and* dependent children) and the 'keep working' generation (as they eschewed the idea of retirement as too ageing, and embraced the concept of 'refocusing' instead).

The contradictory influences that shaped the Boomers

The Boomers' attitudes and values were formed by two powerful but contradictory influences on their early development: the confidence and optimism generated by the post-war economic boom, and the anxiety and pessimism of the Cold War.

The optimism fuelled a big spike in the marriage rate after the end of the war—characterised by some demographers as a period of 'marriage madness'. Young people were not only tying the knot and having babies in unprecedented numbers but were doing it younger: by 1954, halfway through the boom, 60 per cent of women were marrying between the ages of twenty and twenty-four—roughly double the pre-war figure.

The marriage and birth rates had both increased steadily during World War II but exploded when the war ended. The baby boom, like the marriage boom, was a symbolic expression of the post-war spirit of energy and optimism. It signalled a return not only to peace, but also to the prospect of contented, stable family life. 'Home and family' became the focal point of a society that was settling down to the serious business of making the dream of middle-class, suburban prosperity come true, and through the 1950s and 1960s, that dream became a reality on a very large scale.

If the marriage boom was the demographic antecedent of the baby boom, then the economic boom was its cultural cradle. And what a boom it was! A housing boom, a construction boom, a manufacturing boom, a mining boom. Consumerism was born in an enthusiastic rush to buy all the goods and services flooding the post-war market: domestic appliances, kitchen gadgets, wall-to-wall carpets, cars (especially locally made Holdens), women's fashions (the 'New Look', to match the new spirit of the times), confectionery, holidays and travel, even phones (though many people in the 1950s were still walking to the end of the street—including the street I grew up in—clutching their two pennies, to use the public phone).

Unemployment was hardly an issue. There was so much work to be done in the post-war era and so many European refugees looking to start a new life somewhere else that Australia began its massive immigration program. It was partly in response to the humanitarian crisis and partly to help supply the workers needed to fuel the economic machine that was now running at full throttle.

Having braced themselves for the long slog of post-war recovery, the Boomers' parents were astonished by what actually happened: it seemed to them more like an economic miracle than a mere boom. But many of them said later in life that they had tried not to let it 'turn their heads': they maintained the values of prudence and restraint that the pre-war Great Depression and then the war years had taught them: save for what you want; stay out of debt; only buy what you need.

They had hoped to instil those same values into their offspring, but it was not to be. The siren song of materialism was too loud and too seductive! The Boomers became enthusiastic consumers from an early age and then, to their parents' dismay, as they reached early adulthood, they discovered the joys of credit as a way of spending yet more. 'Making the most of it', the Boomers called it; 'living beyond their means' was their parents' verdict.

To the young Boomers, it seemed that the future was rosy, and they would be borne into it on a constantly rising escalator of prosperity.

But all this economic jollity was coexisting with the other major post-war influence: the Cold War. Through childhood and into adolescence, the Boomers lived in the shadow of the atomic bombs that the US had dropped on Hiroshima and Nagasaki and that now represented a threat to human survival. This was not mere sabre-rattling that might have presaged a conventional military conflict: this was the threat of nuclear annihilation on a massive—possibly global—scale. The USSR and the USA were both frantically stockpiling nuclear weapons, and the concept of MAD, or mutually assured destruction, had wide currency, even becoming the title of a satirical magazine that became a Boomer favourite. Its founders never claimed the name had been inspired by the Cold War acronym—that's just my fantasy. ('Let's get sex and violence off TV and back on the streets where they belong' was a typical *MAD* joke from the 1960s.)

Spending their formative years in a Cold War atmosphere, the Boomers were not only absorbing a kind of Armageddon mentality but were also being exposed to all the dark, dystopian material then being published in Cold War espionage novels and films. Spies, not soldiers, were the new heroes. This was a world of moral ambiguity, bleakly documented by writers like John le Carré (*The Spy Who Came in from the Cold*) and Len Deighton (*The Ipcress File*), and treated more flippantly by Ian Fleming's James Bond novels and the popular TV comedy series *Get Smart*.

One of the features of this period was the widespread fear that nuclear war could be precipitated accidentally, by someone badly misjudging a threatening situation or by simply pressing the wrong button. That fear was compounded by the belief that if the Cold War ever turned hot, it would be an unstoppable *danse macabre* of nuclear strike and counterstrike.

***

All of that led to The Big Boomer Question—more intriguing than any question we might raise about any of the generations that followed the boom: how would this rising generation of young Australians reconcile two such utterly contradictory formative influences? On the one hand, there was the promise of endless prosperity and material comfort; on the other was the real possibility of obliteration via a nuclear holocaust.

The answer to that question can be found in the slogan that became the Boomers' generational catchcry: 'We're not here for a long time; we're here for a good time.'

That meant they were in a hurry to do everything, including get married. Thirty per cent of Boomer women were married by the age of twenty—though they didn't have nearly as many children as their parents' generation had. In fact, they cut the birth rate in half, down to 1.8 babies per woman by 1984, the year that mid-Boomers turned thirty. That reluctance to have children was a reflection of their deep misgivings about the future. Getting married was one thing; having children was a commitment of a very different order.

Putting their decision to have fewer kids into practice was greatly facilitated by the introduction of the contraceptive pill in 1961. It was also reinforced by the fact that Boomer women were attaining higher levels of education than their mothers and grandmothers had: as noted in 'The Context', more highly educated women tend to have fewer children than less well educated women.

The Boomers' enthusiasm for higher education transformed the university and TAFE sectors by their sheer numbers. They were in a rush to travel, too, creating an unprecedented 'youth travel' market. They were in a rush to get a mortgage and buy a house. They were in a rush to ascend the employment ladder as quickly as they could.

And they were in a rush to embrace social change. They were turning their backs on their parents' values and way of life. They wanted to be—and were—more radical in their thinking. They wanted the fruits of 'women's lib' to be seen *now*. Older Boomers wanted Australia out of the Vietnam War *now*. In 1972, those old enough to vote were keen to support the switch to the first Labor government in twenty-three years—most of them by then had lived under a Coalition government all their lives.

If you had to choose one word to capture the essence of the young Boomers, it would have to be 'impatient'. And why not? Given those powerful but contradictory influences upon them, who could blame them for feeling some urgency about doing the things they wanted to get done?

They were devoted to the concept of instant gratification. They managed to combine a reluctance to save with an eagerness to spend. The credit card revolution that began in 1974 with the launch of Bankcard was heaven-sent for Boomers. They didn't like to think of borrowed money as a boring 'loan': they preferred the spunkier concept of 'credit'.

By the mid-1990s, when leading-edge Boomers were hitting fifty, one of Australia's most astute economic analysts and forecasters, Philip Ruthven, said of them: 'The Baby Boomers have been the shortest-term thinkers of probably any generation for over 100 years ... And they are our worst savers on record, in terms of saving as a percentage of income.' At the same time, Arun Abey, then the executive chairman of IPAC Securities, described Boomers' reluctance to save with a charitable obliqueness: 'Baby Boomers have a very strong cash-flow need.'

In essence, Boomers were acquiring a reputation for doing precisely what you'd expect people to do if they had grown up with the expectation that all the rosy prospects beckoning from the future could be swept away in an instant, courtesy of The Bomb. How do you live with the simultaneous prospect of a bright future and no future at all? Answer: you run very fast, you play very hard, and you experience all the things you want to experience—sex, travel, prosperity, power—as early as you can. Their goal was not only to 'have it all', but to have it all at once.

Whoa!

Is this one of those reckless generalisations I referred to in the chapter about fake wisdom? It's always hazardous, trying to define generational characteristics because—obviously—there's a huge range of individual differences in any age cohort we might study. Yes, the Boomers shared some mighty powerful influences early on, but like any other generation they had plenty of diversity; they had different parents, grandparents and siblings; went to different schools; and had different personalities and temperaments. Over the years of my research into Boomers' attitudes, I've often encountered Boomers' own resistance to the idea of any generalisations being made about them. As possibly the most extensively studied generation in modern history, they are understandably sick of being under the microscope and then being discussed as if they are 'specimens'. All understood. And it goes without saying that a fifteen-year span is quite a long time: in 1968, for example—the year of worldwide student uprisings with faint echoes in Australia—the oldest Boomers were twenty-two, but the youngest were only seven. Still, I'm not retreating from the broad outlines of this analysis. The facts about the Boomers' generational behaviour speak for themselves.

As time went by, and right up to today, Boomers were gradually forced to accept that, actually, they were here for a long time, after all. And they realised—dammit!—they were not necessarily having the good time that the 1950s, 1960s and 1970s had promised. 'All You Need Is Love', adopted by many of them as a theme song, turned out not to be quite true. Or not true enough. Or not the whole truth.

Nevertheless, they have retained their strong sense of independence, their pioneering, iconoclastic energy . . . and their tendency to self-indulgence. They are still on the front foot, still looking forward in a way their parents were not at this stage of their lives. But it has not been smooth sailing for them, as revealed in some of those generational self-descriptions—'stress', 'sandwich', 'keep working'—I mentioned earlier.

Their children—some tail-end Gen Xers but mostly Millennials (previously known as Gen Y)—have certainly not followed their parents' example, any more than the Boomers followed their own parents', because the formative influences on them were so utterly different. The children of

Boomers did not grow up in the midst of an economic boom; they did not live with the daily fear of annihilation; they felt none of the urgency that drove their parents' generation. In fact, if you had to characterise their generational ethos, it would range from the 'slipstream' approach of Gen X—'The Boomers have paved the way for us; let's relax a bit and concentrate on creating a pleasant lifestyle for ourselves'—to the wait-and-see approach of the Millennials, whose generational catchcry became 'Let's keep our options open'. In neither case was there much sign of impatience.

They might not have followed their parents' example, but perhaps the more relaxed attitude detectable in the Boomers' children was a direct result of living with, and closely observing, the lives of their parents. Seeing the stress that many Boomers have been under, the emotional fallout from messy divorces and the demands Boomers imposed on themselves by their own impatience, perhaps their children have said, 'Not for me.'

Some daughters of Boomers looked at their feminist mothers' 'liberated' lives and said: 'I thought you didn't want to be a doormat to your family, but you're a doormat to your own liberation. If you're free to choose, how come you've chosen to be so out-of-control busy? Yeah, maybe you can have it all, but what makes you think you can have it all at once?'

Now, as they look back on their lives, many Boomers—women and men—are asking themselves the same question.

Boomers are the way they are because that's the hand Fate dealt them. But, in general (warning: another generalisation coming up), they have continued to try to reshape the world to be more to their liking, while still aiming to have the 'good time' their formative years promised. Now in their sixties and seventies, many of them have been gripped by nostalgia for the simpler, more innocent days of yore, but that's hardly unique to them: we're all drawn, from time to time, to reflect on the years when the future seemed full of promise—especially if some of that promise was never fulfilled.

Perhaps because the future, back then, did seem so rosy for Boomers (provided they survived), they are becoming renowned as age-fighters. Reluctant to give up their jobs. Reluctant to admit to the signs of ageing. Reluctant to 'retire' in case that means 'over the hill', they prefer to contemplate the airy uplands of new opportunities that will open up as the need for full-time work recedes. Their famous reluctance to save means that many of them are not as comfortably off as they might have wished—though home ownership is generally seen as the passport to prosperity in old age.

The Boomers will meet the challenges of old age in their own way, as they have brought their distinctive approach to so many other challenges along the way. But what legacy have they left the rest of us? What has been the lasting impact of a generation that cut such a swathe through so many aspects of Australian life?

Here are seven significant culture shifts that I believe form part of the Boomer legacy.

Seven Boomer-driven trends

Boomers invented the 'elastic adolescence' that stretched well into their twenties, and their example has been followed by subsequent generations, right up to today. Back in the 1970s, the Boomers were insisting that 'thirty is the new twenty', believing that, at thirty, they were as 'young' as their parents had been at twenty.

Later, the same obsession with staying young led them to claim that 'sixty is the new fifty'. With eighty just around the corner for leading-edge Boomers, we'll soon be hearing that 'eighty is the new seventy' . . . or perhaps even 'the new sixty'. Boomers have typically thought of themselves as looking younger, feeling younger, dressing younger, eating younger and generally *being* younger than their parents' generation were at all stages of the life cycle. 'My father was old at sixty, but I'm just getting started' is a fairly typical Boomer comment. Now, as they power through their sixties and seventies, their determination to stay young is undiminished—probably a carryover from the period of their lives in which it seemed possible that their youth might be all they would have, so they clung fiercely to the idea of it.

The 'elastic adolescence'—a term I coined in my 1997 book *Generations*—can be observed at full stretch among today's young adults, but the pattern was established by the Boomers. Young people now typically stay at school longer, then undertake tertiary studies, perhaps travel, stay at home with their parents for longer (or come and go in cycles) and postpone parenthood—often until they're well into their thirties—while they enjoy their extended 'youth' to the full. (The proposition that 'thirty is the new twenty' has no real currency today, because the old meaning of 'twenty' is such a distant and fast-fading memory.)

***

They redefined marriage as 'a relationship', not an institution. Facilitated by the new *Family Law Act* of 1975, Boomers briefly held the record for the most-divorced generation in our history. That was one of the more obvious manifestations of the Boomer philosophy 'We're not here for a long time; we're here for a good time'. Their parents' devotion to the idea of marriage as an institution was gradually swept aside in favour of the idea that we should only stick together for as long as the relationship is working for both of us. (Their parents would rarely have used a word like 'relationship' to describe marriage, let alone question whether it was 'working'. 'You're married,' they would typically have said, 'so just get on with it.')

The sense of existential impermanence—the improbability of long-term survival—had been profoundly influential in the formation of Boomer attitudes and values, and it has kept resurfacing in all kinds of settings. Their redefinition of marriage is one of its most visible signs, and one of their most enduring legacies: that's an example their children and grandchildren *have* followed.

***

They redefined parenting as 'admin'. Because Boomer women were so profoundly influenced by the pioneering voices of the women's liberation movement, they adopted paid work outside the home as the most potent symbol of their liberation. The education and training needed to secure work, the job itself and the income it brought all signalled 'independence'. As did the fact that, with wives now entering—or staying in—the workforce in such large numbers, a generation of husbands needed training in home duties, including the care of children.

With time (and energy) for parenting now more limited, compared with the more relaxed and expansive approach taken by their parents' generation, Boomers began to think of child care as one of a number of competing responsibilities that had to be juggled. The term 'Supermum' had brief currency during this early, heady period of social innovation: an expression of the idea that a truly liberated woman needed superhuman energy. Quite apart from trying to combine parenting with housework and a paid job outside the home, there was a widely accepted view among women that they had to *outperform* men in order to be taken seriously in Australia's blokey workplaces. On top of all that, there was a marriage to maintain. Complaints about the effects of the 'have it all' mentality on intimate relationships were frequently aired in my research: 'You can't be a workhorse all day and a show pony at night' captured the essence. Everything—even sex, and certainly child care—was starting to feel like work.

The revolution in child care was facilitated by a combination of compliant grandparents ('We never imagined we'd be looking after littlies again at our age') and the rapid expansion of child care centres (often euphemistically called 'day care', as if it were the day we were looking after, not the child). The days of mothers being *expected* to stay home and look after their children were over: now they were *expected* to pull their revolutionary weight by having at least a part-time job outside the home. In fact, it was the Boomers who effectively institutionalised the two-income family household.

Older women, observing the unfolding scene, sometimes remarked that 'If you try to have it all at once, something has to suffer.' According to the Ipsos Mackay Report, 'Whither the Boomers?' (2005), it was often the quality of the marriage that suffered. If they were guilty of anything in relation to child care, Boomers thought it might be 'overindulgence'. Later in life, they wondered whether a tendency to over-indulge their kids—along with their enthusiasm for the new notion of *quality time*—might have been compensation for the lack of sufficient time and energy to devote to the traditional parenting role. While they typically believed they were more enlightened parents than their own parents had been, the long view from their later years created some doubt about that. Many wished they had tempered their tendency to permissiveness with a little more discipline.

Some now wonder whether their parenting style was too much about administration—organising enough activities to keep the kids occupied, and then racing around taking them to and from everything—rather than spending quiet time simply 'hanging out' as a family. (That rueful question is now raised by many parents from later generations as well.) Some will admit they may have been inadvertently training their children to be even busier than they had been. So that's another legacy that seems to have endured—busyness has become one of the Big Seven drivers of social fragmentation described in 'The Context'.

Many Boomer men have claimed, with some pride, that they were far more *involved* parents than their own fathers had been, yet that was a contested claim. Steve Biddulph, internationally esteemed psychologist and parent educator, described Boomers' children as 'the most under-fathered generation ever'. The gap between those two views can probably be attributed to the relative importance you attach to the *quality* and the *quantity* of time spent with children.

***

They redefined home ownership as 'an investment'. When banks introduced the concept of the reverse mortgage, allowing home owners to borrow against the equity in their home without having to repay the loan (because the bank would own that equity), it was a lifesaver for Boomers. Being reluctant savers meant that many Boomers had come to regard home ownership as the thing that would rescue their financial situation in retirement, especially if house prices kept rising. The real estate market is driven by psychology as well as supply and demand, and the Boomers created a significant attitude shift from the mentality of their parents' and earlier generations who had seen home ownership primarily as a symbol of stability and security for the raising of a family.

But the Boomer attitude has prevailed and become the norm: home owners now typically think of their home as much in investment as symbolic terms, and rising house prices please them greatly (while being bad news for anyone struggling to buy a home). So another Boomer legacy has been the trend for parents who can afford it to be helping their offspring 'get into the housing market'—a quite different perspective from merely 'owning your own home'.

An unintended consequence of this shift in the psychology of housing is that affordable housing is getting harder to come by. There's an obvious link between a housing market overheated by the investment mentality and the fact that more than 120,000 Australians have nowhere to call home.

***

They redefined busyness as a virtue. Given their voracious appetite for life, and for 'getting on with it' (just in case The Bomb was about to drop and—given their wholesale turning away from religion—just in case this life really was all there is), Boomers led the way in elevating 'busyness' to the status of a virtue. A female respondent in one of my research projects said that what she needed was 'tampons with beepers' as she was too busy to remember when they needed changing.

Boomers popularised the view that keeping busy is the best way of staying young, and that chimed with their conviction that they have been one of the 'youngest' generations ever.

***

They redefined retirement as 'a fresh start'. Boomers have tended to resist using the word 'retirement', lest it suggest they might be ready for the scrap heap. Far from it: they antici-pate—or have already discovered—a more liberated way of life once they are unshackled from full-time work. And they've been in no rush to be unshackled, preferring a gradual process of refocusing, if it can be managed. Whereas previous gener-ations might have longed for the 'easing back' of retirement, Boomers are more typically determined to keep moving, one way or another. If they can't stay in their existing full-time job, they might ease into part-time work and begin planning new projects—from volunteering to travel—that will fill their days, retain their sense of life's meaning and purpose and, in the process, keep them feeling young: 'Who wants to quit too young and then sit around like our parents did, waiting to die?'

(All very well, younger people may say, but when are you going to get out of the way and make room for someone else?)

Raising the retirement age was a welcome move for many Boomers. They didn't want to be told, too early, that their working lives were finished. Not for them the gold watch and the farewell drinks party. They have been determined *not* to act their age. And when the time has come for some of them to retire, they prefer to speak of new beginnings rather than endings.

Closely allied to their resistance to the very idea of 'ageing' is their enthusiasm for nostalgia. That's a natural tendency for most people as they age—the pleasure of recalling earlier stages of life that might be associated with more vigour, a keener sense of anticipation of what was to come and, of course, the comfort of knowing that that was a period we survived (unlike the uncertain future).

Boomers might not be ready to admit that their best days are behind them, but their enthusiasm for the very concept of youthfulness does make them vulnerable to the appealing echoes of the past—whether in fashion, cars, music or anything else that evokes the 1960s and '70s in particular.

***

They showed us how to rebel. Perhaps the greatest legacy the Boomers will leave is their demonstration that the world can be at least partly reshaped to suit yourself, that life can be lived on your own terms, that conventions are there to be questioned and can be overturned, and that the shock of the new is good for us. Even the influence of the Boomers' once-revolutionary blue denim has evolved into an accepted dress code called 'smart casual'.

When their parents and others accused them of self-centredness—that old Me Generation label—their defence was that they were simply challenging the old ways of doing things. What might have looked like selfishness was, they argued, more like a rejection of their parents' conservative values and their determination to steer a new, more independent, more liberated course. That defence might have been a trifle disingenuous, given their enthusiastic embrace of hedonism, materialism and consumerism, but it had some validity: in everything from the more casual way they dressed to the way they turned their backs on religion in large numbers, the Boomers certainly did things *their* way.

In that respect, their example has stuck. As the last generation to attend Sunday School in large numbers, the Boomers led a mass exodus from Christian churches and began to show interest in the 'personal growth' movement and, at least for a while, in Eastern spirituality and mysticism. 'Self-awareness' became a quasi-religious term, as many Boomers embraced a vigorous individualism—being yourself, doing it your way, expressing yourself—and sometimes did so at the expense of the sense of responsibility to the community their parents had tried to instil in them.

***

Reflecting on their own experience from the perspective of their middle and later years, Boomers (like most of us) have inevitably become more self-aware and self-critical. Having realised that they are, indeed, here for a long time, some of them rather wistfully wish they hadn't tried to run so fast. And, given the prospect of an easy, comfortable ride that their early years had seemed to point to, some are also asking why it has all turned out to be so hard.

Their parents would have an answer to that last one: 'We started out tough and then had it easy; you started out easy and then had it tough. Wrong way around.' Not that the Boomers had any say in the matter: they didn't choose the year of their birth, and they couldn't be blamed for the economic down-turns of the 1970s and 1980s, or the more severe recession of the 1990s that, with its high unemployment and high interest rates, hit their generation particularly hard.

But Boomers would generally agree with their parents' assessment that they had it easy in the beginning: they typi-cally speak of their own childhood years not as having been consciously dominated by Cold War tensions but as relatively carefree. They believe they had more fun and more freedom than their own children had. Many of them also recall their childhood as a time marked by appalling gender inequality and widespread physical abuse at the hands of family members and institutions ('spare the rod and spoil the child' was still a popular dictum), coexisting with an ethos of near-Victorian prudishness. Yet there remains some wistful-ness in their recollection of having had 'a clearer sense of right and wrong'—sometimes attributed to the role of religion in their formative years, and sometimes to their parents' (and teachers') tougher approach to discipline than the Boomers employed with their own children.

Some Boomers have even wondered whether they were too quick to reject their parents' religious faith. Perhaps, they later thought, 'a bit of religion' might have been helpful in countering their—and their children's—materialism and in encouraging them to spend more time in quiet contemplation of life's meanings, rather than always rushing on to the next thing.

Still, they do wonder why their lives became so stressful. Some of them admit that they had indeed been seduced by the 'have it all' aspiration and by the materialist ethic that led them into the rush to spend and acquire, and the consequential financial stress. More generally, they simply accept that the gender and IT revolutions and the upheavals wrought by the radical economic restructuring of the 1980s and '90s took a heavy toll on them.

There are plenty of contradictions in all this (as there are for any of us trying to make sense of our own and others' lives), but on balance, it would be hard to deny that the Boomers' legacy has been broadly beneficial in encouraging greater boldness in social reform: the generation just ahead of them might have been the pioneers of the gender revolution, for example, but Boomer women added fresh energy to the cause. Their redefinition of marriage has probably reduced the overall level of pain caused by people sticking with marriages it would have been better for them to leave. And their fresh approach to the experience of ageing will set a positive example to following generations and will inevitably transform the aged care market, as the Boomers have transformed so many other markets along the way.

They have their regrets (who doesn't?) and perhaps we can also learn from those. Less materialism would have been good; less indulgence of children, and a combination of more time and more discipline would have been good; and less impatience would have been good—it's probably better to live *as if* there's a future.

Political footnote: The impatience of Boomer prime ministers

What sort of leaders did Baby Boomers make? Here's where any generalisations will be too dangerous, except one: they were impatient for power. (And perhaps a second: they will not go down in history as long-range thinkers.) Australia has had four Boomer prime ministers: Kevin Rudd (born in 1957), Julia Gillard (1961), Tony Abbott (1957) and Malcolm Turnbull (1954). They all came and went in the space of about ten years, a period marked by constantly simmering leadership tensions as, one after another, the four aspirants for the top job lost patience with those who stood in their way.

The first, Kevin Rudd, was elected in 2007. Two and a half years later, he became the first Labor leader ever to be ousted in his first term when he was successfully challenged for the leadership by Julia Gillard. After the following election, when neither Labor nor the Coalition managed to achieve a majority, Gillard put together a government in coalition with the Greens, but before that government's term was over, Rudd's persistent undermining of Gillard paid off and he defeated her in another party-room ballot. His second term as prime minister lasted a mere eighty-three days before Labor was defeated at the 2013 federal election.

On the Coalition side, a similar impatience for power was on display. Malcolm Turnbull, having weighed up the relative merits of the Labor and Liberal parties as his pathway to the long-cherished prime ministership, chose the Libs, entered parliament in 2004, and became their leader (in opposition) at his second attempt, just four years later. Before he could achieve his dream of becoming PM, however, he was ousted in a party-room ballot by another Boomer, the ever-eager Tony Abbott, who ultimately became prime minister at the 2013 election, promising a 'kinder, gentler polity' (having mercilessly savaged Gillard throughout his time as opposition leader). Then, sure enough, Turnbull challenged Abbott for the leadership in 2015 and yet another sitting prime minister was gone.

It all seemed a bit breathtaking and even absurd at the time, with such naked ambition *and* textbook Boomer impatience on display. (This was the period when it was said that para-medics could no longer check a dazed patient's cognitive function by asking: 'Who is the prime minister?')

The Boomer PMs' chaotic run came to an end when the electorate's deep disappointment in Turnbull, reflected in a dismal run of opinion polls, led to another Liberal party-room ballot that deposed the fourth sitting prime minister to fall victim to internecine rivalries within eight years.

(The Scott Morrison story doesn't belong here. He was born in 1968, well after the post-war baby boom, and his ambition was propelled more by opportunism than impatience. There was something of the classic Gen X 'slipstreamer' about the way Morrison occupied the space created by the unresolved leadership tensions between Turnbull and Peter Dutton.)

Reflections . . .

- Like many other researchers, I have found Boomers endlessly fascinating, because their formative years were so utterly different from anything that had come before, and because the results of that formation have been on such public display. In fact, when you compare the young Boomers' social, cultural and economic context with the contexts in which their parents and their children were raised, you realise just how swiftly Australian society has been changing. It's almost as if those three generations represented three quite different Australias.

- I once wrote that impatiens was the perfect flower for Boomers' gardens and stir-fry their perfect meal. I don't know what the favourite flower of today's rising generation of young adults might turn out to be—perhaps climate-proof cactus—but their favourite meal would be 'home delivery'.

- The Boomers' story reminds us that, although family influence is always powerful, the wider world speaks very loudly to us, too. When children are fed a daily diet of information about the imminence of global destruction—by nuclear war, back then, or the effects of climate change today—anxiety about that message will lodge deep in their psyches and become an important part of who they are. In the Boomers' case, all the talk of potential catastrophe was tempered— indeed, contradicted—by the promise of a rosy *material* future to come and by the exuberance of pop culture at the time. It's an interesting question for current and future researchers to study: will today's children and adolescents be influenced even more profoundly than the Boomers were by the relentless bad news, because there's no countervailing promise of a bright future? Some will respond with resignation, some with despair, some with deep-seated anxiety, some with anger and some with urgent activism, but which will be the dominant response?

- Thinking about the Boomers' legacy naturally leads me to ponder the legacy any of us leaves behind us. It would be unrealistic to keep too close an eye on posterity's likely view of us, but it's not a bad idea to speculate, just occasionally, on whether the influence we are having on those around us is likely to be making the world a better or worse place. Every encounter we have with another person is potentially influential in that process: perhaps that perspective might encourage us to modify some of the attitudes and values we would prefer *not* to pass on. We might be the products of our upbringing, but we don't have to be its hapless victims.

6

We worship many gods

'So you're an atheist, you say? Then let me ask you this. What is it that you don't believe in?'

'Come again?'

'Well, you're telling me you're an atheist, so that means you don't believe in something. What is it?'

'God, of course. I don't believe in God. What else?'

'Be more specific, please. What do you mean when you say you don't believe in God?'

'You mean . . . what do I mean by "God"?'

'Precisely. Tell me exactly what it is you *don't* believe in. Let me warn you, though. I suspect you don't believe in a lot of stuff that no self-respecting contemporary theist would believe in, either. I hope you're not going to tell me the God you don't believe in is the one you learned about in kindergarten. Up there with Santa Claus and the Easter Bunny.'

'Don't knock Santa Claus—my Christmas presents used to arrive very reliably when I believed in Santa. But God? Well, I . . . er, I don't believe in the old man in the sky.'

'Neither do I. And I don't know anyone who does. And I'm sure you don't believe in a three-decker universe, either—with heaven up there, earth down here and hell in a fiery basement somewhere?'

'Of course not. I also don't believe in a creator out there somewhere who is gloating over the wonderful world he's created for us to play in. *All things bright and beautiful*, et cetera.'

'And neither do I. By the way, I notice you said "he" as if this god you don't believe in is male. That's pretty weird, for a start.'

'Don't you say "he" when you refer to *your* god?'

'Certainly not. My god is a spirit. Ungendered. We can talk about my god later if you like. Right now, I'm more interested in your non-god. I must say I'm glad you don't believe in an all-things-bright-and-beautiful god. If you did, it'd be a short step to believing there was a god who controlled the weather, plagues and pestilence. War. Cancer. Car accidents.'

'Oh, cancer. When the mother of a friend of mine was dying of cancer, my friend was appalled by the number of people who said stuff like "How could God let something like that happen to a lovely woman like your mother?" It gave him the creeps.'

'No wonder. I even shudder when I think of all the people who pray for rain. Or for the rain to stop. Or ask God to help them pass exams or win football matches or elections. Crazy stuff. Like the people who say things were *meant to be*. As if some out-there entity—some all-knowing life force—had some grand plan for you to be on a certain street corner at a certain time so you'd meet the love of your life.'

'Quite. But I'll tell you something I *do* believe in. Well, *believe in* is probably not the right way to put it. But I do feel a great sense of awe in the face of creation. Or perhaps I shouldn't use the word "creation". Let's just say I feel awe in the face of the grandeur of the natural world. Butterflies, sunsets, mountains, stars, oceans. All that beauty. Even sex. All that pleasure.'

'Of course you do. Who wouldn't? But you wouldn't want to base the case for God on a beautiful world that could shrivel up and die when our sun eventually burns out, or we make the place so *un*beautiful that it becomes uninhabitable. Would that mean your bright-and-beautiful god had ceased to exist? Or would it mean that that god had simply lost interest in this planet and turned its attention to more promising possibilities?'

'You're asking *me*? I'm the one who *doesn't* believe in that god.'

'Just making the point.'

'So we've disposed of the cosmic puppet-master. The supernatural being who controls the weather and makes people sick or well. Decides who'll live and who'll die. So, yeah, I don't believe in any of that and, apparently, neither do you. Who'd have thought! Anyway, I think it's your turn. What sort of god do *you* believe in?'

'Just before we dispose of the creator idea entirely, how do you feel about the proposition that love is the most creative force in the world? Perhaps even the most powerful force in the world?'

'Love? No problem with that, I guess. But what's your point? Love didn't create the daisies and daffodils.'

225

'Of course not. I'm just wondering how you might feel about the idea that God is love. Not out there, but in *here*. Within us all. '

'Hmm. Where are you going with this?'

'You once told me you do yoga. I imagine your teacher finishes up with "*Namaste*". Right?'

'She does. Yes. We have a little ritual. We fold our hands like this and give a little bow and say the magic word.'

'Don't mock it. Has your teacher ever explained the meaning of that word?'

'I might have been away that week. Or I mightn't have been listening.'

'*The divine in me acknowledges the divine in you*. That's the Hindu interpretation, as I understand it, and the Hindus invented yoga, after all.'

'So you're sympathetic to the Hindus? I thought you Christians were pretty sure yours was the one and only True Way.'

'Give us a break. The loving spirit can be nurtured and celebrated in all kinds of ways. All kinds of cultures. All kinds of traditions—religious and otherwise. For most people, the religion you follow—or don't—is an accident of birth. Not everyone, but most people. There'd be no point in denying that.'

***

We'll leave our conversationalists there, though we'll revisit some of the material they were discussing. Meanwhile, here are two provocative statements about God from two of religion's insiders, four hundred years apart.

226

From the sixteenth century, Martin Luther, the man who triggered the Protestant Reformation: 'Whatever your heart clings to and confides in, that is really your God.'

And from the twentieth century, Don Cupitt, the English priest, theologian and founder of the 'sea of faith' movement: 'God is an imaginary focus for the religious life—a projection of the human desire for faith.'

Luther's God was very different from Cupitt's, of course (as yours—if you have one—is probably very different from mine), but what those two widely disparate thinkers were suggesting was that God, however defined, is an expression— or a projection—of our most intense desires, our highest aspirations, our most fervent dreams.

Luther is now regarded by some theological historians as a Christian humanist; Cupitt is certainly that. And why should there be any tension between humanism and religion? Christian humanism—like Christian agnosticism—has become a perfectly respectable position, as humanists and Christians each recognise the overlap between the teachings of Jesus and the teachings of humanism: the dignity and equality of all persons, the right to personal freedom (including freedom from the strictures of fundamentalist religious dogma), loving-kindness and compassion as pathways to social harmony.

Buddhists would be comfortable in that company, too, though they typically reject the label 'religion' because that has been so closely tied to theism. Yet Buddhist teachings on love, and on ways to live more generally, would sound utterly familiar to most Christians, and to most humanists—and, indeed, to followers of most religions.

When you read the teachings of Jesus, as recorded in the so-called Sermon on the Mount and the many parables (most famously, the parables of the Good Samaritan and the Prodigal Son), you realise it's all about how we should *live*, not what we should *believe*. The moral standards Jesus set are revolutionary by the standards of the society he lived in— and, indeed, of the society we live in today. Some theologians would say he was pointing to life in the Kingdom of God; others, including many contemporary Christians and people of other faiths or none, might prefer to say that those standards are radical but not beyond us when we are animated by the spirit of kindness.

But this book is no place for theology—nor am I equipped to go any more deeply into such matters.

Whatever people might claim to believe, the reality is that, in contemporary Australian society, religious observance has been in sharp decline (at least among nominal Christians) and there has been a rise in confidently expressed atheism. Yet I suspect that many of those who think of themselves as non-believers do indeed have a god, according to Luther's definition, even if they don't regard their god as adding a religious dimension to their lives.

Let's have a bit of fun with that idea. No offence intended to any of the twenty-first-century worshippers on the following list . . .

The varieties of non-religious worship

Some people worship Reason. They regard libraries and universities as temples of knowledge where Reason is enshrined and celebrated. They look on the rest of us as something akin to lost souls in our failure to behave more rationally, and they believe that, if only the facts were properly explained to people, they would never believe in God, smoke, eat ice cream, fall in love or make an impulse purchase, since all such behaviour is non-rational. That's a whimsical exaggeration, of course: you could easily argue that pleasure seeking is rational. But the worshippers of Reason, when they are being true to their faith, can be a pretty humourless bunch, since their religion lacks the colour and movement of those that incorporate myths, legends and festivals laden with rich metaphor. They can also be pretty aggressive in their determination to wipe out 'non-rational' religion.

Some people worship Shopping. (I'm not joking.) That's what, in Luther's phrase, 'their heart clings to'. They live for Shopping. They love attending the temples erected for Shopping-worship (especially cathedral-like department stores and malls, but also more intimate, chapel-like boutiques), and they are prepared to devote big chunks of their income to the cause of Shopping—especially luxury items that test their commitment by being wildly overpriced for no tangible additional benefit beyond reinforcement of the shopper's faith. For the true believers, the rituals of Shopping induce a trance-like state. They abandon themselves to the uplift of 'retail therapy'. They relish the feeling of power that committed consumers enjoy— the freedom to choose what to buy and the attentions of retail people who exist only to please them. They love the reassurance provided by the familiar sights, sounds and smells of the retail (especially high-end retail) world; the rush of pleasure when the new stuff is taken home and unwrapped; and the thrill of wearing new clothes or putting new possessions on display.

Some people worship Fashion. This is a more refined, circumscribed version of the Shopping god. Worshippers submit themselves slavishly to the latest dictates from the high priests of the Fashion world—the designers, the celebrity label-flaunters, the social media influencers—and can be seen discarding out-of-fashion items that are still perfectly serviceable but fail to conform to the new dogma. Hems and necklines go obediently up and down. Pants get tighter or baggier according to the latest word from the fashionistas. Waistlines wander. The ritual display of each new season's wardrobe is the way of communicating to fellow believers one's faithfulness to Fashion. Dowdiness (in the form of clothes that are *so yesterday*) is the mark of the unbeliever or, worse, the backslider. As with the worshippers of Shopping, the willingness to make financial sacrifices on the altar of Fashion is the mark of true devotion. There's even provision for the hoi polloi to worship Fashion via the cheap labels that rush to put copies of the latest catwalk revelations into the hands of the masses.

Some people worship Work. They don't merely define themselves by it; again using Luther's words, their hearts cling to it. Their lives revolve around it. Their rituals are as fixed and repetitive as any monk's. Their holy days are uninterrupted work days, not days off—in fact, holidays are resisted as an interruption to the pattern (sometimes called 'the demands') of their Work. They willingly sacrifice other pleasures and, sometimes, even their relationships on the altar of Work. As they gain recognition and rewards for their efforts, their commitment deepens into a quasi-mystical union between themselves and their Work. They *become* their Work, and that feels to them like a sublime state of oneness. (No wonder Work-worshippers report a sense of profound loss when they eventually, reluctantly retire and can no longer define themselves by the job they used to do.)

Some people worship Sport, revering their chosen clubs or players with something close to religious fervour. In his book *A Fan's Life*, Paul Campos adds another quasi-religious dimension to our understanding of Sport-worship by reflecting on the fact that most Sport fans suffer failure and loss most of the time: 'Deep engagement, which makes the entire sports branch of the entertainment industrial complex viable, is not about entertainment at all: it is about suffering.' There are 'sacred sites' all over the country where devotion to Sport can be expressed through the rituals of players and spectators alike, and where a powerfully tribal us-and-them ethos is regularly reinforced. There are even some cathedral-like places (perhaps the Melbourne Cricket Ground chief among them in Australia) where more lavish and elaborate rituals are regularly played out, and annual festivals celebrated, such as the AFL grand final, the NRL State of Origin and cricket's Boxing Day Test.

Some people worship Travel; some Music; some Drugs; some Sex. Some people worship Cars: visiting beautifully styled and perfumed showrooms is an inspiring experience for them, and a vintage car rally is somewhat like a pilgrimage where homage is paid to the sainted classics of the past.

Some people worship less-specific gods, like Pleasure or Excitement or, more generally, Sensation—however it might be induced, from magic mushrooms to bungee jumping.

231

Some people worship Food, not as fuel but as an art form, an end in itself. They form tribes—rather like religious denominations—around particular chefs, culinary traditions or movements. They read cookbooks as if they are Holy Writ—and, as is often the case with Holy Writ, they fail to put most of what they read into practice. A meal at a renowned restaurant is rather like a visit to a shrine, with waiters like guides and chefs hidden away like high priests in the holy of holies (the kitchen). As international tourists, they are really only there for the food; everything else is incidental: 'Oh, you went to Rome? Did you eat at that amazing little trattoria just off the Piazza di Trevi?'

Luckily for authors, some people worship Books. They can't get enough of them. They reread their favourites, as Christians reread favourite passages of the Bible, but are open to fresh revelations in the form of the latest literary sensation or a previously undiscovered author. They persevere to the end of books, even those they aren't enjoying (like sitting through a tedious sermon in church and hoping for better luck next time). They forgive favourite authors who occasionally disappoint them, believing that a bad book is merely a temporary lapse or the sign of a bad editor. Libraries and bookshops are their temples, and they like to be recognised and welcomed by those offering encouragement, support and guidance at their favourite bookshop. Literary festivals are like pilgrimages, with their own rituals and practices: the 'in conversation', the panel, the Q&A, the signing queue, the opening and closing parties and coffee breaks for connecting with fellow believers. Festivals are where Books—and even some writers—are idolised, and where the faithful dream of writing their own. (A cartoon I enjoyed shows two men walking along a pavement. 'I'm writing a novel,' says one. 'Neither am I,' replies his companion.)

Book worshippers revere the demigods: Dickens, Joyce, Proust, Tolstoy, Woolf, James, Hardy, Austen, Orwell, Greene, White, the recently deified Rushdie, to pluck just a few names from a very long list. And they are constantly on the lookout for inspirational figures heading for the pantheon: Barnes, Didion, Ford, Garner ('We love her diaries even more than her novels!'), Malouf, O'Farrell, Strout, Grenville, Williams ('Surely you've read *Stoner*!'), Coetzee, Ishiguro, Morrison, Marquez, McEwan, Winton, Flanagan, Allende. They can't imagine not having at least one book on the go. Rather like so-called 'cradle Christians' who never needed a conversion experience, they seemed to have loved books from the very beginning, and perhaps even to have loved them more than the life unfolding around them. They love the smell of books, as churchgoers love the smell of churches. Though apparently accessible—after all, books are easy to buy or borrow—their god seems both infinite and ultimately beyond reach: there's always more to be discovered, always more to be revealed. Book clubs have sprung up all over the country, meeting— just as the early Christians did—in the private homes of the faithful, though many libraries also provide services that encourage Book-worship.

Some people worship Money; some Power; some Status.

Some people worship individuals—leaders, celebrity actors, singers, preachers—who inspire or delight them.

And then there are the narcissists who have devoted them-selves to the worship of Self. The Me Culture has arisen almost like a religious movement to encourage the belief that 'it's all about me', and that personal identity should be carefully burnished, curated and endlessly celebrated. The problem for narcissists is that the field is becoming overcrowded, with fewer people available to worship them with the single-minded devotion they expect.

I could go on, but you get the idea. Most of us worship something, and whatever we worship becomes like a god, or a whole pantheon of gods.

Most Australians still believe in a supernatural god

Perhaps you don't think of those things as gods. Perhaps you like to worship them while still characterising yourself as an unbeliever, because you think that term applies to your disbelief in one particular interpretation of God—an entity with supernatural qualities like omniscience, omnipresence and omnipotence. Given our cultural baggage, you might think anything called 'God'—capital G—would have to be a mystical being, while still possessing some human-like qualities, like 'mind'. (There's an eternal debate over those qualities: did God create us in his own image, or was it the other way around?) In fact, most cultural traditions—including ours—do incorporate some notion of a supreme being that is greater than ourselves, beyond time and space but still accessible to us in some way.

Throughout this first quarter of the twenty-first century, most Australians have continued to believe in a reasonably conventional, traditional interpretation of God. A 2021 national survey conducted by McCrindle Research for the Centre for Public Christianity found that almost 60 per cent of Australians claim to believe in God—defined in the research as the creator of the universe, or a supreme being—and 70 per cent believe in, or are open to, the idea of the soul. Of those surveyed, 43 per cent said they believe or are open to the possibility that Jesus rose bodily from the dead—roughly the same number as those who identified as Christian in the 2021 Census.

That level of belief in God represents a slight drop from 2009, when the Australian Survey of Social Attitudes conducted by the Australian National University reported that 67 per cent of Australians either believed in God (47 per cent) or in something they preferred to call a 'higher power' (a further 20 per cent). A less nuanced Nielsen poll in the same year reported simply that 68 per cent of Australians believe in God.

To put that in a historical context: in a 1949 Gallup poll, 95 per cent of Australians declared their belief in God.

That 'higher power' concept covers all kinds of poss-ibilities—some religious, some entirely secular. Some people appear to be calling on a 'higher power' almost as a form of *magical thinking*, where they come to believe that their own thoughts, perhaps expressed through little personal rituals, can influence external events, presumably because they have tapped into some higher power—something greater than themselves; something inherently mysterious. Magical thinking can be focused on anything from finding a conveni-ent parking spot to ensuring that the plane you're on doesn't crash, a loved one doesn't die from cancer or your team will win a footy match. In some cases, this represents a belief in the inherent force of our own will or the magical properties of the rituals we have devised ('If I carry a particular handbag . . .'; 'If I play a particular song . . .'; 'If I wear the team jersey, sit in a particular seat in the stand and drink three beers . . .'). In other cases, though, people explicitly claim that they have been able to harness some cosmic influence: 'I put it out to the universe.'

Contemporary Australians who want to call themselves atheists or unbelievers would typically distance themselves from such magical thinking, because they emphatically reject any idea of an 'out-there' entity that has some creative and/or controlling influence on the universe in general and on the life of Earth in particular. But theology has moved on. And so has science. And so has history. And so have the belief systems of many people (including many Christians) who would still want to say they believe in a god that is greater than Work, Fashion, Books or even Reason, but that has no supernatural properties, nor any existence independent of us.

Perhaps this is where Don Cupitt's idea of God as a projection of our desire for faith makes sense. Many people *want* to believe in something greater than themselves, and psychologists like Martin Seligman will tell you that such belief makes an important contribution to our mental health. But they resist any notion of God that entails belief or practices that strike them as little more than superstition.

When I have sought people's understanding of 'God', I have encountered a wide range of responses: God is love, God is light, God is life, God is being, God is now, God is the soul of the universe. Listening to people struggling for words, it soon becomes clear that God, like faith, is a highly subjective product of the imagination. Many people resist any attempt at defining God, preferring vague references to 'something out there', a 'life force', a 'cosmic imperative' . . . or a 'higher power'.

To say that God is a product of the imagination is not to denigrate that idea, nor to suggest that God does not exist—any more than we would say Justice, Beauty, Truth or Love don't exist because they are intangible. My purpose, as a researcher, is simply to try to understand what people mean when they say they believe in God and, equally, what they mean when they say they don't.

In *Beyond Belief* (2016), I reported that Australians' conceptions of God ranged across five broad categories: *something out there*, too mysterious to define; *a supreme being*, with the properties of a creator, ruler and judge; *a heavenly father*, like the supernatural version of an earthly father, characterised by unconditional parental love; *an imaginary friend* we can talk to, bounce ideas off and share experiences with; and *a spirit within and among us* with the 'divine' quality of love that exists within us, rather than coming to us from an external source.

It's impossible to estimate the number of Australians who subscribe to one or more of those interpretations, but when believers talk about God, the idea of 'love' is never far from their minds. They speak of its transformative power (in the same way many non-religious people do)—expressed through kindness, compassion, personal sacrifice and a concern for the wellbeing of others. In fact, that idea of self-sacrificial love lies at the heart of most of the world's great religions. And, as we shall see in the following chapter, that's the only form of human love that doesn't require any emotional engagement.

It's not about affection, or about liking or agreeing with the people we're kind to; it's about a way of being in the world—a way of realising our full human potential by becoming whole (or 'holy', if you prefer the religious version).

***

Take your pick. We all worship something. And, sooner or later, most of us pause to reflect on whether we have been worshipping at the right altar, celebrating and enshrining in our lives the best possible values, encouraging our noblest and finest impulses, and making the world a better place through our worship practices—whether in the workplace, the shopping centre, the bookstore, the kitchen . . . or the church, the mosque, the temple or some other more obvious place of worship.

The deathbed test is a good way of checking whether you're on the right track, god-wise. Imagine you're facing the prospect of imminent death, but there's still time to ponder the meanings you've chosen to invest your life with. It's a cliché that no one on their deathbed ever says, 'I wish I'd spent more time at the office', but, like most clichés, it contains deep wisdom. No one ever does say that. Nor do they say, 'I wish I'd accumulated more stuff', or even 'I wish I'd made more money' . . . or read more books.

No, the more typical deathbed reflections are these: Was I kind enough? Was I loving enough as a partner, caring enough as a parent, attentive enough as a neighbour, faithful enough as a friend? Did I apologise readily enough when I hurt, offended or wronged someone? Did I forgive generously enough when someone hurt, offended or wronged me?

And the questions underlying all that are these: Did I choose to worship the kind of god that encouraged me to be the best person I can be? Did my faith in Reason, perhaps, make me more loving, generous, tolerant and kind? Did my devotion to my work, my status or my possessions make me a better person? Did my chosen god/religion empower me to help to make the world a better place by building social harmony?

Good questions, all. And here's another good one . . .

What is the purpose of religion?

Every society in every period of history has had some form of religious activity at its cultural heart. In contemporary Australia, that is less true than it has ever been, though the religious influences on our culture are still evident, in everything from our ethics to our classical music to our festivals. The reason for the decline of religious observance in Australia is an issue we'll address. But first, this one: why religion at all?

I can come up with three answers based on human psychology and social analysis, rather than spiritual insight.

First, religion has traditionally addressed the mysteries of life and death and tried to illuminate or explain them . . . or show us ways of living with them, unexplained. Why are we here? What happens after we die? Is there an inherent 'meaning' of this life, or must we each invest our own life with its own meaning? Why do some people seem so good and others so bad? Sadly, the question we'd all like to know the answer to—'Is there an afterlife?'—is the only one for which an answer can never be found this side of the grave, but most religions offer one (and, on that point, we're all free to choose what we believe, without fear of contradiction). As one of my

239

research respondents, an ex-churchgoer, said: 'I miss church. I really do. There's nowhere else you can go where people talk about the spiritual life, and I think we all have a need of that.'

Second, religion has typically set out to bolster people's commitment to the social-harmony project by encouraging them to live kindly and compassionately, to attend to the needs of the poor and disadvantaged, and to be tolerant of others. Through its music, its rituals, its formal preaching, its teachings and its festivals, religion *at its best* celebrates and reinforces our noblest impulses, and discourages our darker ones. As part of that function, religion has traditionally addressed the central moral question of 'How should we live?' by offering detailed prescriptions and suggestions about ways to make the world a fairer, more equitable and more peaceful place.

Third, because religion typically involves group activity, it generates faith communities that foster a powerful sense of belonging and mutual support. Even at a time when church attendance in Australia is at an all-time low, many churchgoers persist, in spite of their disenchantment with the larger institution, because of their intense personal connections to their fellow worshippers. Indeed, the research that shows the undeniable health benefits associated with religious faith and practice can probably be partly explained by the positive experience of belonging to a close-knit community of like-minded people.

Those health benefits are not insignificant: I listed them in 'The Context'. According to Harold Koenig and his co-authors of the research-based *Handbook of Religion and Health*, religious involvement is associated with improved wellbeing, happiness and life satisfaction; hope and optimism; a sense of purpose and meaning in life; higher self-esteem; better adaptation to bereavement; greater social support and less loneliness; lower rates of depression and faster recovery from depression; and less anxiety.

Even one of religion's most ardent opponents, the US philosopher Daniel Dennett, noted in *Breaking the Spell* that 'for day-in, day-out lifelong bracing, there is probably nothing so effective as religion: it makes powerful and talented people more humble and patient, it makes average people rise above themselves, it provides sturdy support for many people who desperately need help staying away from drink or drugs or crime'. Dennett also concedes that religious faith often gives people a perspective on life that helps them 'make the hard decisions we would all be proud to make'.

Dennett is quick to point out that there are many wise, engaged, morally upright atheists and agnostics, too, and that it's always hard to be sure that statistical correlations point to causation. In any case, as I have already suggested, studies of the health benefits of religious faith and practice may be reporting the benefits of *belonging* as well as the benefits of *believing*. Health benefits also flow from some of the activities often associated with religious practice, such as singing and meditation. The Buddhist practice of loving-kindness meditation, for example, is designed to induce positive feelings towards others and to transform anger into compassion, and group singing has well-documented therapeutic value.

***

The English Catholic writer G.K. Chesterton is generally credited with the remark that 'when a man stops believing in God, he doesn't then believe in nothing—he believes anything' (though it may have been his biographer Emile Cammaerts who actually wrote it). That could suggest some correlation between the decline of religious faith in the West and the rise of conspiracy theories. But it's apparently not that simple: a 2022 study by Marius Frenken and colleagues, published in the journal *Political Psychology*, found a positive correlation between religiosity and belief in such theories, with right-wing political orientation being a strong linking factor. That research suggests that religious believers from the political right (such as the Christian nationalists in the US) might be 'believers'—more credulous, less sceptical—in a more general sense. It also suggests that sceptics are more likely to be sceptical about everything.

But our growing scepticism about religion might be blinding us to its positive impact on individual believers and its broader positive contribution to our culture. Even among people who have abandoned institutional religion, or never engaged with it at all, my research has revealed a kind of faith envy, a wistful sense that 'something is missing' or that believers are possibly 'better off' in various ways than non-believers. Such sentiments have been expressed in statements like this: 'I admit I'm frustrated by my own lack of faith. I'm quite angry with God for not existing, as a matter of fact. I'm sure life would be better if I had something to believe in.' And this: 'If their faith gives them a reason for living and makes them a better person, then I'm all for it. It's just that I don't have it.'

It would be hard to deny that religion, for all its shortcomings, its follies and its failures, enriches the lives of millions of Australians and encourages them to lead better lives than they otherwise might, even though, through history, it has sometimes done the precise opposite. (As usual, context is everything and generalisations are dangerous.)

The power of myth and metaphor

Every Christmas, we sing carols and read biblical narratives about Jesus being born in a manger in Bethlehem, because there was no room in the inn. We hear, once again, about the virgin birth, the wise men and the angels. Many of us don't accept the literal truth of virgin births—whether of Jesus or other figures from antiquity whose greatness was later explained by the claim of a virgin birth, such as Egypt's Ra, born of the virgin Net. Yet we cheerfully sing about 'the virgin Mary' *as if* it's literally true. Angels on high? A star guiding wise men (possibly kings) to the location of the manger? Many of us accept these as mere poetic flourishes, but we still sing along as if they are an integral part of the history.

When historians assert that the most likely birthplace of Jesus was Nazareth, not Bethlehem, contemporary Bible scholars will ruefully admit that, yes, it was a fudge: Bethlehem was identified as the birthplace in order to line up with Old Testament prophecy. According to the US Catholic priest and writer on the historical Jesus, John Meier, it was a matter of theology, not history. The Roman census that allegedly took Mary and Joseph from Nazareth to Bethlehem was apparently another invention—or, more charitably, a literary device used by the writer of Luke's gospel to explain how the family came to be there.

But does it matter? It matters if you're going to insist that we will only tell such stories if they can be shown to be literally true. But, knowing that Jesus did actually live and die, and knowing a great deal about his teachings, we could simply accept that the mythology surrounding his birth and, indeed, his resurrection is designed to illuminate and amplify his significance. The first gospel to be written—the Gospel According to Mark—didn't even mention the resurrection: that was added later, to line up with the other gospel writers' versions, several of which contradict each other in the details of who saw what, and when.

But does it matter? It matters if you refuse to accept that the power is in the metaphor, not the history. It matters if you're a literalist and a fundamentalist who believes that every word of the Bible is the inspired word of God—even the contradictory bits. It matters if you have an almost idolatrous attitude to the Bible as something to be worshipped with uncritical acceptance.

On the other hand, it doesn't matter if you accept that the Bible is a collection of books written by a diversity of men (yes, all men), some of whom may well have been inspired by the spirit of love, and who had a point to make. The gospel writers were evangelists, not journalists or historians. And the accounts they were recording—up to ninety years after the events might have taken place—were based on stories that had previously only been transmitted orally, with the inevitable additions and subtractions associated with oral transmission across five or six generations. Given the many contradictions, the only sensible way to approach the Bible is to read it selectively: after all, if you go looking, you can find support for oppression of women *and* equality of the sexes; for slavery *and* emancipation; for war *and* peace; for genocide *and* ethnic equality; for hope *and* despair.

Some of those stories have been embraced with more fervour than others, becoming embedded in our language and culture because they have metaphorical power. That's the role of myth, and we diminish our culture when we try to insist that we will only take seriously religious stories that are 'true'.

The value of myth does not rely on historical truth at all. A myth is a particular kind of story that derives its power from some universal truth it conveys—psychological, cultural, moral or spiritual. Reflecting on the work of the French philosopher René Girard, Geoff Shullenberger notes that Girard described myths and rituals as 'entry points into the deep logic underlying the cultures that give rise to them'.

We certainly don't hold back on the transmission of cultural myths and legends to our children: Grimm's fairy-tales, Aesop's fables, Hans Christian Andersen, the stories of King Arthur or Robin Hood—or, indeed, Middle-earth. We don't present these stories to children as historical truth, but they resonate with us—and we keep retelling them across generations—because we think of them as conveying deep cultural, moral and spiritual truths. The Dreaming stories of Australian Aboriginal and Torres Strait Islander cultures, similarly, have long been used to transmit and preserve cultural material.

The Anzac/Gallipoli legend is an example of myth making. Based on a disastrously callous miscalculation of the risks involved in trying to invade Turkey by landing troops on a beach overlooked by a large force of heavily armed Turks, the exercise was doomed from the start. But the inglorious has somehow become glorious: the Anzac legend now portrays the murderous madness of Gallipoli as such heroic sacrifice that it is widely regarded as a crucible of nationhood.

We humans are myth makers from way back. Let's not 'cancel' that aspect of our culture, whether in a religious or any other context. At the same time, let's not pretend that things that could not possibly have happened actually did happen.

**

We are not obliged to believe or disbelieve each other's religious stories, any more than we are expected to share each other's cultural tastes and preferences. Some people think *Lord of the Rings* offers a brilliant allegory; others think it's a rather silly story they can't relate to at all. Some people (including its creator, George Lucas) think *Star Wars* is just a classic Western transferred to space; others think it has quasi-religious significance and have adopted 'May the Force be with you', rather as more conventional theists might say, 'May God be with you'. In a pluralistic, multicultural society like ours, as long as people's religious beliefs and practices don't harm anyone else, then our only obligation is to respect each other's right to choose what we will believe.

Yes, we might wish to engage in vigorous debate about the differences between our assorted beliefs, but such engagement is only valuable when it is respectful. Religious prejudice is as ugly as any other kind, and ridiculing another person's religious proclivities is as offensive as ridiculing their ethnicity (especially since religion and ethnicity tend to be closely linked) or their gender.

Ultimately, the question is not whether any religion is 'true' or 'false', any more than we might question the truth or falsity of art. The question is whether religion is helpful, inspirational and transformative for those who practise it, whether it helps to promote social harmony and whether it encourages wholeness.

Why have we stopped going to church?

'Church' is, of course, a Christian term. And it's church attendance that has been in steady decline for fifty years, leading some commentators to call this the 'post-Christian era'. Hinduism and Islam are continuing to grow steadily and their adherents typically attend places of worship more faithfully than nominal Christians do.

In the 2021 Census, 61 per cent of Australians identified with some religion, so you'd have to say that, at least on paper, ours is still a rather religious nation. We're well below the global average: about 75 per cent of the world's population identify with one of the 'big four': Christianity, Islam, Buddhism or Hinduism. (Incidentally, by the middle of this century, on present trends, there will be more Christian churchgoers in China than in the US.)

Of the 61 per cent of Australians identifying with any religion, by far the biggest group, in spite of their falling numbers, are Christians—44 per cent in 2021, down from

52 per cent in the 2016 Census. Of the other three major world religions, 3.2 per cent of Australians now identify as Muslim, 2.7 per cent as Hindus, and 2.4 per cent as Buddhist. Judaism accounts for 0.4 per cent of the population.

The number of Australians reporting 'no religion' rose from 30 per cent to 39 per cent in the same five-year period. That increase can be partly attributed to the move of 'No religion' from the bottom to the top of the list of options in the Census question about religion. That move was in response to active lobbying from anti-religion groups who thought religion was benefiting from the 'donkey vote' (that is, disengaged people who tend to tick whatever is first on the list) . . . so now, presumably, 'no religion' benefits from the donkey vote.

At the same time as church attendance is falling, enrolments at religious schools continue to climb: about 30 per cent of secondary students in Australia now attend private faith-based schools. There are many reasons why parents are choosing those schools for their children—not least the fact that changes in government funding policy have eroded the resources of public schools, leading to a growing performance gap between public and private. But there is clearly a large number of parents who, while not wishing to attend church themselves, are nevertheless keen for their children to be exposed to religious values, beliefs and practices at school.

We're also happy to look to the churches for charitable work that governments are unable or unwilling to undertake. So we like the work being done by religious institutions in education and social services; we just don't like going to church. Here again, though, are signs of faith envy: 'I don't go to church, but it's kind of reassuring to know that some people still do.'

There are many reasons for the decline in churchgoing, but the main one is that ex- and non-churchgoers simply can't see any relevance of church services to their lives. Perhaps they are content with the gods they are already worshipping. Perhaps they have been 'burned' by bad or disappointing experiences at one church or another. Or perhaps they have been disgusted by the behaviour of religious institutions—denying gender equality, condoning or ignoring the sexual abuse of children, and unfairly exploiting tax laws.

Like all other institutions that receive a 'social licence' to operate, churches exist to serve the needs of our society. When they appear to be primarily serving their own institutional needs, we become justifiably uneasy and cynical—just as we do when banks, trade unions or any other institutions abuse our trust.

Hostility between and within various religious denominations doesn't help, either: to an outsider, it almost appears as if different denominations—or even different factions within one denomination—are worshipping different gods, especially when it comes to their position on the spectrum between love and forgiveness at one end and punitive judgement at the other. Fundamentalists and liberals within the same religion often mock each other in ways that suggest a serious antipathy, if not mutual loathing.

And what is an outsider expected to make of the furious disagreements between Christians? They diverge on matters including the literal versus metaphorical truth of the Bible; the significance of the communion service (a simple

249

commemorative meal, or a sacrament imbued with mystical power?); the doctrine of the atonement (did Jesus die on the cross as a sacrifice for the sins of the world, or does that represent too violent and vengeful a view of God?); and the resurrection (a literal, physical event, or an inspiring myth about the continuing influence of Jesus's teachings and the possibility of spiritual renewal)?

Religious services that seem baffling to the uninitiated are a further impediment. When people try to explain why they stopped going to church, they typically say things like 'boring', 'insult to my intelligence', 'I felt too exposed', 'I couldn't tick all the boxes they expected me to tick', 'I wasn't going to recite a creed I couldn't sign up to', 'I felt as if I didn't belong there' or 'I just didn't get it'.

***

When you look at the broad sweep of history and the contribution religion has made to our culture through music, mythology, festivals, education and, most particularly, the encouragement of loving-kindness, it's perhaps surprising that it is in such decline. What is not surprising is that the decline coincides with the rise of individualism and the erosion of what Martin Seligman calls 'the commons': the sense of community, the sense of a common life, the sense of mutual obligation between us and our neighbours.

There's no shortage of interest in spirituality, however, and the rise of the 'spiritual but not religious' (SBNR) movement in Australia suggests that mainstream churches have drifted away from the communities they are meant to serve. Today,

250

a person in search of spiritual guidance or comfort would be more likely to explore the possibilities offered by yoga, meditation or psychotherapy than traditional religion.

Atheism might be a popular label, but people worship as many gods as they ever have; it's just that conventional Christianity has less appeal than it once did. And yet, for people who claim not to believe in God, the word 'god' now occupies a surprisingly large place in our vocabulary. It makes you wonder what people are referring to when they so habitually say, 'Oh my god!'

Reflections...

- Pondering the gap between religious identity and religious practice in Australia (at least among Christians), and the growing tendency for non-churchgoing parents to send their children to church schools, I'm reminded of Voltaire. Though famously anti-Christian himself, he apparently believed that the moral values of the Christian religion were valuable as a discipline for the masses: 'I want my attorney, my tailor, my servants, even my wife to believe in God, because then I shall be robbed and cuckolded less often.' I'm also reminded of the McCrindle research showing that the overwhelming majority of non-churchgoing Australians like having a church in their suburb or town. Presumably, that's not about architecture; it's more likely to be about the idea that churchgoers might be expected to exert a good influence and do 'good works' in their local community. While most Australians clearly don't want to go to church, we seem to like the idea that other people still do.

- We all live by faith, to some extent. When we board an aircraft, we are putting our faith in the technology, the maintenance crew and the skill of the pilot. When we order food in a restaurant, we put our faith in the integrity of the menu and the hygienic practices of the kitchen staff. We express our faith in each other when we fall in love or when we commit ourselves to any kind of relationship. And faith is a powerful thing. As Martin Seligman and so many others remind us, we benefit from placing our faith in something greater than ourselves, but there's more to it than that. Faith healing is not a fiction: consider the famous 'placebo effect', where some of the people taking part in clinical trials of a new drug form a 'control group' and are given something that looks like the drug but is in fact a harmless substance with no therapeutic efficacy at all. In roughly 30 per cent of cases, people taking the placebo report improvements in their health consistent with having taken the drug. Faith might not be able to 'move mountains' but it can certainly produce positive outcomes for us.

- Doubt is the engine of faith; it is the oxygen that sustains faith's flickering candle. If we had no doubt—if we *knew*—we wouldn't have to *believe*. Even the faith we place in the crew of an aircraft, or the skill of a surgeon, or the integrity of a financial adviser, only arises because we feel the *need* of faith: that's our response to an unbidden doubt or fear about whether this will go well. The test of whether you're a true believer is not whether you have absolute confidence in an outcome; it's whether your confidence sometimes wobbles. Faith doesn't remove our doubts;

it depends on them. Doubt arises from a sense of power-lessness, or at least a feeling of loss of control. That, in turn, fuels our humility and, in my experience, the humble faithful are more attractive to us than the self-righteous, the bigots, the narcissists—or, indeed, those religious funda-mentalists whose convictions are so strong and inflexible, they could scarcely be called 'believers' at all.

- I believe the highest human good is to let the spirit of love grow and prosper within us so that it animates everything we do. Love's work (which for many religious people is synonymous with God's work) can only be done by us, individually and collectively. And love's work is the hardest work of all. Cynicism is easier. Prejudice is easier. Disengagement is easier. Indifference is easier. Even hate is easier. But, however it's expressed, love's work is all that can heal our wounded society.

- Whenever I hear or read 'God' in a sentence, I mentally substitute 'the loving spirit' to see whether the sentence rings true for me. (Try it sometime.) In fact, I wonder whether faith in the power of love is the bridge that can unite theists and atheists.

7

Survival of the kindest

In a 2021 article for *New Scientist*, UK science journalist Kate Ravilious reported the findings of a group of archaeologists who were trying to explain why *Homo sapiens*—that's us—is the only human species to have survived. After all, if you go back far enough—say, 200,000 years—there were at least five different types of humans on the planet. So what was our secret?

Ravilious reminds us that many explanations have been put forward, including superior brain power, our mastery of language or sheer good luck. But according to the latest archaeological thinking, the answer is laden with irony: it is 'our deepest vulnerabilities—being dependent on others, feeling compassion and experiencing empathy—that could have given us the edge'.

It's been tempting to assume that it was our cognitive skills, rather than our capacity for kindness, that ensured our survival. But it appears that some of our human rivals—the

Neanderthals and *Homo erectus*, for instance—were also cognitively competent, having built tools and made drawings on the walls of caves, as we did, and having adapted very well to living in particular parts of the planet. But *Homo sapiens* set itself apart by being more adaptable to variations in climate and environment.

The burning question, therefore, is *how* did we do it? How did we become the masters of adaptability? And that's where 'our deepest vulnerabilities' come in. As reported by Ravilious, Penny Spikins, a professor of archaeology at the University of York, believes that the frailties inherent in our emotional nature have been the making of us. 'Our emotional neediness gave us the drive to connect with others,' she says, and it comes from a long way back—there's evidence of our ape-like ancestor in southern Africa, *Australopithecus*, caring for the sick and injured. But the biggest finding is that *Homo sapiens* developed strong community connections: 'The more we look, the more we see evidence for increased social interactions and wider networks,' says Spikins.

There's a downside, of course, and we know what it is, because our species is still living with it in the twenty-first century: if you belong to an essentially social species, that will lead you to build strong, resilient communities but, as Spikins says, this 'also makes individuals vulnerable to being lonely, depressed and anxious' if they feel excluded from those communities.

Our emotional neediness was our trump card during a period of cataclysmic climate change, around 42,000 years ago, because our desire to connect with others turned us into the cooperative species we needed to be in order to survive.

This takes us back to the central theme of 'The Context'—indeed, to the central theme of this whole book. Because we are born to cooperate, we are also born with the equipment we need to achieve social harmony—the capacity for kindness, compassion, tolerance, empathy. That cluster of traits, when nurtured, brings out the very best in us and, we now know, has actually contributed to the survival of the species.

By contrast, when we concentrate too much on our individuality—our differences, our separateness—that tends to bring out the worst in us and can diminish our capacity to connect with the community we live in. In the 2020s, that has become the core challenge for Australian society: rebuilding our eroded sense of community by restoring our sense of the common humanity we all share. Let's not highlight our differences for dramatic effect; let's refocus on the ways we can promote harmony and cohesion.

It's not just the archaeologists and the neuroscientists who are pointing to this deep truth about humanity's need of community. Ancient wisdom has always pointed to the same thing, often expressed through religion, but also through philosophy and culture more broadly. Versions of the Golden Rule—'Treat others the way you would like to be treated'—appear in ancient Egypt, ancient China and ancient Greece, and in religious traditions ranging from Confucianism, Taoism, Hinduism and Zoroastrianism to the three Abrahamic faiths of Judaism, Christianity and Islam, and in newer religions such as the Baha'i faith. You'll also encounter it in non-theistic traditions like Buddhism and humanism.

Since it now appears from the archaeological record that our capacity for kindness is the secret of our long-term survival, it's hardly surprising that we esteem kindness so highly. And since being kind and cooperative makes so many demands on us, it's no wonder that we sometimes fall short of the gold standard. As I wrote in 'The Context', 'most of the fine and noble aspects of human nature cast shadows' and if you think of kindness—or, in its fuller original form, *loving-kindness*—as being like a light at the centre of our being, that's bound to cast shadows, too.

In his inaugural speech on becoming president of South Africa in 1994, Nelson Mandela said, 'It is our light, not our darkness that most frightens us.' But why would anyone be afraid of the light? Why would anyone who understood the very essence of what it means to be human try to deny that essence, instead of celebrating it and nurturing it? Why would anyone choose to be as unkind as possible—for example, by hurling abuse through cyberspace as an online troll, or by always leaping to the most negative, uncharitable conclusion about other people's motives, or by resorting to bullying as a way of avoiding our inherent responsibility for the wellbeing of others? (That's what the archaeologists and neuroscientists are telling us: it's *inherent*.)

The answers to those questions are likely to vary wildly from person to person, but the common thread is most likely this: for whatever reason, the *capacity* for kindness was not carefully nurtured in them when they were young; an example of kindness was not shown to them by parents or other carers; kindness was not rewarded, reinforced and encouraged when they were in their formative years. Or perhaps some trauma occurred that made them wary of emotional attachment.

Or perhaps they suffered too many experiences of rejection or humiliation.

Or—and here's a surprising one—perhaps they are sleep deprived. New research conducted by Eti Ben Simon and her colleagues at the University of California's Center for Human Sleep Science has shown that even relatively mild sleep loss is linked to a reduced inclination to help others. Describing the research in *Medscape Medical News*, Ben Simon says that

> insufficient sleep represents a causal, yet previously unrecognized, factor dictating whether or not humans choose to help each other, triggered by a breakdown in the activity of key prosocial-brain networks.
>
> The study adds to a growing body of evidence demonstrating that inadequate sleep not only harms the mental and physical well-being of an individual, but also compromises the bonds between individuals.

(Don't you love the way concepts that we think of as *moral*—like altruism—so often turn out to be rooted in biology . . . or illuminated by archaeology?)

When it comes to a want of kindness, no one is a lost cause. Knowing what we know about the nature of our species, we can confidently say that even narcissists and psychopaths were not born that way. The *capacity* for kindness and cooperation is always there. These inherent qualities can be revived—and it now appears that even improved sleep hygiene may help! The nurturing can happen later in life, perhaps in the context of a loving relationship. The influence of a bad example can be gradually replaced by the influence of a good one.

Which is why all of us are charged with the responsibility to show kindness towards the lonely, the disaffected, the marginalised—and the unlovely. Not because we're wonderful people, but because we're human. The species demands that of its members—and we now know it has been doing so for many thousands of years.

What is kindness?

'Define your terms!' people are fond of saying in philosophical debate. Alright, then, let's define kindness . . .

First, a reminder. To understand why kindness is so fundamental to our psychological and physical health, we need to reflect—yet again—on what it means to say that we're members of a social species. It means we yearn to *belong*. The sign that we belong is that other people take us seriously—notice us, acknowledge us, appreciate us, include us. So here's my working definition of kindness: 'anything we do to show other people that we take them seriously'.

Literally, anything.

It might be a smile to a stranger: I recently heard of a young man who had attempted to take his own life by jumping off a bridge. He survived the attempt and said to the person who rescued him: 'If someone had smiled at me, I wouldn't have jumped.' Ponder that, next time you pass a stranger: your smile might be enough to bring that person back from the brink of despair. And even if it isn't as grim a situation as that, then your smile has at least said, 'I see you. I acknowledge you. I greet you.'

It might be a wave to a driver who's stopped for you at a pedestrian crossing. (Yes, I know it's the law for cars to give way, but not everyone does it, so why not treat it as an act of courtesy?) It might be helping a frail elderly person on or off a bus, or across a busy street. It might be calling in for a chat with a neighbour who is at risk of social isolation. It might be offering to share a sandwich with someone who's out of cash, or buying a cup of coffee for a person begging in the street.

Or it might be that glorious, generous, therapeutic act of giving someone your undivided attention by really listening to what they have to say. Nothing says 'I take you seriously' quite as eloquently, or as kindly, as attentive, empathic listening.

Think of kindness—loving-kindness—as a unique form of human love. All forms of human love are wonderful, of course: romantic love energises and inspires us; the enduring power of a loving relationship sustains us; the bonds of familial love can, if we're in the fortunate majority, comfort and nurture us. And where would we be without the richness of the companionate love that connects us to our friendship circles?

All those forms of love have something in common: they are about affection; they involve the human emotions. As do most of our other uses of that magic word 'love'. If I say 'I love chocolate' or 'I love dogs' or 'I loved that movie', you know I'm talking about an emotional response to those things.

But here's how kindness is unique: it's the only form of human love that does *not* necessarily involve the emotions. It's the only form of human love that does not *entail* affection. We might happen to feel affection towards someone we're being kind to, but we might not; it's actually irrelevant. As Samuel Johnson wrote so memorably, two hundred and fifty years ago: 'Kindness is in our power, even when fondness is not.'

261

Isn't it wonderful knowing you belong to a species of which that can be said? Isn't that worth celebrating? Isn't that enough to get you out of bed in the morning? We humans are capable of showing kindness to total strangers, to people we could never agree with, even to people we actively dislike. Our emotional disposition simply doesn't come into it. We are equipped to be kind to each other because we are human.

How else would we be able to cooperate in the Grand Human Project I've mentioned several times—creating and maintaining social harmony? Not by agreeing with each other about everything. Not by always liking each other. Not by feeling we have to please each other all the time. But simply by showing kindness to all comers, without prejudice, without discrimination, without restraint.

That's how we can make sense of an injunction like 'love your enemies', attributed to Jesus of Nazareth. It's not about emotion or affection; it's about this remarkable quality of loving-kindness. It's about showing kindness to everyone, even those who oppose you. (Good lesson there for pollies . . . but also for the rest of us.)

None of this should be taken to mean that kindness implies acquiescence or infinite agreeableness. It's possible to have a robust argument kindly. It's possible to terminate a relationship, discipline a child, or lodge a complaint kindly. Kindness is not to be confused with being soft in the head; it does not turn us into doormats. Being kind—always and to everyone—is a way of being in the world while still being true to yourself.

Kindness should be as natural as breathing. The body can't survive without inhaling and exhaling, and the spirit can't flourish without giving and receiving kindness.

It's not heroic. It's not exceptional. It's not praiseworthy. It's just what humans do when they're being true to their essential human nature.

A friend in her seventies recently travelled interstate and took a tumble in a city street. She landed flat on her face. Momentarily stunned, she lay there wondering how serious her injuries might be. Before she'd had time to process what had happened, a young woman appeared, helped her to her feet, examined her bleeding face and insisted on accompanying her back to her hotel, three blocks away. This total stranger supported her by the elbow and chatted to her all the way, to keep my friend's spirits up and to distract her from the blood trickling down her face. Back at the hotel, the young woman handed my friend over to the reception staff and melted away into the dusk.

Naturally, my friend had thanked her helper profusely because she had been so kind, and because that prolonged act of kindness had detained the young woman from whatever else she had been intending to do at that time. In response to my friend's thanks, she had simply smiled and said, 'Anyone would have done the same.' That was probably not literally true, but it was close to the truth. That's how we humans are programmed to act. There's a person in need of help; I'm here; I'll help. What would be really remarkable would be *not* to help a person in that situation.

Kindness, then, is not only showing another person that we've noticed and responded respectfully to them; it is doing so without qualification. That young woman *didn't* say to my friend: 'Ah! I see you're in strife. I can probably help you out. But first, let me ask you a couple of questions. How did you vote in the last election? Where do you stand on the question of bodily resurrection? Who's your favourite author?'

No . . . there are no boxes to tick when kindness is called for. Those 'better angels of our nature' (in US president Abraham Lincoln's poetic phrase) simply swing into action. And note that Lincoln was talking about our *nature*. Our 'better angels' are part of who we are.

There are less attractive parts of us, of course: our egos, for example. The ego-driven agenda can be the enemy of kindness: our ambition, our selfishness, our rivalries, our jealousies, our prejudices, our vengefulness, our eagerness to judge or control others. All of these can inhibit the kindness impulse by promoting our sense of ourselves as independent individuals rather than members of a family, a neighbour-hood, a community, a society and a species.

Kindness needs to be nurtured

Given that it is our nature to be kind, cooperative, compassionate and caring; given that that's the way we've evolved; given that the long history of our species points to the survival of the kindest, it's a wonder we ever stray from the path our destiny points to.

But we do. Sometimes it's a personal thing: as I've already acknowledged, there are people whose capacity for kindness has either never been developed or may have been diminished by bad experiences. But sometimes an entire society gallops off in the wrong direction, without even knowing why. Just glance again at the seven social disruptors listed in 'The Context'—especially our shrinking households, our high rate of relationship breakdown, our relentless busyness and our uncritical embrace of the IT revolution—and you can see how these trends, taken together, encourage individualism, erode social cohesion and increase the risk of social isolation.

Crises and catastrophes—whether personal or societal—tend to make us pause and reconsider what it really means to be human. We know exactly how to behave towards each other when a fire or a flood or a pandemic or an economic depression or a war cause us to think more about survival than self-indulgence, and more about the importance of social cohesion than the importance of the self. But we don't have to wait for the next crisis; there are things we can do to promote kindness and thereby enhance our health and wellbeing, if not our survival.

The township of Frome in Somerset, England, is an instructive case in what can be achieved when a community wakes up to its compassion and kindness deficit. In 2013, Dr Helen Kingston, a GP in the town, noticed that many of her elderly patients' health problems were being exacerbated by social isolation. In collaboration with local authorities and agencies, Kingston developed a register of community groups that she could direct patients to join. Thus began the phenomenon we now recognise as 'social prescribing', where a doctor doesn't just prescribe medication but also prescribes a pathway out of social isolation. It was the beginning of a larger project that came to be known as Compassionate Frome.

Choirs, community gardens, book clubs, men's sheds, writing workshops . . . these and other activities were prescribed by Dr Kingston and, in time, by other medical practitioners as well. As George Monbiot put it in a 2018 article he wrote for *The Guardian* about Compassionate Frome: 'The point was to break a familiar cycle of misery: illness reduces people's ability to socialise, which leads in turn to isolation and loneliness, which then exacerbates illness.'

What the Compassionate Frome project appeared to show in the first five years of its operation was that, as Monbiot put it, 'when isolated people who have health problems are supported by community groups and volunteers, the number of emergency admissions to hospital falls spectacularly'. 'Spectacularly' is certainly the word for what happened in Frome: preliminary data from a three-year study showed that emergency hospital admissions across the whole county of Somerset rose by 29 per cent while, in Frome, they *fell* by 17 per cent. Monbiot quotes Julian Abel, a consultant physician: 'No other interventions on record have reduced emergency hospital admissions across a population.'

But we're not surprised, are we? Doesn't everything we know about humans point to the crucial importance of community—to the need for us to feel connected, to feel included? Many of us had a tiny taste of social isolation during the lockdowns designed to limit the spread of COVID-19 (though most of us were locked up with one or more members of our household). Did that experience make us more alert and more sensitive to the plight of those in our midst—perhaps in our street—who are at risk of social isolation most of the time? Knowing the health risks associated with social isolation, one would certainly hope so.

A 'compassionate cities' project is spreading around the world as part of the Global Charter for Compassion. Belfast, in Northern Ireland, recently conducted a ceremony for children to plant 'seeds of compassion' in a public garden, and to symbolically rake over the hurts of the past.

In Australia, Ballarat is leading the way in encouraging more compassionate decision-making and action by organisations and individuals in the city. The City of Ballarat, business and community leaders, and local schools are partnering with Compassionate Ballarat to raise awareness of the need for more compassion in all our interactions with each other. Under the leadership of Lynne Reeder, Compassionate Ballarat has become a focal point for people in need of any kind of support. It has collaborated with other volunteer organisations—for example, to help fund a 'sleep bus' that offers overnight shelter for homeless people, and to support the Be Kind Ballarat initiative that was designed to encourage residents to look out for each other during the COVID pandemic lockdowns. Compassionate Ballarat has also established a CEO group comprising leaders from local businesses and other organisations, designed to encourage more compassion-focused leadership.

Ballarat is undergoing a quiet revolution as people begin thinking more habitually about the need to act compassionately towards each other—at work, at school and in the neighbourhood. In the city's annual youth awards, the 'compassion and care' award now attracts more nominations than any other category.

We don't have to wait for formal initiatives to encourage greater kindness and compassion, and to stimulate the sense of community, wherever we live. It's easy to wring our hands about the state of the nation, but not so easy to admit that it's our own behaviour that helps to determine the shape our society is in. To say (as I've heard many people say over the years) that 'we don't know our neighbours'—or even, more brutally, 'I have no interest in getting to know the neighbours'—is to say something deeply sad and deeply troubling about our lack of understanding of our responsibilities towards each other. Architecture plays a role here: people in higher-density housing typically feel a heightened need for privacy, though some people in more traditional house-and-garden suburbs report that it's a struggle to form neighbourly connections.

Forget 'survival of the fittest'. While Charles Darwin successfully explained the origin of many species, he didn't pick the reason why *Homo sapiens* survived and other human species didn't. It's too easy for those of us living in the comfort of the developed world to grab hold of 'the survival of the fittest' as a justification for economic and social inequality and for a dog-eat-dog competitiveness, forgetting that we owe our very survival to those 'deepest vulnerabilities' that encourage cooperation, kindness, tolerance, compassion and empathy.

Everything we know about the price we humans have to pay for inequality (ask the French), for aggression (ask the Ukrainians, the Afghans or the Sudanese, among many others), for prejudice (ask the Jews) or for unbridled competitiveness (ask the Americans) should alert us to the need to respect our species' heritage. It worked for us 42,000 years ago; it can still work for us. A kinder, more cooperative, more compassionate and more egalitarian society would benefit us all. The alternative is a descent into chaos.

Kindness is a way of being in the world that changes the world and changes us. When we dream of a better world isn't that always a dream of a kinder world? We help to make that dream come true simply by being kind—always and to everyone—and, in the process, our life takes on a richer meaning. No one can guarantee that a life lived for others will bring you a deep sense of satisfaction, but it's certain that nothing else will.

To conclude this chapter, here's an extract from my 2021 book, *The Kindness Revolution*:

Everyone is in need of kindness because everyone walks with shadows—the bereaved with their grief, the arrogant with their deep-down insecurities, the believers with their doubt, the lonely with their ache for connection, the uncherished with their fear of insignificance, the ambitious with their vulnerability to failure, the siblings with their rivalry, the bullies with their repressed self-loathing, the errant with their guilt, the anxious and depressed with their dark yearnings . . . and all those living with the pain of disappointment, frustration, humiliation, rejection or loss. Kindness is the universal balm for troubled souls; the gift that says, 'I understand your need for kindness, because I share it'.

Reflections . . .

- In order to be properly equipped to show kindness to others, we need also to be kind to ourselves. We need to devote some time in every day to self-care—especially through periods of quiet solitude, either sitting alone in a meditative state, or reading, writing a reflective journal, walking, gentle swimming, playing or listening to music, or anything else that helps to recharge the batteries. We need emotional and physical energy to stay kind.

- Kindness also implies patience, tolerance and forbearance. It's not just a matter of saying or doing kind things; it's also a matter of giving other people the space to be themselves and the time to find the words that will express what they'd like to say to us. Impatience, like busyness, is the enemy of kindness.

- Kindness is a pure, selfless thing. It's only ever about our response to other people. Try not to sully it by wondering what you're getting out of it. Don't assume it's transactional, as in 'If I'm kind to this person, I'll receive kindness in return'. That's self-serving, not kind. And don't assume that being kind will make you feel good: sometimes it will and sometimes it won't, but that orientation is all wrong. If I'm being kind in order to feel better about myself, then, again, it's all about me, not the person I'm being kind to. And don't act kindly out of a desire to *appear* kind: that, too, diminishes the generosity of the act. Keep it simple; keep it pure. *Just be kind*, for no reason except to be true to those 'better angels' of your nature and, as a result, to improve the lives of those on the receiving end of your kindness.

- Thinking about the archaeological record might also remind us that we humans are part of a larger whole— our survival as a species doesn't only depend on how we treat each other, but also on how we treat the other species we share this planet with, and how we treat the planet itself. Kindness is not only a socially desirable quality; it's ecologically desirable as well.

8

It's time to hone our listening skills

During the long transition from an oral communication culture to the present online digital culture, there has been a steady erosion of our listening skills. As we gradually came to attach more significance to the written word, we began to listen less carefully.

Now, in the 2020s, our ever-increasing reliance on screen-based messages—and the cascading oversupply of those messages—has further encouraged the habit of not listening as attentively as we once did. At the same time, as mentioned in 'The Context', our attention spans have shrunk alarmingly—and that's bad news for listening, too.

Does it matter? Of course it does! We might be relying more and more on our digital devices to inform (or misinform) and entertain (or merely distract) ourselves, and even to communicate with each other but, in the end, we're human. We need that all-important face-to-face interaction. We need eye contact.

And we need to be heard! Our sanity depends on it.

The following chapter is less about social analysis and more about finding ways to sharpen our listening skills; less about *the way we are* and more about *the way we need to be* if we are to repair our damaged social fabric. Of all the skills required to strengthen our personal and working relationships, restore our sense of community and address the problems of loneliness and social fragmentation, listening is the pre-eminent one.

Some years ago, I heard of a newly appointed school principal who took great pride in her ability to read problem situations quickly and come up with workable solutions. Shortly after arriving at her new school, she was chatting to the school counsellor about Oliver, a troublesome fourteen-year-old in Year 9. Several teachers had mentioned that Oliver was becoming inattentive in class, late with his homework, reluctant to play sport and generally rather disengaged. He was regarded as one of the most promising musicians in the school, but had recently withdrawn from the choir and was showing signs of the lack of piano practice. The counsellor felt she was making some progress with Oliver but the principal was determined to act decisively in response to those teachers' complaints.

'Sounds like a classic case of Year Nine Malaise. Send him to me. I'll put him on weekly report for a while and I'll simply tell him choir is compulsory for all music students. He can go on the gardening roster for a month. I might pull his parents in for a chat, as well—an apple never falls far from the tree.'

The counsellor looked at her and smiled.

'Why don't you just listen to Oliver first?' she suggested.

How can we ever hope to understand what's going on in another person's head—let alone try to change their behaviour—without first hearing their story? A so-called 'problem boy' like Oliver is more than a boy with a problem: he is a complex bundle of his genetic inheritance, his social conditioning (including the influence of his family life, his neighbourhood, his school community, his peer group), his exposure to media content, plus all the learnings he has acquired through his own experience . . . to say nothing of the bruises he might be carrying as a result of disappointments and disenchantments along the way. What of the dreams he might have dared to dream and the pain and humiliation he might have suffered by sharing those dreams with unsupportive parents or unsympathetic friends?

And how does a promising young musician deal with daily humiliation at the hands of a music teacher who has clearly developed an intense personal dislike of him and, much to the amusement of his classmates, addresses him scathingly as 'little Ollie'? Or with the frequent taunts about his 'unnatural' musical tastes from his mother's new partner? Or with the pain of separation from his father who has now moved interstate and will see him only in school holidays?

'Why don't you just listen to Oliver first?' Indeed.

The courage to listen

Really listening to someone else is an act of courage because, when we listen attentively and with empathy, we run the risk of being changed by what we hear. To press the point a little further: if we're *not* running the risk of being changed—influenced—by what we hear, then we're not really listening;

273

we're merely hearing the words being said. The pioneering US psychotherapist Carl Rogers has written that when we truly listen to another person, we inevitably make ourselves vulnerable to change and that this risk of being changed is one of the most frightening prospects most of us face.

No wonder it takes courage to listen!

You might think it's all very well for a professional psychotherapist like Rogers to talk about listening in such a committed, attentive, non-judgemental, empathic way, but what about the rest of us, going about our daily lives? In fact, there's no real difference between the professional and the rest of us when it comes to listening. Whether you're a parent, a partner, a friend, a neighbour, a colleague, a teacher or a stranger at a bus stop, if you're going to give someone the gift of your undivided attention, that will be a beneficial experience for them. Actually, it will be received as a precious gift.

If you doubt the therapeutic value of listening, just think about the unspoken message we send each other when we refuse to listen, or only half-listen, or appear distracted and uninterested or, worst of all, refuse to make eye contact. Without needing to put it into words, this is the message we're conveying: 'Sorry, I don't take you seriously enough to bother listening to you. I'm not even prepared to entertain your ideas.' Would you ever say that to a partner, a child, a colleague, a friend or neighbour? Of course not: it would be too hurtful and offensive. Yet when we withhold the gift of attentive, empathic listening to someone who *needs* us to listen, that's the impression we give.

When it comes to listening (and, indeed, relationships in general), everyone's a therapist and everyone's a client. Of course

I don't mean that we are all equipped to offer each other therapy in the professional sense. My point is simply that all of us have a deep need to feel that we are valued and, when that need is being met, that's therapeutic for us. And since being listened to is one of the most potent of all the signs that we are valued, it's one of the most therapeutic things we can do for each other.

In most healthy relationships, we are constantly switching the roles of 'therapist' and 'client': when you need me to listen, I'm the one offering the therapy; when I need you to listen, I become the client. It's not that neat or formal, of course, but one of the reasons why it's so much easier to talk than listen is that the talker is the one receiving the therapy and the listener is the one giving it.

Many people describe a trip to the hairdresser as 'therapeutic'. It's not just that they come out looking better than they did when they went in; it's also that they often feel they've been attentively listened to. (Hairdressers should really get more credit for the contribution they make to the mental health of the nation!)

What do we most need on those occasions when we might pay to see a professional therapist? We need an attentive, patient, listening ear; the reassurance that we are valued; and the confidence of knowing that, whatever approach to psychotherapy the therapist happens to take, and wherever this encounter may lead us, at the very least our story will be heard.

Imagine the impact on young Oliver of having that school principal give him her undivided attention: it might well have changed his whole sense of engagement with the school and, over time, changed his own behaviour as well. When we are listened to with empathy, it is as if someone is saying, 'I am prepared to put my own interests and concerns on hold; I am putting you first; I am going to entertain your ideas, and try to see things from your point of view.' Therapy indeed!

That's why 'R U OK?' is such a great question to ask. Without being intrusive, it is at once an expression of concern and a declaration of our willingness to listen. 'How are you travelling?' can work well, too, for the same reason.

***

A listening-as-therapy tip: if you accept the idea that being a committed listener will, in effect, cast you in the role of 'therapist' from time to time, here's a tip that might be useful. When someone really needs you to attend to something they are telling you about their own behaviour, never seek an explanation for that behaviour; never ask, 'Why?'

It's so tempting to say, 'But why did you do that?' By asking 'Why?', we are making two unwarranted assumptions. First, we assume there must be a (preferably rational) explanation for the behaviour in question; second, we're assuming the person concerned knows what that explanation is. Both assumptions are problematical. We often act in ways that are quite irrational and therefore hard to explain in any reasonable terms, and we are often quite unaware of the factors that have led us to do something. When it comes to human behaviour, not everything can be explained . . . or needs to be.

In the case of children, in particular, the demand for a sensible-sounding explanation can simply cause a child to clam up, or lie, rather than admit that what they did was stupid, thoughtless, pointless or likely to cause harm. But whether child or adult, to be asked 'Why?' is bound to provoke a defensive reaction because it feels like an assault.

Instead of asking 'Why?', simply say, 'Can you tell me a bit more about that?' Or perhaps, 'Okay, what happened next?' Or even, 'Go on . . . I'm interested.'

You're only being asked to listen, remember, not to interrogate, judge or explain. If someone *asks* you to help them understand their own behaviour—to help explain them to themselves—that's a different matter.

Really listening or merely hearing?

There's a big difference between the physiological act of hearing and the psychological act of listening. Hearing is involuntary: it simply means that your ears are in working order and that the sounds you hear are being transmitted to your brain. No interpretation. No processing, apart from the unavoidable physical process that goes on in your brain and central nervous system as a result of hearing a noise.

That's why it can be deeply irritating when someone says to you: 'I hear you.' It can sometimes sound rather dismissive, as if they're saying, in effect: 'I have no actual interest in what you're saying. I'm not even trying to understand what you're saying, let alone deciding what I think about it. This is either a subject of no interest to me, or else it's a subject on which I've already made up my mind. I'll go through the motions of hearing you out, but I won't bother attending seriously to anything you say that might challenge my entrenched position.'

What an insult! And what a declaration of that person's lack of courage! On the other hand . . . let's acknowledge that, in some circumstances, 'I hear you' can actually be intended to convey a quite different, much more sympathetic message: 'I've listened to what you have to say, and I hear you.' In other words, 'I've really taken it on board.' (Yes, context is everything.)

Listening is the art of entertaining another person's ideas. Imagining what it must feel like to be them. Trying out the things they are saying, to see if we could accommodate them within the framework of our existing knowledge, attitudes, beliefs and convictions. Perhaps even making some modifications to that framework *in order to* accommodate them.

Suppose I point to a coat that's hanging on a peg on the wall over there.

'Go on,' I say to you. 'Try on that coat.'

And suppose you say: 'Oh, no. I can see it wouldn't fit. It wouldn't suit me at all. Wrong colour. Wrong style. Wrong length. No, it's just not my kind of coat.'

Wouldn't I be entitled to say to you, 'Hey, you can't say that. You haven't even tried it on. Go and try it on first, and then tell me if it suits you'?

Listening—deep listening, attentive listening, empathic listening—is like trying on the coat. Yes, it might well turn out that it doesn't suit you at all, but you don't know that until you've tried it on. Seeing the coat is there, simply because your eyes are working, is like hearing what someone is saying, simply because your ears are working. The question is whether you're prepared to run the risk of trying it on in case—*horrors!*—it might actually fit after you've so confidently declared it wouldn't.

Personal relationships are essential to human flourishing, and conversations are a vital ingredient in the process of building relationships. But what's the point of conversation if we don't listen to each other? And what's the point of listening if we don't open ourselves up to each other?

It's only by listening that we qualify ourselves to agree or disagree with each other. It's only by listening that we start to bridge the chasms that threaten to divide us. It's only by *deep* listening that we can begin the process of healing our troubled, fragmented, wounded society . . . one conversation at a time.

Why are we so scared to listen? Why are we so reluctant to entertain another person's ideas? Why are we so afraid of the possibility of being changed by what we hear? There's a simple answer . . .

Prejudice is a very comfortable prison

Ever since the stage in your development when you started laying down permanent memory traces in the brain—for most of us, that's around the age of three—you have been gradually constructing a personal framework for making sense of the world. As you acquire each new piece of knowledge, as you begin to adopt particular attitudes and reject others, as you come to believe in certain ideas and not in others—based partly on your direct experience and partly on the influence (especially the example) of parents, teachers, preachers, friends, enemies, books, movies, poems, plays, video games and social media—that framework becomes more complex and more resilient.

Just for a moment, try to imagine it as a physical framework: think of yourself (and everyone else) as walking around with your head enclosed in a kind of psychological cage. A mind-cage. The bars of that cage are all the attitudes, values, beliefs and convictions you have acquired up to this point in your life. You might find the word 'cage' a bit unattractive, a bit intimidating. Yet it accurately conveys the idea that we are both the beneficiaries and the prisoners of our knowledge, attitudes, beliefs and prejudices.

Some of the bars of our mind-cage are undeniably valuable and useful. 'One plus one equals two', for example. Can't argue with that—could come in handy in all sorts of contexts, from shopping to planning a space flight. Good, solid stuff. *Click*—into the mind-cage it goes. 'Wash your hands before handling food.' Sound, evidence-based advice, always worth remembering, so—*click*—in goes another bar of the mind-cage. 'The Earth goes around the sun.' Helps to explain a lot of other stuff. *Click*—store it up for later use. 'Treat other people the way you'd like to be treated.' Easy to grasp the point of that, even though it's hard to put into practice sometimes, but—*click*—add it to the framework as an ideal, at least.

Some of the conclusions we draw from our experience are not so useful, and some of the reckless stuff we choose to believe—like the prejudices we pick up from family or friends or media propaganda—can be downright dodgy. 'Black people are inferior to white people.' 'You can't trust traditional media—you only learn what's *really* happening on social media.' 'All religions do more harm than good.' 'All politicians are corrupt.' 'The Labor Party/Liberal Party is out to wreck the country.' If we incorporate ideas like those into our mind-cage—perhaps because we had no other reference points for judging them at the time we first heard them, or because peer-group pressure made it seem necessary to go along with them—they may become as entrenched as any other, more legitimately acquired attitudes and we may cling to them just as tenaciously. (Remember the Dunning–Kruger effect I described in chapter 2?)

Once acquired, a prejudice can feel no different from knowledge. A conviction, no matter how outrageous it might seem to others, can feel to the person who holds it like a perfectly reasonable, rational insight—if not a certainty, then at least a strong probability.

Don't get me wrong: the mind-cage is, generally speaking, a good thing. Necessary. Couldn't function without it. Vital to our sense of mental and emotional security. It's the mechanism that equips us to understand and interpret what's going on around us, by bringing our existing knowledge and experience to bear on every new situation. But when it comes to listening to each other . . . well, it's hardly surprising that what we *most* love is listening to people who reinforce the bars of our own mind-cage. People whose prejudices match our own. People who see the world in much the same way we do. That's why we love watching ads for products we are already using (especially if those ads are justifying the crazy prices we pay for high-end cosmetics, cars or watches). We love listening to politicians or religious preachers who confirm what we already believe. When it comes to music, we mostly prefer familiar classics to edgy experimental stuff. 'Preaching to the converted' feels wonderful to the converted.

But we're humans . . . remember? We are joined together in the noble task of creating and maintaining social harmony. That's our mission. That's our destiny. And that's why we need to rise to the challenge of listening to others. I'm not, for one moment, suggesting that we should change our minds in response to everything we hear from political opponents, religious extremists, conspiracy theorists, zealots of any kind . . . or even people who support a different football club, or have wildly different cultural tastes and preferences from ours.

All I'm saying is that social harmony depends on us finding the courage to be more attentive, empathic listeners, prepared to acknowledge what is being said, *especially when our own prejudices are being challenged.* In ninety-nine cases out of a hundred, nothing will change. In ninety-nine cases out of a hundred, the strength and resilience of our mind-cage will serve us well and we won't only emerge from the encounter unscathed, we'll actually find that our own prejudices have been reinforced by the experience of having them tested, if not actually attacked. In fact, *reinforcement* is the most likely outcome of any assault on our mind-cage. Except when we're very young, we are the very opposite of blank slates!

There's nothing like persecution to build up the faith of a particular religious or other minority group. Minorities naturally hate being the victims of other people's prejudices, but their convictions about the validity of their own position will usually be strengthened—not weakened—by the experience of others' disapproval or mockery.

The viewer is part of the view. How could it be otherwise? We don't just see what's out there; we see it through the filter created by the complex interlocking bars of our mind-cage. This is why we tend to see what we're looking for; why our expectations are so often met; why we tend to see and hear some things, but miss or misinterpret things that other people (from within their own very different mind-cages) see or hear quite clearly. And it's why we're so good at twisting what we see or hear—often quite unconsciously—or conveniently misremembering it, to make it fit within the framework of our existing mind-cage. Psychologists call this 'selective perception'.

Nowhere on earth is as comfortable and secure as the inside of your own mind-cage. After all, it's your very own construction. It's your life's work, the fruits of your very own experience (give or take a few prejudices you borrowed along the way from someone you admired or perhaps feared). Yet, to be a good listener is to step outside the comfort and security of your own mind-cage—even fleetingly—as you try to imagine what it must be like to inhabit the mind-cage of the other person. Not so you can adopt their view of whatever subject you're discussing. Not so you can take their beliefs, ideas or prejudices on board. Simply so you can get what they're really saying; so you can *entertain* their ideas; so you're in a position to comprehend and appreciate their point of view.

You can see why it needs a certain amount of courage to listen to someone whose view of the world might turn out to be very different from your own. The challenge is not necessarily to accept what they're saying; the challenge is to accept that they do seriously hold these views, and to understand them as well as you can, even if you find them abhorrent, batty or simply inconceivable. You'll have your chance to say all that—if it needs to be said—once you've heard them out. It's the cardinal rule of good listening: *receive before you react*.

A person in the audience at one of my recent lectures asked me this: 'Are you seriously suggesting I'm supposed to listen attentively to some extreme right-wing nutter? Wouldn't that be dishonest—wouldn't I just be pretending?'

My answer was the obvious one: by all means listen even to extremists spouting their views, because then you've qualified yourself to disagree. Only then can you say, 'I think I get what you're saying. You're saying the state should get right out of people's lives and just leave everything to the market. Survival of the fittest. Is that broadly it? Okay, well let me put a different point of view, and see if there are some points where we might agree. And, by the way, it doesn't really matter if we disagree. Lots of people see the world differently from me.'

Social harmony is always the goal, even when the differences are irreconcilable. You don't have to like what you're hearing. But the more attentively you listen, the more likely it is that you will be listened to in return.

I'm not unrealistic about this: I accept that some situations are impossible; some attitudes are too vile to respond to, and you don't want to risk reinforcing them by appearing to take them seriously. And some views are so extreme there's no possibility of finding common ground. But it's possible to show respect to a person without showing any respect for their opinion about something. In any case, those extreme situations are pretty rare. Hearing your grandmother telling you to keep things in perspective and reminding you of the hardships she endured living in London through the Blitz might strain your patience, especially if you've already heard it many times before, but how hard is it to hear her out and to say something supportive and sympathetic that proves you've been listening? At that moment, you're the therapist and she's the client. Do your job!

Equally, how hard would it be for politicians of all stripes to get together and say, 'From this day on, we are going to civilise the process of parliamentary debate. We are going to respect the fact that each of us has been legitimately elected to this chamber. We are going to listen respectfully to each other's points of view and try to learn from them. We are going to *receive before we react*. We are going to value compromise and consensus above coercion and control. We are going to refrain from personal attacks or remarks designed to ridicule or belittle our opponents. In fact, we're going to stop calling them our "opponents". Whether we're in government or opposition, we are all colleagues engaged in the same crucial task of making laws for the betterment of the society we all live in.'

Unrealistic? Not at all. Not once you realise that listening respectfully to each other is the first step towards serious progress, and the necessary ingredient in the cooperative process. After all, there's a huge difference between respect for the person and respect for their views. I might not respect the views you are expressing at all, but I owe you my *personal* respect as a fellow member of this parliament, this organisation, this neighbourhood, this family . . . this species.

***

It's no wonder we fear the possibility of being changed by the experience of listening to someone: changing our minds is not a simple, straightforward, painless business. It may involve a bit of work on our own mind-cage—a changed attitude, perhaps, or a modified belief, or some other shift that now seems necessary in the light of this new information or new insight. And that can be a challenge to our complacency. Which is why it's helpful to remind yourself, occasionally, that your own strongest beliefs and convictions look like prejudices to people who think differently from you.

A touch of humility—a little room for doubt—never goes astray when it comes to becoming a better listener, and a good starting point is simply to acknowledge that whether the issue is abortion, tax reform, nuclear power, child-rearing practices, the resurrection of Jesus (historical fact or metaphorical myth?) or the West arming Ukraine, people whose views differ from yours are probably not malevolent, misguided fools. Their experience has led them to draw different conclusions from the ones you happen to have drawn. There's always room for debate, but harmony is impossible if your starting point is that 'those people are simply wrong' (especially if that's precisely what they also think about you).

Beware of catching the wrong train (of thought)
It's not just the influence of the mind-cage that can inhibit our effectiveness as listeners. We must also deal with another human characteristic: our *thought-speed*.

In so many ways, our capacity for rapid and complex thought is a huge asset: we can think about several things at once; we can size up a tricky situation in a moment; we can think of a number of possible solutions to a problem almost as soon as the problem emerges.

Take driving in traffic. A sudden emergency arises—a car comes out of a side street, for instance, going too fast and failing to give way to you, even though you have the right of way. You size up the situation in an instant and take evasive action, managing to avoid hitting the offending vehicle and another one that's in the process of overtaking you. It's a complex task you've just performed—calculating the relative speeds and distances involved, and taking into account your vehicle's braking capacity and the limited opportunities available to you to avoid a collision. But you do it. And you perform similar high-speed thought leaps all day long.

A mother is listening to her nine-year-old enthusing about a YouTube video he's just seen while deciding what to put in his school lunch, what to have for dinner that night, whether to trust that her husband has taken the clothes out of the dryer, and what to say at the management meeting she's called for nine o'clock this morning to deal with a crisis in morale caused by the sacking of a colleague who had turned out to be dishonest. Piece of cake—in the lunch box, and metaphorically.

Thought is a puzzling process—for a start, we're not even sure what consciousness is—but we know the process of thinking is both complex and unpredictable. And we know it sometimes happens in words and sometimes it doesn't. If I ask you to imagine the smell of roses, can you do it? I'll bet you can. That's a good example of a non-verbal thought process, as is visualising fireworks lighting up the night sky.

It's hard to measure the speed of thought but, inevitably, researchers have had a go at it. Broadly, their conclusion is that *when we think in words*, most of us have the capacity to think at a rate of up to about five hundred words per minute. Impressive, but also a problem when it comes to listening, since most conversations plod along at the rate of about a hundred and twenty-five to a hundred and fifty words per minute. (Formal speech—like lectures or the reading of news bulletins—is typically delivered at an even slower rate than that.)

You see the difficulty. If you're talking to me at about a hundred and twenty-five words per minute and I have the capacity to be thinking at about five hundred words per minute, how will I avoid jumping on one or two other trains of thought while still listening to you? The danger, of course, is that one of those trains of thought might turn out to be an express, carrying me off at high speed in a direction that has nothing to do with what you're trying to say to me.

The signs of a distracted listener are obvious: the person whose eyes glaze over while you're talking to them; the person who is smiling and nodding at precisely the wrong moment; the person who fails to register that you've stopped talking; the person who suddenly changes the subject without realising you're only halfway through the point you were making; and the person who is staring at a smartphone while saying, 'Go on. I'm listening.'

What's the solution? Should we all try to talk more quickly in the hope of using up the listener's capacity for thought? (Speed reading is based on that principle, by the way, so we can train ourselves to read so quickly that there's no room for distraction. How often have you read a page of a book and then realised you hadn't retained any of it because you were thinking of something else?) No, that's not the answer. It's unrealistic, anyway—just try it sometime. The challenge of thought-speed is a challenge for the listener, not the speaker—though the speaker has some obligation to be interesting, engaging, relevant . . .

To be a good listener, it's not just a matter of stepping, however briefly, outside the comfort and security of your own mind-cage. It's also a matter of finding ways to harness your thought-speed in the interests of fully attentive listening.

It can be done, and the best place to start is by concentrating very carefully on the *total* message you're receiving—starting with the words and the music. When it comes to the words, try to see the point of what's being said. Try to keep connecting the dots. But have some fun, too. Count the clichés. Spot the non sequiturs. The exaggerations. The obvious fabrications. Watch out for the things linguists call 'non-lexical speech sounds'—the *ums* and *ahs*—plus the little verbal tics and habits of speech that people develop to fill in the gaps when they're stuck for the next word: *I mean*; *so to speak*; *to be honest*; *y'know*; *oh my god*; *as well*; *so yeah . . . nah.*

So much for the words. What about the music? The speech music. The tone of voice. The rate of speech. The sounds and the silences. The accents and cadences. The pauses and hesitations. The sighs. The throat clearings. The emphases.

How much of the speaker's meaning is being conveyed by the words and how much by the speech music is a moot point: the relative weights of meaning constantly shift, according to the circumstances. Back in the 1960s—a golden age of communication research—Albert Mehrabian undertook

289

a series of experiments designed to test people's reactions to the sound of the human voice in a situation where the words themselves were made unintelligible. Mehrabian discovered what the parents of young children soon learn: that we can attach some degree of meaning to the sound of a voice—speech music—even when it is not speaking 'proper' words. Mehrabian also showed that when there's some incompatibility between the words and the music (he called them verbal and vocal messages), the music always wins: tone of voice often says it all. Even 'I hate you' can be said in such a way that it conveys precisely the opposite meaning to what the words seem to be saying. A message can seem boring, urgent, amusing, poignant, loving, tragic or routine . . . simply because of how it sounds.

It's a rich field of study, speech music. That incomparable wordsmith David Astle once used the example of the sentence 'I never said she stole my money' to show how the apparent meaning of a sentence can be utterly changed by a shift in emphasis. There are seven words in that sentence. Say the sentence seven times out loud, stressing a different word each time, and see how you seem to be conveying a series of seven quite different meanings.

While you're weighing up the relationship between the words and the speech music, you'll also be noting the messages embedded in the so-called *body language* of the speaker. I've heard the words; I've heard the music. Now what are my eyes telling me? What can I read into that facial expression? Into those shifty eyes? Into those defiantly crossed arms, or that wagging finger, or those legs being nervously crossed and uncrossed? Was that a tear I saw forming in the corner of your eye? Why are you shrugging your shoulders so much? Stroking your chin? Pulling your ear lobe?

'A picture is worth a thousand words.' Never have truer words been spoken. The eye beats the ear every time. Visual messages don't merely outweigh verbal ones; they swamp them. Think back to that near-miss in traffic. If you'd had the car radio on while you were dealing with that emergency, you wouldn't be able to recall a word of what was being said while your mind was fully engaged with the potential crisis unfolding in front of you.

If you're giving a lecture and you want to use visual aids, make sure they don't distract your audience by competing with the words you're saying, because when they're looking at the pictures—or even the words on a screen—they're not listening, or they're only half-listening to you. If you've ever watched the *Q&A* program on ABC TV, you'll know that if you read a tweet streaming across the bottom of the screen, you probably won't hear whatever is being said in that moment.

You want to become a better listener? Practise using up your mental capacity by concentrating on the total package—words, music, visual images—so all those other potential trains of thought can leave the station without you. To keep yourself on track, be constantly asking yourself, 'What's this all about? What is this person trying to say, and why are they saying it?' Even if you can't immediately answer those questions, it's helpful to speculate. G.K. Chesterton once wrote: 'There is no such thing on earth as an uninteresting subject; the only thing that can exist is an uninterested person.' You can train yourself to be interested!

How do I get other people to listen to me?

The main point of these reflections has been to encourage you to take listening to a higher level; to screw up your courage for the risky business of entering into the world of the other; to accept your social obligation to acknowledge and value other people, regardless of their opinions and attitudes; to pay them the respect of listening to them when they need you to.

They might not always need you to, by the way. Sometimes, people just need to talk to work out what they think—listeners are irrelevant, except as a source of encouragement to keep talking. Talking is not always about communication; sometimes, it's principally a matter of self-expression. But it can be hard to pick the difference: I was once accused by a friend of listening too intently to something she was saying. 'It's not that important,' she said. So I tried to appear less interested and let her keep talking . . .

As speakers, though, we can increase the chances of people attending to us when we want them to. The first and most fundamental thing to remember is that the things we say—and write—to other people are like empty vessels that those people will fill with their own meaning. What we say or write will be *interpreted* by our listeners or readers. They'll make their own sense of it. (That's if they judge it to be worth interpreting; otherwise, they'll simply ignore it.)

It's so tempting to think the reverse—that our messages *contain* the meaning we want to convey to someone else. But 'meaning' isn't like that: it's not in the words, but in the mind—the *intention*—of the person using the words and in the mind(s) of whoever might be hearing or reading those words and making their own sense of them. Dictionaries don't tell you the meaning of words: they record the ways people have *used* particular words to convey particular meanings. They are like museums of meaning. Pedants (like me) might cling to the idea that words have specific meanings but, when it comes to language, usage is the final arbiter—language is a living, changing thing. Just think of the recent changes in the way we use words like 'random', 'oversight', 'enormity' and 'disinterested' . . . to say nothing of 'virtual'. (And whatever happened to 'underestimate'? It's now routinely used to mean the very opposite of what it says, as in: 'the importance of this can't be underestimated'. Surely the people who say that mean 'can't be *over*estimated' . . . but that's language for you.)

What do you take to be the 'meaning' of that well-known proverb 'A rolling stone gathers no moss'? If you know the proverb, you know the meaning, right? Okay, then; what does it mean? Ah, you might say, it obviously means that if you keep moving, you won't stultify; you won't go mouldy. But now I hear someone else objecting: 'Hey! That's not right. In fact, that's practically the opposite of what the proverb means. To me it means that a shiftless, restless person will never prosper.'

Take your pick. I suspect that, these days, the first meaning has a bit more currency than the second, thanks in part to Mick Jagger et al. If you're interested in the *origins* of the proverb, it came into popular usage at a time when 'moss' was slang for 'money'. It turns out that, yet again, the right question is not 'What does *it* mean?' The right question is 'What do *you* mean when you say it?'

But you said . . . can be a very cruel response to another person's statement, especially if it was made when that person was in an agitated state. It's never about what a person *said*.

It's always about what they *intended* to say—what they *meant* by what they said.

***

Lesson number one in attracting another person's attention is really the same as lesson number one in listening: *remember the mind-cage!* Try to relate your message to the mind-cage of your audience. As we've already seen, people are not blank slates waiting for us to write our messages on them; they are pulsating bundles of knowledge, convictions, contradictions, attitudes, values, prejudices, experiences, thoughts, feelings, sensations, aspirations and expectations. They are active, not passive, in what they bring to their encounter with you—whether in a private conversation, in a classroom, at a meeting, around a meal table, or in any other setting. Unless we can ensure the relevance of our message to our audience, there is very little chance that they will listen.

The biggest trap in human communication is the failure to learn the lesson our experience teaches us, time after time: people pay most attention to those messages that directly concern them, and that relate to their own needs and interests at that time. And even when they do listen, they will listen in their own way because, unless they are being very generous, they will be filtering your message through the bars of their own mind-cage.

I mentioned the deepest truth about human communication in chapter 2, but here it is again: it's not what the message does to the audience but what the audience does with the message that determines the outcome.

Communication is not a matter of 'injecting' a message—like a drug—into someone's brain via the eye or ear or both, and then hoping that, just like a drug, the message will do its magic work of persuading the other person to accept what you're saying. If that were how it worked, what a mess we'd all be in! We'd be swayed by every message 'injected' into our unwitting brains. Rather, it's a matter of evoking a response from someone, based on the way they interpret the message we send them. To return to the empty-vessel analogy: they will fill our message with their own meaning.

But the 'injection' model is seductive because we secretly *wish* that's the way communication worked. If only I could develop a powerful enough message—if only I were eloquent enough—people would not only get my message but would *buy* it. Nagging is one of the surest signs of an 'injectionist'. When a person keeps repeating the same message, over and over, you know they have blind faith in the idea that, sooner or later, the magic drug will do its work; they just have to keep increasing the dose.

When an exasperated parent or teacher says, 'If I've told you once, I've told you a hundred times,' what they're actually saying is: 'Hey! I've come up with a message that never works! I've said it ten times, twenty, thirty . . . a hundred times, and it still doesn't work! But I'm not discouraged. It's what I really want to say, so I'll just keep saying it.' (Popular definition of insanity: doing the same thing over and over, and expecting a different result.)

The corollary of the principle that *people do things with messages, rather than messages doing things to people*, is obvious: if you want someone to listen to you, first get to know the shape and structure of their mind-cage. How else can you be sure that what you're saying will be relevant to them? Like it or not, that's the framework within which you're going to be operating. How can you tailor your message to your audience if you don't know your audience?

***

A man once gave a lecture about music in which he concentrated on the idea that all musical instruments make distinctive sounds and that each demands of its player a particular set of skills.

As the lecture drew to a close, he opened a trunk on the platform beside him and offered to demonstrate the different sounds of the different instruments. 'I will begin with the rich and powerful sound of the trumpet,' he announced.

He reached into the trunk, withdrew a violin, looked at it rather quizzically, then pressed it to his lips and blew. Nothing happened, of course. The audience stirred uneasily.

'You see my difficulty,' he said. 'I seem not to have brought my trumpet, but that's the sound I really want you to hear, so I'll just blow a little harder into this violin and see how we go.'

He blew again. And again. He became red-faced with his blowing. Still nothing happened.

The audience began laughing and heckling him. 'You're crazy,' they shouted.

But was he any crazier than a person who thinks they can get a response from someone else just because they want one?

We need to work out whether we're dealing with a trumpet or a violin before deciding whether to blow or bow.

***

When we offer someone the gift of our undivided attention, we are reassuring them that they are valued—even if we can't accept their views—and, by that act of generosity and kindness, we are helping to make the world a better place.

Listening when it isn't comfortable to listen, listening when we'd rather be doing something else, and listening because someone needs us to—even when we might not particularly like the person or their message—are personal sacrifices that we make for the common good. We don't strive to become better listeners because we're heroes; we strive to become better listeners because we understand what it means to be human.

If you take nothing else away from this chapter then, at the very least, I'd encourage you to be prepared to take more risks in entertaining other people's ideas. Each person you encounter is the product of the accident of their birth—into *this* family and not *that* one; into *this* cultural milieu and not *that* one; into *this* postcode and not *that* one—as well as their upbringing, their family dynamics, their education, their formative experiences and, in particular, their struggles with life's inevitable frustrations and disappointments. Nothing is perfect, for anyone. Life is messy. Relationships are complex. Outcomes are uncertain. People are irrational . . . and that is as true for you as it is for everyone you meet.

When there's a gulf between you and someone else, they will see you as being just as 'other' as you see them; your prejudices will seem as irrational and unjustifiable to them as theirs do to you; they may hope you'll move in their direction, just as you may hope they'll move in yours. 'But the difference is that I'm *right*,' you might say (just as they might), and that is no basis for building social harmony.

We will never all agree about everything, and wouldn't the world be a dull and dreary place if we did! Listening— *deep* listening, *risky* listening—to each other's points of view doesn't mean that we'll change each other's minds: it simply means that we'll understand each other better and be more likely to find ways of accommodating our differences.

In 'The Context', I suggested that the Grand Human Project is to create and maintain social harmony. *Harmony*, not unity. As the many different voices in a choir blend into a harmonic whole, so the many different voices in a society can blend into social harmony. We don't have to 'sing with one voice'. What we must do is listen attentively to each other's distinctive voices and learn to sing in harmony. Harmony-builders are always great listeners. And even some occasional dissonance can enrich and enliven the process of reaching harmonious resolution.

Reflections . . .
- Everyone's story is interesting. Every life is a journey of discovery and you only have to listen attentively to realise that each of us has made our own discoveries; each of us has something to teach the rest of us. Though we share a common humanity, everyone's story is uniquely their own.
- Everyone's story includes shadows—tragedies, disappoint- ments, sadness and loss. The moment when someone needs

you to listen might be the moment when your therapeutic act of listening can restore their sense of hope, or their faith in the goodness of other people, or even their confidence in themselves.

- Under the influence of information technology—especially social media posts and our endless texts—we are at risk of seriously blunting our listening skills. Given the crucial importance of eye contact in interpersonal communication and the huge contribution made by speech music and body language to the listening experience, we need to be aware of how much richness and subtlety we are losing when we go online. If we are losing our skill as attentive and empathic listeners in everyday life, that would help to explain the record demand for professional psychotherapy.
- Everyone needs to tell their story to someone who will listen . . . and if I won't listen, who will?

9

Sometimes the dream is enough

It was a warm spring morning on the south coast of New South Wales. I was standing on the balcony of a rented holiday apartment, overlooking a secluded beach. Ever since I was a small boy, I have relished moments like this— watching passers-by from the concealed branch of the tree across the street from my family home; standing at the first-floor window of the school library, watching the activity in the playground below; and now, far enough away from the beach to be unobtrusive, but close enough to be able to watch the movements of a family (I assumed it was a family) at the water's edge.

It would be wrong to say I preferred watching other people's families to being part of my own, or that I was standing in that school library because I was a friendless isolate. It's just that I've always enjoyed imagining what other people's lives must be like; trying to interpret the situations I observe; wondering where that person who just got off the bus might be going, who he will meet when he gets there, what kind of reception he'll receive. I play the same game in restaurants.

Idle curiosity? Perhaps. But I managed to make a career out of it. Observing, listening, interpreting ... and always imagining what else might have been said; what dreams my research respondents might have chosen to keep to themselves; what disappointment, pain or loss might lie behind that fleetingly clouded face. In my most recent novel, *The Therapist*, the psychotherapist Martha Elliott says to a colleague: 'I sometimes wonder if I'm in danger of being overwhelmed by all the things I don't hear.' I know what she meant. It's the researcher's nightmare, too: what am I missing?

The sea was calm. The family on the beach comprised (more assumptions) the father, the mother, two girls aged around six and eight, and a younger boy, perhaps two years old. The father was now in the water, not quite up to his waist, frolicking with his daughters. The younger one had her arms around him and was kicking her legs in the gentle swell, laughing whenever a wave rose high enough to bring her face level with his. The other girl would swim a few strokes away, then turn and swim back to grab her father's hand.

The mother was in a loose cotton dress. A pair of sandals dangled from her hand. Her son was down on his haunches beside her, digging in the wet sand. Occasionally, one of the girls would come out of the water and give her mother a damp hug, then splash back in and swim the few metres to her father. At one point the older girl seemed to be trying to coax her little brother into the water, but he was firmly stuck beside his mother and was going nowhere. Eventually, the father emerged from the water, scooped his son up in his arms and took him into the shallows, where he leaned over and dipped the boy into the water, with much wriggling and giggling.

Soon the boy was returned to his mother who wrapped him in a towel, picked him up and held him against her. The father swam out into deeper water but the squeals of his daughters brought him back into their comfort zone. They were not strong swimmers. This didn't look like a beach family.

I watched them for twenty minutes, and the joy they were so obviously experiencing reached me and warmed me. Even thrilled me a little. The love between them was obvious, even to a stranger standing on a balcony, too far away to hear any of the words they said to each other. They displayed complete trust in each other. They wanted to be nowhere but together. It looked to me like a perfect moment in the life of this family and I wondered what else would happen to them that day.

It wouldn't stay perfect. But such magic moments are precious because they give us a glimpse of perfection; they fuel the dream of perfection; they remind us that perfection can be as fleeting, and as memorable, as a splash or a squeal at a beach.

Perhaps they went off to have fish and chips for lunch, and one of the girls panicked when a bone got briefly stuck in her throat. Or perhaps the children squabbled about who would get a turn in the front seat of the car. Or perhaps the parents exchanged cross words about the father's failure to have remembered the sunscreen—or about his over-long phone call to his office over lunch. Perhaps they weren't even a family. Perhaps the woman's husband had left her and her new partner was trying his best to ingratiate himself with her daughters. Or perhaps they were *his* daughters and the boy was her son, and this was the first time they'd all been to the beach together.

It was a fine day. But the weather wouldn't stay as sunny as this. It would cloud over. There would be a storm. It would rain. It always does, eventually. As someone remarked to a fellow cyclist who had fallen off his bike on a mountain trail: 'We're all just between crashes, mate.'

But, for those twenty minutes or so, it was fine. They were fine. Both the day and the family were beautiful to behold. Did I dream it? Did I make all that up?

Perhaps I exaggerated. Perhaps I over-interpreted (another occupational hazard of the researcher). Sometimes the dream is enough.

***

A few months later, I was walking on a bush track behind another family (another assumption). As I caught up with them, I could see a girl of about twelve looking intently at her parents. Her mother had her arm around her husband's waist, her face turned to him. The impression was of an intense conversation going on. As I overtook them on the path, I heard the mother say, 'You've still got us.'

'You've still got us.' Beautiful. Maybe even perfect. Four magical words. Possibly the only thing that man needed to hear at that moment. To be reminded that, whatever else was going on, he still had a loving family. Perhaps he'd unsuccessfully applied for a job he really wanted. Perhaps he'd been retrenched. Perhaps he'd just lost a beloved parent. The wife's tone sounded serious, tender, gentle. It wasn't a flippant remark.

It was absolutely none of my business, of course. Simply a remark overheard. Possibly misheard. But it was such a loving remark, and such a loving tableau, it evoked the same response in me as the sight of that family at the beach. It reminded me, yet again, that moments of perfection might be all we have any right to expect, but they are like rocket fuel for our dreams of glory. If that woman could say that to her husband at a time when (let's say) he needed such an explicit expression of his family's loving support, then there must be millions of women and men, all over the world, who can rise to the occasion in the same way. People don't just do and say wonderful things—loving things, reassuring things, kind things, gentle things, forgiving things—in books or movies; they say them all the time in real life. Those books and movies can only offer us a pale imitation of the real thing.

Most of us probably don't say such things as often as we could, or should. What holds us back? Shyness? Complacency? Familiarity to the point of contempt? A fear of being laughed at, or not being taken seriously enough?

Magic moments can be created by a tender touch, a revelation of some point of vulnerability, an assurance that the love between us is secure. Such moments bring us close to perfection, but it would be greedy, and unrealistic, to imagine that every moment will be like that. We just need enough of them to sustain our faith in each other.

Yes, we might well wish for more. We might dream of a life that's richer, more fulfilling, more explicitly loving, less restrained, more creative than the one we have. Those are good dreams, as long as we don't turn them into yearnings. They are the kind of dreams that can carry us from one magic moment to the next—even 'borrowed' moments, like that family at the beach or the fleeting sense of intimacy between that woman and her husband on the bush track, and the intensity of their daughter's appreciation of what was passing between them.

Such moments, whether experienced or merely glimpsed, can encourage us to generate more of them than we otherwise might. Sometimes, even the dream of magic is enough to inspire and motivate us—not to make the dream come true, but to do something that just might bring our life, and the lives of those we encounter, closer to the dream. In fact, dreams don't have to come true to do their powerful motivational work.

Even the experience of observing those two vignettes of family life was enough to make both those days seem perfect *for me*. Yes, I thought with gratitude, people can behave like this. Yes, people can be this kind to each other. Yes, families can play uninhibitedly at the beach. Yes, couples can create a moment of tenderness and intimacy on a bush walk with their daughter. Such reflections stayed with me; they inspired the dream of a life lived more lovingly, more spontaneously, more generously.

***

As a researcher who has spent a large chunk of my working life sitting in people's homes listening to their life stories, my most vivid recollection is the buoyancy I usually felt when I emerged from an intense one-to-one interview, or from observing a group discussion between friends, neighbours or work colleagues. (I explain how I did that work in the Technical Appendix.) Sometimes, inevitably, it was a bit dispiriting if the respondent had been in a sour mood or a negative frame of mind, or if I had been listening to the expression of prejudices that made me feel personally uncomfortable. But the far more general impression I received was not just positive, but energising and even inspiring.

I think I can sum it up best by saying that most people, regardless of their circumstances, were doing their best. To say they were 'living the dream' would sound trite and dismissive, and yet it *was* something like that. Not that life was a bed of roses—it hardly ever is—but simply that they had dreamed of how life could be, and they were not going to let it go. The dream didn't have to be coming true. The vision, the possibility, was enough to spur them on.

Parents seemed generally determined to persist, even in the face of discouraging setbacks, in their desire to be the best kind of parent they could be. People wanted to be good neighbours to each other, and they had a sense—a dream—of how that could work. Even if they hadn't yet made it work in their own street, they still wanted it to happen and hoped it would. People mostly wanted to be good employees, good colleagues, good citizens. They wanted to be 'good', more generally. They wanted to be well regarded by those they loved and those they worked with. They didn't expect actual praise for any of this; they just wanted to do the best they could, given the situation they were in.

Dreaming? Hoping? What's the difference? And what, after all, is the difference between hope and faith? If we have faith in a better future, that's another way of saying we hope that's how it will turn out. And none of that is very different from saying we dream of a better future. If we have faith in each other, that means we believe we'll be able to rely on each other . . . and part of that belief is the hope that our faith will be justified.

Faith. Hope. Dreams. Don't you find it inspiring to see the power of such things in our lives? People fall in love and decide to get married, propelled by the dream of a future together that *feels* more like certainty than faith—why else would they take the plunge? We see a bride looking radiant on her wedding day, and sense that the dream of undying love is alive in her.

And imagine deciding to have children! What a declaration of faith, of hope and of our capacity to dream! (That's why there was both a marriage boom and a baby boom in the years following the end of World War II. That was certainly a time for dreaming of a better world, and all those babies were a symbol of it.) Parents hold their children's hands—literally and metaphorically—in the hope of protecting them from all ills. They can't do that, of course, but that's the dream that changes them from being people who only have to look after themselves to parents responsible for another life they have created.

People enrol in a course of study in the hope of being both inspired and equipped for a life—or, at least, a job—that will bring them closer to their dream of the kind of person they'd like to become. They may not become that person: the course might disappoint them; the dream job might elude them; life itself might derail their plans. But the dream was enough to propel them into an experience that, in most cases, they will judge to have been worthwhile, and possibly even life changing.

Let me remind you of Edgar Allan Poe's most famous lines: 'All that we see or seem/Is but a dream within a dream.' No, it isn't, though philosophers have had a field day playing with the idea. Personally, I'd only go so far as to say that if we want to make sense of a life, we need to know the dreams that have animated and shaped it. Life is not about dreams coming true; it's about daring to dream and then choosing to follow the path illuminated by that dream. Or it's about *not* daring to dream and forever wondering if there was another path that might have led us to a better place.

Will the path you chose take you where you dreamed of going? It might and it might not. Some people do speak of having found their 'dream job', while others can only say 'it's a job' or, perhaps more wisely, 'there's more to life than work' and dream of other satisfactions. Some romantic relationships feel, in the beginning, like a dream come true; later, the dream might become blurred by the onrush of life.

But then we catch a glimpse of magic in our life, or even in the lives of others, and we're reminded that, yes, we *can* dream; that our dreams can inspire and sustain us; and that, sometimes, the dream is enough.

TAKING ACTION

What can one person do?

In a 1987 interview with *Woman's Own* magazine, the British prime minister Margaret Thatcher said: 'There is no such thing as society. There are individual men and women, and there are families. And no government can do anything except through people, and people must look to themselves first. It's our duty to look after ourselves first and then also to look after our neighbour. People have got the entitlements too much in mind, without the obligations.'

There's no such thing as society? That remark provoked outrage at the time, especially from sociologists and social psychologists (like me). It was like saying there's no such thing as the sea—there are only drops of water, and waves, and currents. Or there's no such thing as a choir—only individual singers singing their own part. It sounded like a classic case of 'you can't see the forest for the trees': in other words, you can only see the individual trees, the leaves, the trunks, the branches, but you can't appreciate the forest as a whole—the synthesis, the *Gestalt*.

I certainly thought, for a long time, that 'there's no such thing as society' was one of the silliest things Thatcher had ever said. And it still sounds pretty silly, taken out of context, though it was no doubt very deliberately intended to be provocative. Thatcher knew full well that there is indeed such a thing as 'society', just as she knew there is such a thing as 'the electorate', though she could equally have argued that 'there are only individual voters'.

But, to be fair to Thatcher, there was also deep wisdom in her implied assertion that social action can only occur through the efforts of individuals. People must indeed 'look to themselves' and look after their neighbours, if we are ever to create the kind of society we'd all like to live in.

When you're in the thick of it, it can be hard to appreciate the complexity and diversity of a community—or a society. It's always tempting to think that everyone else's experience must be pretty much the same as ours. (*Wrong!*) Yet it's our sense of society that produces our moral sense: we act out of kindness, altruism, courage or compassion precisely because we do feel ourselves to be part of a larger whole—joined by that 'shimmering, vibrating web of interdependence and interconnectedness' I described in 'The Context'. (I daresay Margaret Thatcher would have said, 'There's no such thing as a web. There are only strands . . .' Metaphor, Mrs T., *metaphor!*)

But it's true, as Thatcher implied, that if we are to enrich this thing called society, we must examine the ways we are acting *towards each other*, rather than trying to think of ourselves as actors on some vast stage called 'society'.

It always comes down to our personal relationships and interactions, in the end. Unless we've been helplessly seduced by the siren songs of individualism and materialism—*It's all about Me! I just wanna be rich! Let me do whatever I want!*—then our relationships with each other are likely to be the richest source of our life's meaning and, indeed, its purpose. That's how we make our mark. That's how we contribute to the transformation of society. That's how virtue flourishes—through action. Indeed, action is the only way you can discern virtue.

There's not much point in sitting in a tower—ivory or otherwise—thinking beautiful thoughts and bestowing blessings on the hoi polloi struggling to survive in the heat and dust below. You have to get out there and *act*. To repeat the key message of 'The Context': *you need the community and the community needs you.* That's the glory of being human, but it also defines the burden we must all carry and the contribution we must all make.

And don't imagine I'm talking primarily about your *work*. When people remember you—if they do—it's highly unlikely your work will be the focal point of your legacy. You might be a carpenter, a musical-comedy star, a dentist, a university chancellor, an IT whiz-kid, a minister of either religion or state, a bricklayer, a poet, a fashion designer . . . and, yes, some of your work might survive in a recognisable way, in a building whose bricks you laid, or in a lovely set of teeth you helped maintain (at least until its owner died). If you're supremely talented, one of your poems might appear in anthologies for generations to come (that's if anthologies continue to appear for generations to come).

But most of the ways we help to make the world a better place do not rely on having done this or that job. Far more

313

important than any of that is the way we manage our personal relationships—including those within the workplace and beyond it. The question is not, in the end, 'Was this person a brilliant accountant?' The question is: 'Was this person the kind of neighbour that could always be relied on for a smile, a sympathetic ear, or support in a crisis? The kind of colleague who always had time for a chat? The kind of parent who listened? The kind of partner who was loving and loyal through thick and thin?'

William Wordsworth was one of those rare poets whose work *has* survived, but spare a thought for the millions whose work you've never heard of. Wordsworth described the goodness we've contributed to the world as our 'little, nameless, unremembered acts of kindness and love'. Unremembered, quite possibly, but still influential and likely to reverberate into the future through the acts of kindness and love performed by those whose lives we touched—by those who were influenced by our example.

There's nothing grandiose about this: in fact, if you set your sights too high—changing the world, for instance, or getting a teenager to think like a parent—you might be defeated by frustration and discouragement. But if you seek ways of helping to make the world a better place through the nature of your personal influence, then deep life-satisfaction awaits you.

Being communitarians by nature, communication is not only our currency; it's our social life-force. You could think of society as being like a power grid, humming with energy. We must tap into it if we are to draw power from the community, but when we connect, we must also contribute our own

energy—if we only take without giving, the grid will ultimately lose its force.

It has been the recurring theme of this book that we are
born to cooperate, communicate, connect and contribute.
When we deny those natural impulses, we diminish ourselves.
In its essence, being human is a shared experience, not an
individual one. When we cling to our infantile narcissism,
or surrender to feelings of enmity based on religious, ethnic,
social, cultural, political or other prejudice, we inhibit the
full flowering of the richest and noblest human possibilities
within us. When we embrace materialism and enshrine it as
a core value—as Australia has been in danger of doing, along
with the rest of the West—we don't only let 'the economy'
obscure our view of 'society' but we encourage the crazy idea
that our wealth defines our worth. (If that's true, more is
bound to be better, so put this book down and get back on the
treadmill, *now!*)

Given the many challenges facing us—including all those
arising from the looming impact of climate change and species
extinction—what can an individual, or even a small group,
hope to achieve?

When it comes to mitigating the effects of climate change,
we know that it's not only up to governments and big cor-
porations to act. We ourselves must take all possible steps to
contribute to the global effort: buy only what we need; buy
things that will last and keep them for as long as possible;
recycle everything we possibly can; minimise our non-essential
flying (since jet aircraft deposit their carbon emissions
directly into the stratosphere and upper troposphere); never
make a non-essential car trip (and switch to an electric or

hydrogen-powered car as soon as possible); use public transport as much as we can; drastically reduce our consumption of red meat; limit our total energy consumption. We know all those things; now we need to *do* them.

And what about mitigating the effects of *social* change? Every step we take, every move we make, helps shape the kind of society we will become. To repeat a point made in 'The Context': the state of the nation starts in your street. Your example counts as much as anyone else's. Every ripple travels . . .

You'd like to see a more peaceful world? Join a peace march, by all means, but first make peace with your family, your friends, your neighbours, your colleagues. You're appalled by the idea that 32 per cent of Australian adults report feeling lonely, and that loneliness is associated with so many other health issues ranging from anxiety to sleep deprivation? You groan inwardly at the thought of a lonely person dying at home, undetected for days? Check whether anyone in your street is at risk of social isolation and establish contact with them.

You think we're being overwhelmed by mediated information—via social media and elsewhere—at the expense of our personal relationships? Cut down on screen time and spend more of every day listening to members of your family, neighbours, friends, colleagues . . . and strangers whose paths you cross.

You're concerned about the threat to our humanity from the influence of artificial intelligence? Be grateful for the things we humans can *uniquely* do—things that machines can't replicate. Limit your personal use of chatbots and, where you are in a position to influence organisational decisions about replacing humans with AI, always weigh the technology factor against the human factor. And always remember, in your personal or professional life, that it is we humans who must monitor the accuracy of AI, and it is up to us to decide where to place limits on its influence.

You're worried about the rise of doctrinaire fundamentalism—in religion, economics, geopolitics and elsewhere—and about the dangers of a creeping puritanism in gender issues and 'cancel culture'? Reject facile answers and resist the tug of simplistic certainties. Remember we exist at a point in history where, like people at every other point in history, we're tempted to think we have emerged into a new state of enlightenment. Maintain a healthy scepticism about that. Maintain a healthy scepticism about *everything* (everything but loving-kindness: abandon yourself to that).

You're distressed by bullying and by sexual abuse? Speak up, every time. (And, once justice is done, be prepared to forgive.) You despair over homelessness, disadvantage and poverty? Ring up any of the charities struggling to respond to those problems, and ask what resources you can contribute, in time or money, or both. They might want you to peel spuds, sort clothes or serve meals for a few hours a week. They might want you to help young people improve their literacy skills or migrants learn English.

You worry that individualism is eroding our sense of community? You think society is suffering from too much busyness, too little courtesy, too little eye contact? Or that, post-COVID, people again seem reluctant to make personal sacrifices for the common good? You think it's outrageous

317

that so many people don't even know their neighbours' names?

There's no magic wand. You exist in a circle. Join the dots.

***

That's not my final word, since our understanding of these things is always imperfect and incomplete. My final word, therefore, is: *and . . .*

TECHNICAL APPENDIX
How I did my research

**Not everything that counts can be counted,
and not everything that can be counted counts.**
Albert Einstein

When, in the late 1950s, we first heard about the 'depth research' being conducted by Dr Ernest Dichter at his Institute for Motivational Research in the US, most of us in the fledgling Australian public opinion research industry were inclined to be sceptical or dismissive. It sounded unscientific and faddish.

Ours was, exclusively, a world of quantitative research. But it was about to change. By the early 1960s, several Australian researchers had begun tentatively experimenting with qualitative techniques—ranging from projective tests such as sentence-completion or word-association tests, to unstructured interviews and small-group discussions. My first personal experience of qualitative research was a 1962 study of family TV viewing I conducted for the audience research department of the ABC, based on direct, in-home observation of the dynamics of program choice and viewers' reactions.

What encouraged this push into the previously uncharted waters of non-statistical, exploratory, diagnostic research?

Two things: first, researchers' frustration with the limitations of conventional, questionnaire-based surveys when it came to the exploration of human emotions and motivations; second, a growing belief that a new development in psychotherapy— the so-called 'encounter group'—may have something to offer the public opinion researcher.

There was a sense of excitement and energy in the industry at that time. The pioneering work of Joseph Klapper at America's CBS network was challenging traditional views about the process and effects of mass communication (Klapper, 1960), and Marshall McLuhan had burst onto the scene with his radical reappraisal of the cultural role of mass media (McLuhan, 1962 and 1964). Fresh interest was being shown in the very concept of attitudes and the relationship between attitude change and behaviour change: both Leon Festinger's theory of cognitive dissonance (Festinger, 1957) and Martin Fishbein's later work on prediction (Fishbein, 1967) were regarded as revolutionary. Later, some of this work would be challenged by Jozef Nuttin and his 'response contagion' theory that persuasion is often a consequence of social pressure to conform (Nuttin, 1974). All this stimulation encouraged practitioners in the field of attitude research to become more adventurous in their development of new methodologies.

Although there have been times during the past sixty years when qualitative research has been regarded as nothing more than a 'quick and dirty' form of quantitative research—a kind of mini-survey—or perhaps nothing more than a preliminary to 'proper' (i.e. quantitative) research, its origins were quite different. The early experimentation with qualitative methods in social research was driven by the conviction that this was a quite different form of research that would complement—not supplant—traditional quantitative approaches.

Good medical practitioners use qualitative data—such as a conversation with a patient that yields some insight into the person's personal history and present circumstances—to enrich and deepen their understanding of their patients. Such understanding equips a doctor to make a more enlightened interpretation of quantitative data from medical tests (weight, blood, urine, scans, etc.), before deciding on a diagnosis and prescribing the most appropriate treatment. In the same way, qualitative research is designed to expand our capacity to interpret and explain quantitative data about human behaviour. Quantitative research may tell us the birth rate is falling, or households are shrinking, or voting patterns are changing; qualitative research can tell us why.

The case for qualitative research

In any form of research, it is critically important to find a method that is compatible with the kind of thing we are trying to investigate. When it comes to human behaviour, quantitative methods are often best. For example, if we want to know how many people visit a particular place—or how often they go there, or how much money they spend per visit, or what they do while they are there—then a method which relies primarily on direct observation or an examination of records will be the most appropriate. All such data can be quantified.

If we can't directly observe what people are doing, we might have to rely on an indirect research method, such as a questionnaire-based survey, to get an approximate idea of their pattern of behaviour based on their own recollections or claims about what they did. Again, the information will be quantifiable, though less reliable.

Similarly, if we want to examine the extent to which certain information is known within the community (for example, the name of Australia's biggest trading partner, or the percentage of the Australian population born overseas, or the policies of the major political parties on a particular issue), we can measure the extent of such knowledge by means of a structured questionnaire.

When we venture beyond the realm of quantifiable behaviour and 'concrete' knowledge into the more complex and subtle question of *why* people behave as they do or how they *feel* about what they're doing—the area of motivations, aspirations, values, beliefs, dreams and fears, as well as 'attitudes'—the task is not so straightforward. Although a great deal of quantitative research is undertaken to 'measure' attitudes, it generally takes the same form as the surveys of more obviously quantifiable data: that is, simply asking people a series of questions designed to elicit the required information. This temptation to try to measure everything is based on the widespread conviction in the scientific community that 'if it exists, we can measure it' and that if we can't measure it, that just means we haven't yet defined it carefully enough.

Our personal experience suggests otherwise. We can observe the excitement of a child at a birthday party, but can we measure it? (Neuroscientists may well say, 'Not yet!') Can we measure the security of a loving relationship? The fear of a jobseeker? The despair of unemployment, or homelessness, or poverty? Our response to a poem or a song that moves us? The private pain of divorce? The anguish of a parent over a troubled or underachieving child? Can we measure anything as subjective as 'wellbeing'? (Many researchers are trying—it's become big business!)

Serious difficulties arise for the social researcher in treating all data as quantifiable and employing the same kind of questionnaire-based survey—or any other 'rational' instrument—for the conduct of all our research. For a start, every time you ask a question you are likely to receive an answer, and it is tempting to believe that the answer has told you what you wanted to know. But what if the answer only exists *because* the question was asked? Answers are, inevitably, the 'creatures' of questions. This is a classic example of every scientist's nightmare: the experiment effect. Is my data being unduly influenced by the way I've conducted my experiment?

If we were to ask a set of questions in a different order, we would almost certainly obtain somewhat different responses. If we varied the wording of the questions, the answers would also be likely to vary. Researchers know that it would not be hard to predetermine the outcome of a survey by carefully controlling the way the questions are asked.

Yet another uncertainty is inherent in questionnaire-based attitude research: when a set of structured questions is used to investigate attitudes, we can never be sure whether there are other potentially significant attitudes—feelings, thoughts, motivations, desires, dreams—that lie beyond the scope of the particular questions we asked. What *else* do people feel about a particular subject? What *else* have we failed to elicit because we didn't ask enough questions, or the right questions?

I mentioned this in chapter 8, but it's worth re-emphasising here: 'Why?' is the most hazardous question of all, because merely asking it implies that there *should* be an explanation for the behaviour or the attitudes under investigation, *and* that the respondent should be aware of that explanation. Once that expectation has been created, the respondent will be tempted to offer a reasonable-sounding explanation (which may be a mere rationalisation, or may even be pure fabrication) in order to satisfy the apparently rational demands of the question. 'Why did you marry that man?' 'Why did you stop going to church?' 'Why did you vote for that candidate, or buy that car, or choose to live in that house?' All such questions assume there's a 'reason' for doing those things, yet we do many things for no reason at all—or, at least, for no logical or easily explained reason that we are aware of.

We still *want* to find out why, of course, but experience suggests there are better ways of eliciting information about the motivations for human behaviour than asking direct, head-on questions.

***

Qualitative research takes many forms and embraces many methodologies: participant observation (drawing on the traditional methods of anthropology and ethnography); so-called 'projective tests' such as word association and sentence completion, and variations on the Thematic Apperception Test (using ambiguous pictures to be interpreted by the respondent); in-depth, unstructured personal interviews; two-person conversations in the presence of a facilitator; and small-group discussions ranging from highly structured group interviews to loose, freewheeling, non-directive conversations.

To increase our confidence in the quality of data we are generating, it's advisable to combine at least two methodologies in one qualitative project: for example, non-directive group discussions combined with unstructured personal interviews, or a conversational method (group or individual) combined with a projective test or some direct observation, in order to increase our prospects of gaining the widest and deepest possible access to people's attitudes and motivations.

One great advantage of conversational methods—especially the group discussion—is that they generate non-verbal as well as verbal data. In addition to the words being spoken, a rich source of complementary data is to be found in all the non-verbal signals that might help the researcher interpret what is meant by what is being said: rates of speech, tones of voice, postures, gestures, facial expressions, pauses, hesitations, eye-rolls, laughter (nervous or otherwise), subtle signs of awkwardness or discomfort, and so on. Such material should be regarded as integral to the data-collection process. It should also be taken as seriously as the verbal data, especially when the tone of voice or other non-verbal cues appear to contradict what is being said. (By the way, the potential significance of non-verbal data is one reason why online methods should be avoided for qualitative research projects. The lack of eye contact between participants is a crucial weakness of online methods, as is the researcher's inability to sense the 'energy' in the room.)

***

Unfortunately, in the drive for speed, efficiency and profit, 'qualitative research' has become almost synonymous with 'focus groups' among many contemporary marketing and political strategists, and among many academic and commercial research practitioners as well. Focus groups typically comprise a collection of individuals who don't know each other (indeed, typically *must not* know each other), assembled in a central location unfamiliar to them, and led by an active, interventionist moderator following a predetermined discussion guide, rather like a questionnaire. Some focus groups comprise people drawn from similar demographic and socioeconomic backgrounds; some deliberately seek to 'mix up' the participants in terms of age, sex, etc., treating each group as a miniature cross-section of society.

Because focus groups are artificially constructed for the purposes of research, the method is peculiarly vulnerable to the experiment effect. Strangers in a strange place can say strange things! While its advocates argue that the focus-group method is appropriate for particular purposes ('horses for courses'), any philosophical defence of the method must first address that core problem: in what way is this method designed to enhance the validity of the data it generates?

The non-directive, unstructured, 'affinity' group discussion

This method—the polar opposite of 'focus groups'—has been in continuous use in Australian research for sixty years, and was the first qualitative method to undergo serious development here. It involves naturally occurring social groups, sometimes known as 'affinity groups'—typically five to eight friends, neighbours, work colleagues, etc. who spend enough time in each other's company to be at ease with each other—meeting together in the home of one of them, or a club, or workplace, or wherever the group feels comfortable, to engage in informal, free-flowing conversation about the topic of the research.

In the relaxed and permissive atmosphere of a group of people who already know each other and are used to talking to each other, the discussion ranges widely over any aspects of the subject that interest or concern the members of the group—there is no agenda and no predetermined topic outline. The moderator's role is essentially passive—in a typical group discussion of this type, the moderator will introduce the topic and say nothing else (or very little) for the duration of the discussion.

Some group members will talk a great deal; some will say very little or, occasionally, nothing at all. The discussion will proceed rather like any natural conversation between a group of friends or colleagues. There will be leaders and followers; those who are dominant and those who are submissive; agreements and disagreements; sidetracking and wisecracking.

In the ebb and flow of natural conversation, the attitudes, values and beliefs will gradually emerge (often involving ambiguities, inconsistencies and even contradictions). It is the dynamics of natural group interaction that generate the information we are seeking.

To be successful, the method should meet three rigorous criteria:

- The groups should be natural (i.e. pre-existing) groups whose dynamics are well established.
- The discussions should be conducted in the 'natural habitat' of the participants.
- The conversation should be allowed to proceed freely and spontaneously, without any interference, structure or leadership being imposed on it by the researcher.

The method has its limitations. It is unsuitable for eliciting the kind of information people might be reluctant to discuss in company, even among their friends or workmates. And it obviously excludes people who are socially isolated. Unstructured personal interviews should therefore be part of the standard repertoire of qualitative researchers, and should ideally be incorporated into every project, to provide a check on—and to potentially enrich and extend—the scope and depth of group-generated data.

How many groups/interviews would you need to conduct to establish some conclusions you can have confidence in? That depends largely on the size and diversity of the population you are studying. With qualitative sampling, the key point is that we need to conduct enough fieldwork to be sure we have captured the maximum possible diversity within the cohort we are studying (e.g. people turning forty, the mothers of teenagers, people on the brink of retirement, etc.). If you're studying attitudes to work among people in a small organisation, you can probably talk to everyone!

The twenty-five-year social research program I ran from 1979 to 2003, *The Mackay Report*, employed the non-directive group discussion as the central method, though almost always supplemented by unstructured personal interviews. A typical project involved the conduct of sixteen group discussions and thirty individual interviews, spread across three capital cities and at least two regional areas.

If you're interested in the detailed practicalities of conducting non-directive group discussions and unstructured interviews, and analysing and interpreting the data, see my article 'The "unfocused" group discussion technique' (Mackay, 2012).

One reason why I have relied so heavily on the non-directive group discussion technique is that the process of data collection is as *natural* as we can possibly make it, and the asking of potentially influential questions is bypassed altogether.

A further safeguard has been my reliance on the team approach, designed to minimise the risk of personal biases and preconceptions intruding into the analysis and interpretation of data. Typically, three or four researchers would work independently on the fieldwork and analysis, only coming together for the process of drawing conclusions about the findings.

I therefore conclude this Appendix by acknowledging the colleagues who worked most closely with me on the development of qualitative methodology, particularly in the period from the early 1960s to the mid-1980s, listed here in alphabetical order: Margie Beaumont, Ian Cameron, Peter Copleston, Marilyn Elfverson, Barry Elliott, Peter Kenny, Prue Parkhill, Penelope Paterson, Yvonne Repin, Patrick Shanahan, Libby Turnock and Maggie Wilkins.

REFERENCES

Abey, Arun, quoted in Debra Jopson and Greg Lenthen, 'Baby Boomers: Who'll Pay When They're Grey?', *Sydney Morning Herald*, 12 July 1994

Adichie, Chimamanda Ngozi, *We Should All Be Feminists*, Anchor Books, New York, 2015

Ahsan, Sanah, 'I'm a psychologist—and I believe we've been told devastating lies about mental health', *The Guardian*, 6 September 2022, www.theguardian.com

Alcaraz, Kassandra, 'Social isolation directly affects health by causing changes in the body such as inflammation', *American Journal of Epidemiology*, October 2018

Armstrong, Karen, *A Short History of Myth*, Text Publishing, Melbourne, 2005

Astle, David, '"I never said she stole my money." Amazing . . .', X (formerly Twitter) post, 18 January 2023, twitter.com/dontattempt/

Baggini, Julian, 'The philosophical meaning of equality', *Prospect*, 25 January 2023, www.prospectmagazine.co.uk

REFERENCES

Banerjee, Robin, '"Are we going to be snapped back into individuality? That's up to us . . ."', *The Psychologist*, October 2022

Beard, Mary, *Women and Power: A Manifesto*, Profile Books, London, 2017

Ben Simon, Eti et al., 'Sleep loss leads to the withdrawal of human helping across individuals, groups and large-scale societies', *PLOS Biology*, 20(8), 2022

Biddulph, Steve, quoted in Mike Safe, 'Boys to Men', *The Australian Magazine*, 2–3 August 1997

Burnard, Philip, 'A method for analysing interview transcripts in qualitative research', *Nurse Education Today*, 11(6), 1991

Campos, Paul, *A Fan's Life: The Agony of Victory and the Thrill of Defeat*, University of Chicago Press, Chicago, 2022

Centre for Public Christianity, 'Easter 2021 survey', 26 March 2021, www.publicchristianity.org

Chesterton, G.K., 'On Mr. Rudyard Kipling and making the world small', in *Heretics*, John Lane, London, 1905

Collier, Paul and John Kay, *Greed is Dead: Politics After Individualism*, Penguin, London, 2021

Cox, Eva, 'Feminism has failed and needs a radical rethink', *The Conversation*, 8 March 2016, theconversation.com

Cupitt, Don, *The Sea of Faith*, British Broadcasting Corporation, London, 1984

Dalgarno, Paul, *Prudish Nation: Life, Love and Libido*, Upswell Publishing, Perth, 2023

Darwin, Charles, *The Descent of Man*, John Murray, London, 1871

Davies, William, 'The reaction economy', *London Review of Books*, 2 March 2023

Dennett, Daniel C., *Breaking the Spell: Religion as a Natural Phenomenon*, Allen Lane, London, 2006

References

Eliot, T.S., 'Choruses from The Rock' in *The Rock,* 1934, republished in *Collected Poems 1909–1962,* Faber & Faber, London, 1963

Ending Loneliness Together, *State of the Nation Report: Social Connection in Australia 2023,* Ending Loneliness Together, Sydney, 2023

Evans, Rachel Held, *Inspired: Slaying Giants, Walking on Water, and Loving the Bible Again,* Nelson Books, Nashville, 2018

Festinger, Leon, 'Informal social communication', *Psychological Review,* 57(5), 1950

—— *A Theory of Cognitive Dissonance,* Stanford University Press, Stanford, 1957

Fishbein, Martin, 'Attitude and the prediction of behaviour', in Martin Fishbein (ed.), *Readings in Attitude Theory and Measurement,* Wiley, New York, 1967

Ford, Richard, 'Our moments have all been seized', *The New York Times,* 27 December 1998

Forstater, Mark (ed.), *Meditations: The Spiritual Teachings of Marcus Aurelius,* Hodder, Sydney, 2000

Frenken, Marius, Michał Bilewicz and Roland Imhoff, 'On the relation between religiosity and the endorsement of conspiracy theories: The role of political orientation', *Political Psychology,* 44(1), 2023

Galbraith, John K., 'Recession economics', *New York Review of Books,* 4 February 1982

Gallop, Geoff, 'Substantive equality—The missing link', paper presented to Australian Council of Human Rights Agencies, Sydney, 28 February 2023

Gigerenzer, Gerd, *How to Stay Smart in a Smart World,* Penguin, London, 2022

Gilder, George, *Life After Television: The Coming Transformation of Media and American Life,* W.W. Norton, New York, 1985

REFERENCES

Gillard, Julia and Ngozi Okonjo Iweala, *Women and Leadership: Real Lives, Real Lessons*, Penguin, Sydney, 2021

Glaser, Barney G. and Anselm L. Strauss, *The Discovery of Grounded Theory: Strategies for Qualitative Research*, Aldine, New York, 1967

Goebbels, Joseph, *The Goebbels Diaries: 1942–1943*, trans. Louis P. Lochner, Doubleday, New York, 1948

Goodwin, Kristy, *Dear Digital, We Need to Talk*, Major Street Publishing, Melbourne, 2023

Gordon, Allison and Pamela Brown, 'CNN Surgeon General says 13 is "too early" to join social media', CNN, 29 January 2023, edition.cnn.com

Greer, Germaine, *The Female Eunuch*, Paladin, London, 1971

Harkien, Chris, 'Leaving the door open—interview with Chris Harkien', *CASE*, 66, 2023, www.case.edu.au

Harrison, Pam, 'Social isolation directly affects health, ups risk of death', Medscape, 20 November 2018, www.medscape.com

Holt-Lunstad, Julianne, 'Loneliness: A growing public health threat', Paper delivered at the 125th Annual Convention of the American Psychological Association, Washington Convention Center, Washington DC, 5 August 2017

Hutchings, Paul B. and Katie E. Sullivan, 'Gender: How stubborn are the stereotypes?', *The Psychologist*, April 2023

Johnson, Mark, 'Developing human brain functions', *The Psychologist*, British Psychological Society, November 2009

Jung, C.G., *Memories, Dreams, Reflections* [1961], Fontana, London, 1983

Kagan, Jerome, *Surprise, Uncertainty and Mental Structures*, Harvard University Press, Cambridge, Mass., 2007

Kale, Neha, 'Lally Katz', *The Saturday Paper*, 18 February 2023

King, Richard, 'Machine learning', *The Monthly*, April 2023

References

Klapper, Joseph T., *The Effects of Mass Communication*, The Free Press, New York, 1960

Koenig, Harold G., Dana E. King and Verna B. Carson, *Handbook of Religion and Health*, 2nd ed., Oxford University Press, New York, 2012

Kruger, Justin and David Dunning, 'Unskilled and unaware of it: How difficulties in recognizing one's own incompetence lead to inflated self-assessments', *Journal of Personality and Social Psychology*, 77(6), 1999

Lim, Michelle, 'Is loneliness Australia's next public health epidemic?', *InPsych*, 40(4), August 2018

—— 'The misconceptions of loneliness', *Health Voices*, 27, November 2020, healthvoices.org.au

Luther, Martin, *Luther's Large Catechism* [1529], trans. John N. Lenker, The Luther Press, Minneapolis, 1908

Mackay, Hugh, *Reinventing Australia*, Angus & Robertson, Sydney, 1993

—— *Why Don't People Listen?*, Pan Australia, Sydney, 1994

—— 'Can we know too much? Information & morality', St James Ethics Centre Annual Lecture, Sydney, 7 November 1995

—— *Generations*, Pan Macmillan, Sydney, 1997

—— *Advance Australia . . . Where?*, Hachette, Sydney, 2007

—— 'The myth of an Australian spirituality', St George's Cathedral lecture, no. 16, Perth, 2009

—— 'The "unfocused" group discussion technique', *Australasian Journal of Market & Social Research*, 20(2), 2012

—— *The Good Life*, Pan Macmillan, Sydney, 2013

—— *Beyond Belief*, Pan Macmillan, Sydney, 2016

—— *Australia Reimagined: Towards a More Compassionate, Less Anxious Society*, Pan Macmillan, Sydney, 2018

——*Right & Wrong: How to Decide for Yourself, Make Wiser Moral Choices and Build a Better Society*, 3rd ed., Hachette, Sydney, 2019

——*What Makes Us Tick: Making Sense of Who We Are and the Desires That Drive Us*, 3rd ed., Hachette, Sydney, 2019

——*The Kindness Revolution: How We Can Restore Hope, Rebuild Trust and Inspire Optimism*, Allen & Unwin, Sydney, 2021

Macleod, Emily et al., *Australian Psychologists in the Context of Disasters: Preliminary Report on Workforce Impacts and Needs*, Australian National University, May 2023

Manne, Anne, *The Life of I: The New Culture of Narcissism*, Melbourne University Press, Melbourne, 2014

Marchiano, Lisa, 'Collision with reality: What depth psychology can tell us about victimhood culture', *Quillette*, 27 December 2017, quillette.com

Mark, Gloria, *Attention Span: Finding Focus for a Fulfilling Life*, Hanover Square Press, London, 2023

Maugham, W. Somerset, *A Writer's Notebook*, Heinemann, London, 1949

McAllister, Ian, 'Does pork-barrelling actually work? New research suggests it's not a big vote winner', *The Conversation*, 31 January 2022, theconversation.com

McLuhan, Marshall, *The Gutenberg Galaxy*, Routledge & Kegan Paul, London, 1962

——*Understanding Media: The Extensions of Man*, Routledge & Kegan Paul, London, 1964

Mehrabian, Albert, 'Communication without words', *Psychology Today*, 2(9), 1968

Meier, John P., *A Marginal Jew: Rethinking the Historical Jesus*, Bantam Doubleday Dell, New York, 1991

References

Melville, Nancy A., 'Sleep loss linked to reduced generosity, even at a neuronal level', *Medscape*, 30 August 2022, www.medscape.com

Miller, George A., 'The human link in communication systems', in *The Psychology of Communication: Seven Essays*, Basic Books, New York, 1967

Monbiot, George, 'The town that's found a potent cure for illness— community', *The Guardian*, 21 February 2018, www.theguardian. com

Moore, Thomas, *The Care of the Sou: Twenty-fifth Anniversary Edition: A Guide for Cultivating Depth and Sacredness in Everyday Life*, Harper Personal, New York, 2016

Nuttin, Jozef, *The Illusion of Attitude Change: Towards a Response Contagion Theory of Persuasion*, Academic Press, London, 1974

O'Donnell, James, *Mapping Social Cohesion 2022*, Scanlon Foundation Research Institute, Melbourne, 2022, scanloninstitute.org.au

O'Hagan, Andrew, 'Off his royal tits', *London Review of Books*, 2 February 2023

Overington, Caroline, 'How our kids' reading future is being rudely interrupted', *The Weekend Australian*, 18 March 2023

Palmer, Benjamin, 'The Bell Curve Review: IQ best indicated poverty', student paper EC 970, Department of Economics, Harvard University, 2018

Polidoras, Alexis et al., *State of the Older Nation 2023*, COTA Australia, April 2023, cota.org.au

Postman, Neil, *Amusing Ourselves to Death: Public Discourse in the Age of Show Business*, Penguin, New York, 1985

Ravilious, Kate, 'The last human', *New Scientist*, 27 November 2021

Rawls, John, *A Theory of Justice*, Harvard University Press, Cambridge, MA, 1971

REFERENCES

Richardson, David and Matt Grudnoff, *Inequality on Steroids: The Distribution of Economic Growth in Australia*, The Australia Institute, 2023, australiainstitute.org.au

Robinson, Jennifer and Keina Yoshida, *How Many More Women? Exposing how the law silences women*, Allen & Unwin, Sydney, 2022

Rogers, Carl, *On Becoming a Person: A Therapist's View of Psycho-therapy*, Constable, London, 1967

Rossiter, John R., *Measurement for the Social Sciences: The C-OAR-SE Method and Why It Must Replace Psychometrics*, Springer, New York, 2011

Rothwell, Jonathan, 'You are what you watch? The social effects of TV', *The New York Times*, 25 July 2019

Russell, Bertrand, *Principles of Social Reconstruction*, G. Allen & Unwin, London, 1916

——'The triumph of stupidity' [1933], in *Mortals and Others: Bertrand Russell's American Essays, 1931–1935*, vol. 2, Routledge, London, 1998

Ruthven, Philip, quoted in Debra Jopson and Greg Lenthen, 'Baby Boomers: Who'll Pay When They're Grey?', *Sydney Morning Herald*, 12 July 1994

Ryan, Michelle K., 'Addressing workplace gender inequality: Using the evidence to avoid common pitfalls', *British Journal of Social Psychology*, 62(1), 2023

Sandstrom, Gillian, 'Why you should talk to strangers', *The Psychologist*, June 2023

Schramm, Wilbur, Jack Lyle and Edwin B. Parker, *Television in the Lives of our Children: The Effects of Television on American Children*, Stanford University Press/Oxford University Press, Stanford/London, 1961

References

Seligman, Martin, 'Why is there so much depression today? The waxing of the individual and the waning of the commons', in Rick E. Ingram (ed.), *Contemporary Psychological Approaches to Depression: Theory, Research and Treatment*, Plenum Press, New York, 1990

Shullenberger, Geoff, 'René Girard and the rise of victim power', *Compact*, 10 December 2022, compactmag.com

Spong, John Shelby, *Unbelievable: Why Neither Ancient Creeds Nor the Reformation Can Produce a Living Faith Today*, HarperCollins, New York, 2018

Srivastava, Ranjana, 'Complicated lives—taking the social history', *New England Journal of Medicine*, 365(7), 2011

Suzuki, David and Amanda McConnell, *The Sacred Balance: Rediscovering Our Place in Nature*, 2nd ed., Greystone Books, Vancouver, 2007

Toussaint, Loren L. and Everett L. Worthington Jr, 'Forgiveness', *The Psychologist*, British Psychological Society, August 2017

Twenge, Jean M., 'Have smartphones destroyed a generation?', *The Atlantic*, September 2017

Vallejo, Irene, *Papyrus: The Invention of Books in the Ancient World*, Hodder & Stoughton, London, 2022

Wilkins, Roger, Matthew Fischer-Post and Nicolas Herault, 'Unequal? Our analysis suggests Australia is a more equal society than has been thought', *The Conversation*, 14 April 2023, theconversation.com

Wilson, James Q., *The Moral Sense*, Free Press, New York, 1993

Wodehouse, P.G., *Summer Lightning*, (originally published under the title *Fish Preferred*), Doubleday, Doran, New York, 1929

Zielinski, Chris et al., 'WAME recommendations on ChatGPT and Chatbots in relation to scholarly publications', *Pan-American Journal of Ophthalmology*, 5(1), 2023

ACKNOWLEDGEMENTS

CONSULTANT PUBLISHER
Richard Walsh

SENIOR EDITOR/JUNIOR COMMISSIONING EDITOR
Tom Bailey-Smith

COPYEDITOR
Emma Driver

PROOFREADER
Pamela Dunne

PUBLISHING ASSISTANT
Allegra Bonetto

COVER DESIGNER
Mika Tabata

SENIOR PUBLICITY MANAGER
Ali Hampton

341

ACKNOWLEDGEMENTS

I am particularly grateful to Richard Walsh and Tom Bailey-Smith for their guidance, encouragement and support throughout the development of *The Way We Are*, and to the entire team at Allen & Unwin for their professional skill and personal engagement with the project.

Many people—family, friends, neighbours, colleagues, total strangers—have contributed richly to my thinking about the issues raised in this book, but the truth is that everyone I have encountered, every relationship, every conversation has stimulated, illuminated or influenced me in some way. I am therefore grateful to everyone I've ever met; everyone who's told me even a little of their story. And that includes, most especially, the thousands of research respondents who, over the years, have agreed to let me and my colleagues into their homes to share their thoughts and feelings on almost every imaginable topic. Their generosity has made my research possible; their frankness has given it its integrity.

Truly, as the book's subtitle says, mine has been 'a lifetime of listening' and that's been a rare privilege. Thank you, all.

INDEX

INDEX

INDEX

cognitive behavioural therapy 41,
   117
cognitive dissonance 118, 320
Cohn, Harry 160
Cold War 200–2, 204, 216
Columbia Pictures 160
commitment 18–19
communication
   contrasted with data transfer 65–7,
      71
   mass communication 66, 101, 320
   meaning and intention in 292–5
   see also listening
community
   essential nature of 7, 10
   in times of catastrophe 45–6, 265
   loss of sense of 65
   neighbourhood communities 45,
      48, 75, 316
   relation to sense of responsibility
      75
   role of the individual in 313
   sense of in religious communities
      240–1, 250
   Thatcher's view of 311–12
   ways of maintaining 31, 48–9
community gardens 31
compassion 172
Compassionate Ballarat 267
Compassionate Frome Project 265–6
competence, relation to ignorance 81
competitiveness 8, 33, 35–8, 119,
   268
compulsive behaviour 117
computers see information
   technology
conformity 320
Confucianism 257
connectedness see interconnectedness
consent 167
conspiracy theories 79, 242
consumerism 199, 215
contraception 18, 116, 202
conversations 279, 324

convictions 280–1, 286
cooperation 8–10
Copernicus 82
COVID-19 pandemic 1–2, 22, 45–6,
   93, 174, 195, 266
Cox, Eva 149–50
creation myth 51
credit cards 203
criminal behaviour 126–7, 166
culture, cancelling manifestations of
   168–72, 246, 317
Cupitt, Don 227, 236

Darwin, Charles 81, 268
data transfer 65–7, 71, 109
Davies, William 53
Davis-McCabe, Catriona 42
Dawkins, Richard 97
de Beauvoir, Simone 167
Dear Digital, We Need to Talk
   (Goodwin) 112
deathbed test 238
Deighton, Len 201
democracy 86
Dennett, Daniel 241
depression
   among clinical psychologists 42
   as part of a mental health crisis
      33
   ignoring the causes of 43
   link to screen time for teenagers
      114
   lower incidence of in faith
      communities 21, 241
   resulting from social isolation
      38–41
depth research 319
desire see social desires
Dichter, Ernest 319
disabled people 183–4
disadvantaged people 10, 193–4
disasters 45–6, 83–4, 92–4, 265
divorce 15, 17, 209
domestic help 191

346

Index

Index

Index

INDEX

Index

Index

INDEX